To Gerry Tasiace
Hope you will enjoy
reading this book.
Anna Stern-Bay
Nov. 2010

(Please share with the staff)

THE GOLDEN AGE AND ITS IMPLOSION

Emil Steinberger

authorHOUSE®

AuthorHouse™
1663 Liberty Drive
Bloomington, IN 47403
www.authorhouse.com
Phone: 1-800-839-8640

First published by AuthorHouse 10/11/2010

ISBN: 978-1-4520-7714-7 (sc)

Library of Congress Control Number: 2010913949

Printed in the United States of America

This book is printed on acid-free paper.

ACKNOWLEDGEMENTS

This final volume of trilogy, "THE JOURNEY", was penned by a retired physician and newspaper columnist. It couldn't have been published without the help of several individuals who made many valuable suggestions and devoted innumerable hours to editing and proof-reading the volume. Before this book was ready to be published, Emil Steinberger lost his battle with cancer, and it was up to these caring individuals to make it happen as they felt it was important for the book to become available not only for those in the health professions but for the general public.

My foremost gratitude goes to Dr. David Rodbard, a professional colleague and good friend of Emil, for his help with biomedical terminology and names of professional institutions referred to in the text. Another physician- colleague, Bill Powell, M.D. was invaluable in improving the flow of the text, particularly in the proper usage of the English language.

A significant contribution to the book in the afterward was made by Barbara Sanborn, Ph.D., who wanted to share some of her experiences of over ten years as a faculty member and research collaborator in Emil's department at UT Medical School.

Many thanks go to Dr.Cheves McCord Smythe who, as the first dean of the newly created University of Texas Medical School in Houston, was responsible for recruiting Emil Steinberger, M.D.and his wife, Anna Steinberger, Ph.D. to the faculty and the great state of Texas! He and his wife Polly offered useful suggestions for text revisions and language clarity.

I want to acknowledge also, with much gratitude, the contributions of our daughters: Inette Brown, an attorney whose excellent command of the English language was instrumental in proof-reading/editing of the text, and Pauline Solnik, a graduate from the Pennsylvania Academy of Fine Arts, for using her artistic talents to design the book cover.

I will forever be indebted to all these individuals for their invaluable help in getting this book ready for publication.

Anna Steinberger, Ph.D.
Professor Emerita,
University of Texas Medical School in Houston

CONTENTS

FOREWORD

"The Golden Age and its Implosion" is the third volume of a trilogy, "The Journey", penned by Emil Steinberger, MD after retiring from a long and successful career as a clinician, teacher and medical researcher.

The author thoughtfully analyzes various aspects of medical training, health care delivery and the evolution of insurance coverage for patient care from a historical, economic and personal point of view. Considering the sweeping changes to health care adopted by the current administration in an attempt to provide better insurance coverage for more Americans and the huge controversies these changes have generated, the contents of this book could not have been more timely and relevant.

There is fervent praise for the explosion of scientific research after WWII, stimulated by the highly motivated young men and women entering the field under the GI Bill as well as increased government funding for research through the National Institutes of Health, which had been recently created by the US government.

In the first volume, "Between the Devil and Deep Blue Sea" the author related his personal experiences during and shortly after WWII. The second, "The Promised Land – Woes of and Immigrant", details his experiences after arriving in this country as a penniless 18-year old trying to learn a new language, find a job and continue his education. This final volume recounts his professional development and achievements, made possible by the unlimited opportunities of this country, woven into the events of his reach personal life.

Unfortunately, Emil (my husband of nearly 58 years) was diagnosed with non-operative lung cancer in December 2006 and despite heroic efforts was too ill to finish the book. Being strongly convinced this volume contained much valuable information and assured fascinating reading, I felt compelled to finish his story by writing the final chapter and assuring the book is published.

The afterward was written by Dr. Barbara Sanborn, Professor

and Head of the Department of Biomedical Sciences, Colorado State University, Fort Collins, Co. who wanted to share her experiences of over 10 years as a faculty member and research collaborator in the Department of Reproductive Medicine and Biology, chaired by Dr. Emil Steinberger at the University of Texas Medical School in Houston.

My hope is that these additional contributions will help the reader gain a more complete picture of Emil's passionate life-long striving for new scientific knowledge and improved patient care as well as his incredible zest for life!

Anna Steinberger, PhD
Professor Emerita,
UTMS- Houston

CHAPTER 1
THE NAVY - EARLY EXPERIENCES

The big day for my departure had arrived. My two daughters, Pauline nearly five and Inette three years old, were crying. My wife Ania was trying bravely to smile and I didn't know how I felt. It had been decided that I would take two days for the car trip from Detroit, Michigan to Portsmouth, Virginia where I was to go through induction training for the Navy. It was August 2nd, 1956 and I was to report on the 4th. I had two full days for this trip and there was no reason to hurry.

After graduating from medical school and completing one year of internship at the Detroit Receiving Hospital (DRH), I had volunteered to serve in the Navy. This was my way of repaying this country, in some small way, for the opportunities it had offered me after I had emigrated from Europe in 1948.

The morning of my departure was sunny and humid. I had packed only a small bag with a few pieces of clothing since I anticipated that regulation uniforms, shoes and underwear would be issued once I got to the Base. After that, there would be no need for civilian clothing except on some rare occasions.

In no time, I was heading towards Toledo, Ohio. As luck would have it, the new Ohio Turnpike was not scheduled to open until some time in the fall so I decided to head south towards Columbus. As I drove Highway 30, I couldn't help but smile. Some six years earlier I had driven this highway to New York to get married. Today, I was driving it to join the Navy, but there was a big difference between these two days. Now I was a married man, a full-fledged doctor and a trained scientist with two sweet daughters and a wife with a Masters degree! These thoughts certainly put me in a good mood. The weather was perfect as I drove the beautiful highways in my new Oldsmobile musing again about how this great country had allowed me to accomplish so much in such a short time.

Early that afternoon I entered Columbus, a rather old city spanning the Scioto River, but no points of interest I wanted to stop and see. From here I headed to Charleston, West Virginia. The hilly country made for a pleasant drive, but by the time I reached Charleston, it was early evening and I was hungry and tired. After checking into a small roadside motel I drove to a local drive-in, ordered a 'chicken in the basket', and began to feel sorry for myself because I was missing Ania and the girls.

On the next day I arrived in Portsmouth. It was only mid afternoon of August 3rd when I pulled up at a row of parking spots in front of the Portsmouth Naval Hospital. My early arrival gave me an opportunity to report for duty that day and to be assigned to the BOQ (Bachelor Officers Quarters) for that night.

The following morning I reported to the hospital. The main structure was an imposing building. The entrance was flanked by at least ten Greek columns which extended from the entrance terrace all the way to the top of the building. The building was surrounded by carefully groomed, colorful flowerbeds and there were smaller buildings scattered around it along the slow flowing Elizabeth River. The entire compound was situated on attractive, well-tended grounds.

A receptionist advised me to see the Chairman of the Department of Internal Medicine and after several inquiries I found his office. There, I was immediately ushered into a small room filled with regulation green filing cabinets and a small desk. A rotund man who was sitting behind the desk stood up as I walked in and quickly walked over with a big smile on his face and extending his hand in greeting. "Welcome to PNH, the Portsmouth Naval Hospital. I've been waiting for you impatiently, please have a seat," he exclaimed, while gesturing to a straight-back chair in front of the desk. I sat down, pleasantly surprised by this warm greeting, and directed a questioning gaze at him.

"I'm Doctor Rodney Cottrell, Chairman of the Department of

Internal Medicine at this hospital and you are Doctor Steinberger, the new Internist who just joined the Navy, correct?" I looked at him blinking my eyes and not knowing how to respond. Before I could open my mouth, he continued:

> For the past several weeks I've been hearing that you had been assigned to a post here and last week I was informed that you would indeed be arriving today. It's great to see you but you may be surprised when you hear what I have to say. Let me go back and describe the situation to you from the very beginning. I was honorably discharged from the Navy at the end of WWII after eighteen months of service. Subsequently I joined the Department of Medicine at the University of Arkansas, Medical School and couple of years later, was appointed Dean. In this capacity I started a major reorganization of the Departments in the school and began to implement significant curricular innovations. In January of this year, in the midst of these major changes, I got a letter to report for active duty, in other words I was drafted.
>
> You see, after my discharge from active duty with the Navy I remained in the Naval Reserve. Apparently, anyone who served in the Armed Forces for less than twenty-four months remained eligible for the draft to complete that stint. After a series of appeals failed I ended up here and the medical school began to founder. Finally, after further appeals, I prevailed with the brass and was granted a discharge from active duty, effective in August, after the arrival of my replacement. Well, here you are! So, after spending a few days familiarizing you with some details of the job, I'll be returning to Arkansas.

I sat there petrified, not believing what I'd just heard. I couldn't in the farthest reaches of my imagination have envisioned this scenario. My mind went blank. I had no idea how to respond. Dr. Cottrell, realizing that his statements must have shocked me, came from behind his desk and put his hand on my shoulder saying, "Let's go to the Commissary for a cup of coffee". He led me out of the building, across a manicured lawn with beds of colorful flowers, into a two-story structure that housed what I considered a very elegant restaurant. "This is the officer's club and the commissary building," he explained. "The PX (Post Exchange, a supermarket type of a store for military personnel) is also located in this building." I looked around in awe; the room was a sea of tables covered with heavy snow-white linens, and set with beautiful silverware and white china edged with red and blue stripes. At the center of each table was a tall crystal vase full of fresh flowers. This officers club looked like the finest restaurant I had ever seen. However, I should admit that my previous experience with fancy restaurants was quite limited.

The instant we sat down, a waiter wearing a white starched jacket and navy blue tie came over to take our orders. Dr. Cottrell looked at me and asked, "Would you like breakfast?" Actually I was very hungry since I had no time to eat that morning and hadn't known where to find breakfast. I was embarrassed and didn't know what to say. Rodney instantly figured out what was happening and turned to the waiter saying, "I'll have a cup of coffee and the Lieutenant will have two eggs, sausage, ham and toast". Turning to me he added, "Will you have coffee or something else to drink?" "Thank you, coffee will be fine," I responded.

Commander Cottrell sipped his coffee while looking at me with a thoughtful gaze and said:

> I know that this is something of a shock for you, I also know your current interests and background from your correspondence with the Navy Department. During the next six weeks I know you will learn a great deal about the Navy and the Naval Medical Corps (NMC). In addition, I must tell you that you'll be performing another very important duty until the arrival of the permanent Chief of Internal Medicine. You will serve as the 'interim' Chief of the Department of Medicine at the Portsmouth Naval Hospital.

I had just spent a year during which the most unexpected, inconceivable situations had been thrown at me but this certainly topped them all. I looked at the Commander in disbelief. I was to serve as the interim Chief. The words wouldn't even pass trough my throat; only some croaking sounds. Finally, I pulled myself together and said with astonishment "But there must be someone else here with greater experience or higher rank. I've only just finished the internship part of my training." Dr. Cottrell only shook his head and in a quiet, controlled voice he proceeded:

> Please let me explain, the doctors currently serving on the Medical Service at our hospital have completed only their internships, they are considered GPs (general practitioners). In addition to the GPs we usually have several Boarded or Board Eligible Internists but by chance they have all either left the Service or been reassigned to other duties in the past few days. We will be getting an appropriate replacement but not for several weeks. As far as the medical care on the Wards is concerned I foresee no problems. Although the GPs have just completed their internships, they've had considerable clinical experience and can adequately manage the wards.

> We are required to appoint the doctor who has the highest level of formal training to be the interim Chief. At this moment that would be you. You have completed your internship, one month of Internal Medicine training and have earned the equivalent of a PhD (Doctor of Philosophy). Therefore, you have the most training and should be the most senior officer. This is the least complicated solution to the problem and most closely follows the 'rule book'.

I sat listening to Dr. Cottrell trying to comprehend what he was attempting to convey to me; it didn't make any sense. He, however, paid no attention to my consternation:

> This isn't 'boot camp' for you; it's not supposed to be training camp for regular naval service. Since you'll be a doctor in the Navy your training here will focus primarily on learning naval regulations, traditions and the ways of the Service. Most of it will be classroom work for a few hours in the

morning. The rest of the time you'll be able to spend on the hospital wards supervising the physicians and nurses.

As he continued explaining the situation, instead of becoming more relaxed I was getting tenser. Dr. Cottrell must have realized that I was overwhelmed with the avalanche of information and indeed I felt pretty shell shocked. He then suggested that we visit the wards so he could introduce me to the other doctors. I finally realized that all of this was real and that I must accept the situation and try to make the best of it.

Some of the physicians on the internal medicine service were general practitioners, only recently drafted into the Service, and they impressed me as knowledgeable and pleasant individuals. Two had been in the service only one month, having been drafted straight from their internships. The nurses were also very personable and appeared to be quite competent. Thus, my initial contact with the staff was very positive. Dr. Cottrell thought I should skip the morning's induction class and instead go to an "Army Store" in town to order my uniforms. So I suggested we convene a staff meeting that afternoon to discuss work plans for the ensuing weeks. I had already been provided with materials explaining the coverage needs for the wards and the physicians' schedules.

The next several days went by in a blink of an eye and I was still a bit in shock. My formal induction training sessions took only three hours each morning. I could spend the remaining time learning about the organization and activities of the Service, taking care of patients on the wards, and handling whatever little supervision was required to keep the medical service viable until the arrival of a permanent Chief. I soon realized what Dr. Cottrell had had in mind. The Department could really run itself for a short period of time. The staff was competent and he had had exhaustive discussions with them concerning my brief appointment. He hoped that I wouldn't be pressed to "fix" any broad problems and felt confident that I would not "break" anything while acting as interim Chief.

The demands on my professional and leadership skills were indeed relatively minor. The majority of the patients presented simple medical issues, and most were young men who were highly motivated to recover and rejoin their units or return to their ships.

One initial problem was to organize the duty rosters to accommodate my naval induction training courses. Since these started at 8:00 AM the morning rounds had to be completed by 7:30; thus we had to commence at 6:30 and sometimes earlier. It also meant a reorganization of nurses' and other doctors' schedules. Fortunately, I had no classes in the afternoon so the afternoon rounds could be extended.

I developed a routine of dropping in on the wards in the evenings to check on any problems that might have arisen. During my very first week on the Service, the evening routine commenced with a slight disaster. I had just acquired my first summer "working khaki" uniform and couldn't wait to wear the jacket with my Lieutenant Senior Grade gold thread bars on the shoulder boards. Although it would have been quite appropriate and well within service rules to wear only the uniform shirt, I couldn't resist dressing for the evening visit to the wards in my beautiful new uniform; this in spite of the sweltering August temperatures.

As I started walking through ward A between two rows of beds, Barbara, the head nurse, came running over to me, whispering, "We're having a problem with a transfusion in Ward D, could you come and help?" I nodded my head as we began running toward Ward D. There at the far end of the ward, two nurses were bending over a patient next to an I.V. stand that had a bottle of blood hanging from it. One of the nurses was holding a rubber tube, which was attached to the bottle at one end and had the I.V. needle attached to the other end. As I bent over the patient to get a better look at him, she must have given the tube a slight tug, inadvertently detaching it from the bottle. Blood poured all over my head and my beautiful crisp new uniform jacket.

I dejectedly sat in the nurse's station dressed in a hospital gown ruminating over these events while Barbara attempted to restore my uniform to normalcy. I was worried because I had to wear it to class the following morning. However, the next day, as I sat in class in my spotless uniform, no one would ever have been able to tell that just few hours ego it had been covered with blood. I still can't figure out how Barbara accomplished this feat.

Ron, another newly baked medical officer, brought to my attention the Officers Club in Virginia Beach, a twenty-minute drive from the Naval Hospital, and offered to go there with me. After the afternoon rounds I picked him up in my clean Oldsmobile wearing my clean uniform and we took off for the beach. It was a glorious day and the club was a dream; it sat on a beautiful Atlantic beach with huge rolling waves foaming onto a golden sandy beach only yards from the restaurant. For the next several weeks visiting the club was my favorite past time.

All these new experiences began to sink into a routine. There were few medical challenges on the wards and the induction training lectures dealt with some new concepts but nothing unexpected. They were designed primarily to familiarize medical officers with the regulations and routines of the Naval Medical Corps. However, one session focused our attention sharply. We were taken to the Portsmouth Naval Station and lined up next to a contraption consisting of parallel steel rails a few stories high and positioned almost vertically, with a metal seat that rode on the rails.

We were told that as medical officers we may have to travel in fighter craft and use an ejector seat. This exercise was designed to familiarize us with that experience. One by one, we were strapped to the seat and it was catapulted up the rails as if ejected from a plane. Our pulse and blood pressure were measured prior to and after the "ride" and a medical history taken for possible symptoms. One of the officers simply refused to participate because he didn't think he could do it and another became violently seasick. While I was not particularly concerned, I certainly was scared. The experience lasted only a few seconds but it created the sensation of one or two G's pushing me against the seat as it was catapulted up the rails. That day we were let out early to relax, and everyone went straight to the Virginia Beach Club.

I was getting very lonely for Ania and the girls and decided to drive to Detroit for a weekend. It was approximately six hundred miles one-way and, unfortunately, the roads were not the best. I figured I could make it in twelve to fourteen hours plus a couple of hours for meals and rests. Having arranged for medical coverage, I was permitted to leave the BOQ by five PM on Friday and was to return Monday morning. Although leave of this length did not require "leave of absence" documents I knew that going as far as Detroit did theoretically require formal permission. However, I decided to take the chance and go without these documents. I was planning to drive through Richmond, Virginia, and Ron, who had family there, asked to join me.

We left Portsmouth in the early afternoon and were working our way towards Richmond when, some fifty miles out of Portsmouth, a police officer flagged us down. I knew that I had been traveling slightly over the speed limit, about sixty MPH on a highway with a fifty-five MPH speed limit. The officer asked for my driver's license and after noticing that it had been issued in Michigan immediately asked, "Are you going to Michigan?" I reflexively answered "'yes". He glanced at our uniforms and said with a pleasant smile, "I'm certain that you gentleman have leave passes from your posts?" Ron shook his head and responded, "No, but I'm only going to Richmond". The police officer closed the little book he had pulled out after coming over to our car and, while returning to his patrol car, said curtly, "Please follow me to the Justice of Peace". Ron looked at me and started roaring with laughter. "We're in trouble," he announced.

The cops keep a sharp eye out for cars with passengers in uniform because military personnel don't want any problems with traffic police when they are outside the base, especially if they're unauthorized for travel. You're going to get fleeced but don't put up a fight, just pay the speeding ticket on the spot.

I wasn't certain what he meant by this but soon found out. We followed the patrol car over some country roads for about fifteen or twenty minutes and entered, according to a sign on the road, the town of Waverly. The police officer led us into the office of a Justice of Peace and handed him a copy of my traffic ticket. The Justice glanced at it and announced with a severe expression on his cleanly shaven face, "You drove fifteen miles over the speed limit. The fine is $35, no checks!" I quickly calculated that I had only a total of $75 cash in my possession and tried to convince the official that I was going less than fifty-five MPH, the posted speed limit. He looked at the ticket again and said curtly, "The fine is now $45." Ron was tugging at my sleeve, knowing I was about to object again, but as I opened my mouth the Judge looked at me, squinted his eyes and said slowly, "One more word from you and the fine will be $60!" By then Ron was not simply tugging my sleeve, he had almost ripped it off. I reached for my wallet, took out $45 and handed it to the Justice of Peace, who shook his head and said, "Go to the person in the front office and pay her".

When we walked out of the office, I was shaking. "Ron," I whispered, "I only had a total of seventy five dollars with me. This little episode will leave me with only $30 dollars, not enough in case of an emergency." "Relax, don't worry," said Ron with a smile as he pulled out a $50 bill from his wallet and handed it to me. "I'd like to pay half of the fine, so you only owe me $27.50." We spent the rest of the trip to his house joking about this episode and telling stories of our past experiences with law enforcement agencies. I decided not to bring up any of my early experiences in Germany, Poland or the Soviet Union.

After dropping Ron off in Richmond, I decided to take Interstate 64, an excellent highway heading due west. By ten o'clock, the West Virginia Turnpike, illuminated by headlights, loomed in front of me. I turned north and in a few miles I came to a small town called Mabscott and decided to have some supper. Unfortunately, none of the restaurants were open that late in the evening. Only one gas station had its lights on. A sleepy attendant suggested that if I wished to get something to eat I should drive to the town's outskirts where he said there was a 'Dairy Queen', open until midnight. The place was easy to recognize since it was lit up like a Christmas tree and sported on its roof a huge beige cone filled with a twist of frozen ice cream. The tiny parking lot was full of cars with young people playing their radios at maximum volume. They must have been tuned to the same station since I could hear from every car window the song, "Your Cheating Heart" by Hank Williams. Unfortunately the only food choices were chocolate or vanilla "softies" but by this time I was hungry enough to eat anything.

The rest of the trip was uneventful. Dawn was breaking when I reached Columbus, Ohio and I stopped in an all-night café for breakfast. I was so sleepy I dozed off with my head on the table in front of me; however, by midmorning I was hugging and kissing my three girls. That afternoon our friend Junka hosted a huge barbeque in her back yard for our close friends. It was a very happy reunion.

The time in Detroit flew by much too fast. After discussing our immediate plans, Ania and I decided that after completing my Portsmouth stint, I would go directly to Bethesda, Maryland where my permanent assignment station in the Navy would be. I would find an apartment or house to rent and then return to Detroit to pick up the family on the day the movers arrived to pick up our meager belongings.

After my return to Portsmouth, the remaining weeks at the Naval

Hospital passed quickly and by the end of September I was informed that my billet in Bethesda had been secured. My permanent replacement, an Internist named Commander Derek Stokes, arrived and instantly took over the Chairmanship of the Department. One week later, I drove north to report for duty at the Naval Medical Research Institute (NMRI), an arm of the National Naval Medical Center (NNMC) in Bethesda.

My travel orders included an expense account and two days leave to make the trip. This gave me the opportunity to take a leisurely "mini vacation" during the drive to Bethesda, a suburb of Washington, D.C. Looking at the map it appeared that I could drive to Washington through the Shenandoah National Park and it was early October, the perfect time of the year to make this trip. The weather would probably be ideal and the forests would be dressed up in their famous crimson and gold fall colors.

It was a glorious day the last time I drove out of the Portsmouth Naval Hospital and found my way to the Interstate. In no time, I passed through Richmond and stopped at a diner for lunch. Driving east for a few short hours I reached the Appalachian Mountains and the small town of Waynesboro. The town was about five miles from the Blue Ridge Parkway and very close to the Rock Fish Gap Skyline Drive entrance. I decided to check into one of the motels on the main highway as staying here overnight offered a good starting point for the Skyline Drive tomorrow.

That evening I had dinner in a tiny, family owned restaurant in town. The owner, a small, slim man with a thick shock of white hair was happy to talk and in no time I learned a great deal about Waynesboro's colorful past. He talked to me for well over an hour recalling the distant past when the area was called Teasville and many of the fathers of our nation, including George Washington, Thomas Jefferson and others had stayed over night in the Teasville Tavern. The town had been renamed Waynesborough after the important victory of General Anthony Wayne at neighboring Fallen Timbers and officially recognized by the State of Virginia in 1801. I also learned that on March 2, 1865, Waynesboro had been the site of the last Civil War battle fought by the confederate General Jubal Early. When this battle was lost, the entire Shenandoah

Valley was relinquished to Union General Philip Sheridan. This was my first meaningful lesson about the Civil War.

The next morning after a hearty breakfast, I made my way to the Rock Fish Gap Park entrance station. From here, the Skyline Drive weaves north for one hundred and five miles through magnificent mountain ridges to Front Royal, Virginia where the road becomes the Blue Ridge Parkway. As I entered the Drive, masses of turning foliage assaulted my senses and the undulating peaks and valleys were mesmerizing. Within a view minutes I reached the Calf Mountain outlook. It offered an incredible 360-degree view with the almost three thousand-foot Calf Mountain on the Piedmont side to the east and the luscious Shenandoah Valley to the west. I sat in the car drinking in the sights and wishing that Ania and my two girls could be here to enjoy these majestic and superbly peaceful sites with me.

Driving the Parkway was an easy and pleasant experience because its speed limits forced law abiding and nature loving drivers to maintain a pretty leisurely pace. The drive through the Appalachian Mountains provided an endless kaleidoscope of views with parallel ranges connected by cross ranges and scattered hills. One arrived almost imperceptibly at the end of the Appalachian Ridge at Front Royal, a town with an intriguing history. It was settled as early as 1738 and originally known as Lehewtown; however, it was also referred to as "Helltown" due to the mountaineers and river travelers who came there looking for alcohol and women. In 1788, it was incorporated as Front Royal but the origin of that name is uncertain. It was a quaint town with beautiful and historical clapboard houses. I wished I could spend more learning about its history and visiting the fabulous caverns near by.

As I approached Washington, D.C. highway 66 became the Custis Memorial Parkway. Pulling off at a gas station to fill up, I realized it was getting late. I needed to get to NNMC in time to check into the BOQ so any sightseeing would have to be postponed. I proceeded across the Potomac to Bethesda and turned onto Wisconsin Avenue where the Medical Center was located. One couldn't miss the NNMC; it was a sparkling white complex of buildings with a high tower at the center, dominating a huge, lush, green lawn with clumps of trees that separated it from Wisconsin Avenue. A long winding drive brought me to the front entrance at the center of the complex. I parked my car, pulled out my orders and entered the building.

A young sailor behind a desk near the entrance looked up as I handed him my orders. He glanced at them and instantly stood up, saluted crisply and said with a smile on his face, "Sir, NMRI is the complex of buildings behind the NNMC. Please drive around the Medical Center, follow the road and you can't miss it." Following his directions I had no trouble finding the buildings.

As I walked in, I spotted a window on the left side of the room with a non- commissioned officer sitting on the other side:

Oh yes, we were expecting you. I'm Chief Petty Officer Bill Dixon; I'll be working with you. You've been assigned to the Endocrine Division under Dr. Vollmer. First, we'll assign you to your housing so you can move in today. The BOQ is right across the street. Report here tomorrow morning and you'll be introduced to Dr. Vollmer and then meet with the executive officer.

My room was furnished simply but had all the basic amenities and a common bathroom down the hall. Unpacking took me only a few minutes, as I did not have much with me. It was getting late and was time for supper. A little exploration led me to the Officer's Mess where a number of the officers were engaged in lively conversation. The mess was very nice and, as I soon discovered, the buffet was both delicious and extensive. Looking around I noticed a man sitting by himself at one of the tables. He was a slim, almost lanky, young blond fellow with lieutenant's bars on his collar. I introduced myself indicating that I was a new staff member at NMRI and would like to join him for dinner.

I learned that his name was Hugh Van Liew and that he was billeted at NMRI working in the Department of Physiology. Soon we were exchanging information concerning our research interests. His primary interest at that time centered on mechanisms of gas transference across connective tissue membranes using rats as experimental models. He was particularly interested in the mechanisms for permeability of gases through hyaluronic acid, chondroitin sulfate, and collagen components of connective tissue membranes.

My ears perked up. "Hyaluronic acid" I asked. "Yes, why did this catch your attention?" Eagerly I responded: "In my earlier studies, I had to measure the concentration of the enzyme hyaluronidase in testicular tissue. This enzyme, as you know, is depolymerized hyaluronic acid." Well, once we got to talking about research topics, they had to kick us out of the mess at 9:00. When we parted, I promised to look Hugh up in his laboratory as soon as I got organized.

The next day was a whirlwind of events. After I had formally reported to the research institute, I was taken to the Division of Endocrinology on the second floor of the front building. There I met the Director of the Division, Dr. Vollmer. He was a slim man in his fifties, about my height (five foot ten or so). We developed positive feelings towards each other almost instantly. I kept talking and he kept listening; I think his willingness to listen was a strong factor in my liking him so well. He encouraged my enthusiastic flow of research ideas but ultimately stopped me and said something that I had never forgotten during my entire career. "Emil," he said, "ideas are dime a dozen. Its how you bring them to fruition that counts."

With this he got up and said, "Well, let me deposit you back into the capable hands of Bill Dixon, he is a Chief Petty Officer and an excellent laboratory assistant. He knows the Navy and the Naval Regulations book forward and backwards. If there's anything that can be procured in the Navy, he is the one to get it." Dr. Vollmer got up and I followed him out of the office. I'd already met Bill yesterday when checking in and he had looked and acted friendly at that time. However, now I felt a little apprehensive about working with an "old Navy man" and was a little unsure how to manage this situation.

We walked into a huge laboratory where Bill sat at a small desk. When he noticed us, he jumped up and saluted; after a few seconds I realized that I was to respond in kind. Dr. Vollmer laughed saying "Relax fellows, carry on appropriately but don't get carried away". You see, Dr. Vollmer was a civilian employee of the Navy, not an officer. "Bill," he said, "This is Lieutenant Steinberger, he'll be in charge of the laboratory and you'll be his first assistant. Please show him around and introduce him to the rest of the staff. I'm certain he'll want to settle down and bring his family. Let's meet in one week's time at which point we should plan some of our immediate work."

After Dr. Vollmer left, Bill took me around, showed me the laboratory and introduced me to three other sailors who were chemists and laboratory technicians. Once we were done with the 'rounds', he showed me a corner in one of the smaller laboratories with a big desk by the window. "This is your desk and the filing cabinets by the wall will be for your use." "Obviously," he continued, "if you wish to make any changes please let me know and I'll arrange everything to your satisfaction." I had no comments, but I noticed that he kept on casting side-glances at my feet. Finally, I realized that he was looking at my shoes. I looked questioningly at him and he briefly averted his gaze. However, ultimately, he said haltingly, "Sir, in the Navy we keep our shoes polished." For an instant I was taken aback not knowing how to respond to this comment. It is true that over the past few days while I was traveling, I had neglected my shoes. Usually I kept them reasonably clean although I'm certain they were never as shiny as a Marine sergeant's boots. By this time I had had a few weeks experience with the Navy and sensed that I may have a "rank problem". I was now Bill's immediate superior and would have to follow the rules of naval rank. This thought pushed me to make up my mind suddenly.

Kicking off my shoes, I said to Bill with a smile, "Chief, you are absolutely correct. During my travels from the PNH I haven't have a chance to keep my shoes in proper shape, please polish them for me. I'll wait here." I could see that now it was Bill who was taken aback. He looked at me with astonishment, but in a few moments, his face crinkled up in a huge smile. He straightened up, saluted and said smartly, "Yes Sir!" He was back in ten minutes with my shoes in hand and they were shining like a brightly polished frying pan. From this point on our relationship was clearly established and within a few months we became very close friends. This friendship lasted for years after I was discharged from the Navy.

That afternoon I also reported to the Executive Officer of the Institute, Captain Van der Aue. He was a very tall, thin man who exuded friendliness and concern. His interest was in submarine/diving physiology and he had a large and very active program of research in this area at NMRI. This was just a brief formal visit to present myself to the upper echelon. I later became well acquainted with the Captain because we shared some common research interests.

The next day I visited the Personnel Department for advice about housing for my family. My finances were limited. Although I was now earning far more money then ever before in my lifetime we still had to be very careful. We had decided that Ania would stay home with the girls for the two years of my Naval Service so she would no longer be earning a salary. However, we both felt the girls, only three and five years old, would benefit greatly from having their mother with them full time.

I was advised that Bethesda was very expensive but Rockville, Maryland, less than ten miles to the north on Rockville Pike had very adequate housing at more reasonable prices. A real estate agent drove me to Rockville and showed me a number of houses on quiet streets with nice front lawns and back yards. One appealed to me instantly; a red clapboard house with a white porch, a backyard with a swing for the kids, and a huge oak tree. As I was inspecting the house, a neighbor came over with her two sons. The boys were approximately our daughters' ages and they seemed very friendly. Soon after, her husband joined us and he also seemed very nice and intelligent. This tipped the scales. I put down a deposit and we became the proud tenants of a small three-bedroom house. These neighbors, the Weigles, did in fact become very good friends and our daughters loved playing with their sons.

When the time came to move the family from Detroit to Rockville I applied for a week's leave and took off for Detroit. Ania had arranged for a company to handle our few belongings and our move became more of an exciting vacation trip than a chore for us.

CHAPTER 2
WILL I MAKE IT?

Ania and the girls loved the new house and our lives quickly settled into an easy routine. I was finally able to turn my entire attention to the job at hand, the biomedical research at NMRI. My indoctrination to the Institute was quick and simple; I had to formally sign in and out every day and one or two nights a week I had to stand watch, make rounds and be the Officer of the Day. I was expected to wear a uniform every day when on duty and when traveling outside of Bethesda on Navy business. Otherwise, life was casual and I was conducting research at my own pace.

The subsequent week was filled with meetings. I again met briefly with Captain Van der Aue and mentioned to him one of my research interests, the effect of heat on sperm production. He expressed some interest in this topic, particularly in view of his specialization in the physiology of individuals exposed to the often hot environment of submarines. Later I was introduced by Bill to Dr. Jack Christian, a renowned Population Ecologist and former naval officer, who was currently employed at the Institute as a civilian scientist. He was interested in the effects of "population pressures" caused by overcrowding on the physiology of individual members of the population. He had coined the term "population pressure" and pioneered the evolution of this area of investigation. We rapidly developed good feelings towards each other and soon became research collaborators. The rest of the day was spent with Dr. Vollmer discussing the various research directions I could pursue at the Institute. I summarized for him my general research interests, the former directions I had pursued and possible research avenues to be followed at NMRI.

The research results of my latest studies had been presented the previous spring at a scientific meeting. I could not do it personally because of time conflict with my internship so the paper was presented by my colleague Anthony, a graduate student and collaborator in this study. The work dealt with a chemical compound, a thiophen, that we had learned had a similar effect on the testes as ionizing radiation. We were very excited to find a radiomimetic chemical (a substance with effects on tissues mimicking those of x-rays, or ionizing radiation) that affected the testes. This could serve as an experimental model for the study of mechanisms dealing with effects of ionizing radiation on the testes.

I was interested in demonstrating specificity of response to different noxious agents in cells of the germinal epithelium of the testes. My hypothesis of cellular specificity of response could lead to a better understanding of the mechanisms involved in sperm formation, and possibly lead to the development of new methods of treating men whose testes are incapable of producing adequate sperm to affect fertilization. It might also suggest a way to safely and reversibly inhibit sperm production at will, possibly leading to the development of an effective male contraceptive. I had been pursuing these concepts with my graduate school advisor, Professor W.O. Nelson (W.O.), while still in medical school. There were so many ideas to discuss with Dr. Vollmer; however, the day was coming to an end so he suggested we continue our discussion the next morning.

Returning to the laboratory, I was surprised to see Bill still lingering there. He was obviously curious, "How was it?" he asked, "Did the boss tell you what experiments to run?" I was amused but pleasantly surprised by his personal interest. "Well," I responded, "we had a long talk. I described some of the research avenues I've followed in the past and some of my underlying ideas. However there is still a lot to talk about, no decisions of any kind were made." As we talked, Jimmy, a young sailor with the rank of Seaman and Bill's right hand man, walked in. I was surprised to see him there so late and asked Bill why everyone was still there. As I asked, the second laboratory assistant, John, a Seaman Apprentice also came in. I couldn't contain myself; I started laughing and asked, "What gives, fellows? Is this an after hours symposium?" Bill, speaking for the others said "Sir, we all are very curious to know how you got along with Dr. Vollmer and are looking forward impatiently to learning what direction the research will take. As you have probably learned by now, Dr. Vollmer is a man of few words."

I tried to put everyone at ease, repeating that nothing had been decided and that he and I were to meet again the following morning. It was a pleasure to see that good will, cooperation and interest in and anticipation of doing exciting research was developing. Everyone seemed to relax a bit and I suggested we meet the next afternoon to begin planning some of our joint activities.

When I returned home, I was in no mood to play with the girls; I wanted to talk to Ania. They; however, had other plans. They started talking excitedly about their great adventure - a trip to the center of our little suburb. Rockville is one of the oldest towns in Maryland, dating back to Colonial America. During the Revolutionary War, it was known as Hungerford's Tavern. In 1801, the Maryland General Assembly changed the name to Rockville, probably because of its proximity to Rock Creek. It remained a small sleepy town of a few hundred families until the late 1940s when the National Institutes of Health (NIH) and the National Naval Medical Center were established. After that its population began to grow rapidly.

For the girls, a trip "downtown" to visit the few stores there was a treat and Ania loved being able to take them around, to show them their little world and to participate in their lives with intimacy and enthusiasm. Until now, she had directed much of her energy and attention to either school or work at the laboratory. But for the next two years she could devote her time almost exclusively to the family.

By the time the girls finally settled down I was too exhausted to discuss my experiences at the Institute with Ania but I couldn't fall asleep. Memories of medical school in Iowa and my internship in Detroit were on my mind as I tried to evaluate today's experiences at the Institute. I began developing a deeply rooted feeling that, despite my training and interest in interacting with patients, my main direction in life should be basic biomedical research. The down side of course would be the associated economic sacrifices. I had wrestled with this decision earlier during medical and graduate school as well as during my internship. However, today's discussion with Dr. Vollmer and the brief interaction with Bill and the two Seaman made me wish for an exciting future in research. While these thoughts were crystallizing in my mind, other thoughts began to surface and develop into more coherent ideas.

Interactions with my colleagues and professors at school and in the various hospitals, as well as with scientists at national meetings, had opened my mind to the fact that something enormous was evolving in this country; something I could only identify as the inception of a "golden age" in American Medicine. I also perceived that this golden age was being ushered in by the burgeoning number of knowledge-hungry, research oriented young people entering the field who were willing to make personal sacrifices for the progress of science and medicine.

Unquestionably, the G.I. Bill of Rights had had a significant impact on this issue by allowing many who could not do it before, join the ranks and experience the success and intoxication of science! With these thoughts swirling in my mind, I must have fallen asleep because the next thing I remember was Ania's repeated attempts to wake me up in the morning. During breakfast she brought me out of the clouds to focus the realities of daily life. The Jewish high holy days were coming and she felt strongly that we should invite our parents to celebrate with us in our first real home since we had married.

The next several weeks flew by in a dream. I met Lee Greenbaum, a Lieutenant Commander involved in underwater physiology and Connie, a whiz in metabolism. He was particularly involved with studies related to carbohydrate metabolism, its biochemical pathways, and the 'Krebs Cycle' and oxygen consumption. I also met Marshall Nirenberg, also a 'metabolism man', and Connie's colleague from the University of Michigan where both had received their PhD degrees in the same department. However, at that time the most influential person in my life was to be Lieutenant Hugh Van Liew. When I'd met him initially in the Officers' Club I hadn't foreseen this. Within the next couple of weeks we met several times and I became fascinated with his membrane diffusion studies, particularly with his ideas on the use of hyaluronidase to speed up diffusion through membranes and a hyaluronidase inhibitor, like hesperedin, to block it.

We learned that field studies were being conducted to administer whole blood into the abdominal cavity for the purpose of transfusion under military field conditions. We proposed that it would be of great benefit to transfuse blood in this way to soldiers on the front lines and to be able to either speed up its absorption with hyaluronidase or slow it down temporarily with a hyaluronidase inhibitor, depending upon the patient's clinical condition and the circumstances in the field. We proposed to conduct studies in rats to learn if our hypothesis would work. This was my first project at NMRI and it quickly came to fruition.

At the 1957 national spring meetings of the Federated Societies, we were able to present our preliminary data dealing with the mechanisms of red blood cells absorption from the peritoneal cavity of the rat. I was elated; this was my first work totally independent of W.O., my advisor and mentor. He was the man responsible for my acceptance to graduate and medical schools, which allowed me to complete my education. He had become one of the most important influences in my life and I remained deeply grateful to him throughout my life.

While working on the membrane permeability project, I initiated several other studies directly related to my original research interests involving the testes. First, I decided to pursue an investigation on the effects of "radiomimetic" substances on the testes. One substance that I found particularly intriguing was triethylene melamine (TEM). It had a destructive effect specifically on immature germinal cells, the spermatogonia, in the testes. Having a testes model with normal development of germinal cells leading to the formation of mature and fertile spermatozoa, but whose least mature, ' mother type' germinal cells were absent, provided a very desirable research tool. Everyone in the laboratory was excited about working on this project. Jimmy, in particular, found the project to his liking and soon I was able to let him conduct most of the experimental work.

Another project I was very eager to initiate dealt with the effects of heat on the testes. The issues dealing with this project were complex, however, not only from a technical viewpoint but also due to political considerations. It had been demonstrated in the past with a reasonable degree of certainty that even relatively mild elevations of the intra-testicular temperature produced damage to its germinal epithelium. I wondered whether the relatively high temperatures in submarines might be sufficient to cause an adverse effect on the crew. Naval personnel immediately asked what degree of elevation in temperature would cause damage but to date there was no data to answer this question with any degree of precision. I was advised to approach the issue experimentally and design appropriate studies in lower species. This appeared to me to be a reasonable request and when I discussed it with Bill I was pleasantly surprised that he became excited about the project and was full of ideas about how to proceed.

I also had an idea that would call upon Bill's "connections" in order to find the most effective approach. I was vaguely familiar with 'thermocouples', tiny devices used to measure temperatures in places inaccessible to customary thermometers. When I mentioned this to Bill, his eyes lit up:

> Sir, I have just the thing we may need! The Bell Telephone Company recently developed tiny thermal resistors they named Thermistors. These devices can measure temperatures with exquisite precision. They can be placed in a tiny area and will generate a signal and transmit the information about temperatures in this area to an electronic device at a distance.

I was ready to jump up with joy and hug him. "Are these devices sufficiently small to be mounted inside the tip of a tiny hypodermic needle?" I asked. "I think so," he responded, "however, I'll have to run down to the machine shop to get the information."

The high holy days arrived and so did our parents. They admired our new rental house and enjoyed the girls, repeating constantly, "They grew so much! They are delightful young ladies, not babies any more!" We both enjoyed having our parents with us and particularly enjoyed observing their happy interaction with their granddaughters. This was our parents' first trip to Washington and since they stayed with us through two weekends, I had an opportunity to show them Washington D.C. and the Capitol.

Although I had been there before, it didn't minimize my awe as we entered the Capitol Rotunda. It was wonderfully impressive despite the fact that the building was overrun by tourists and Congress was not in session. After a brief visit to Capitol Hill, we meandered slowly to the Washington Monument, the Reflecting Pool and later to the Lincoln Memorial. Everyone agreed that the soaring Washington Monument, with its expanse of white marble glittering in the sun, was one of the most beautiful sights we had ever encountered. However, no one volunteered to climb the eight hundred and ninety eight steps to the top of the obelisk.

The weather was perfect, the sun was shining, and there was essentially no wind. The surface of the water in the reflecting pool was almost still, rendering the image of the Monument with almost perfect fidelity. We sat on the grass enjoying the view. Even the girls sat still, mesmerized by the sights. At the opposite end of the Reflecting Pool, we could see the Lincoln Memorial, also of white marble, glittering in the distance. We got up and slowly walked towards it. As we got closer, we could clearly discern the classic lines of a Greek Doric temple. The rectangular structure was surrounded by a row of stately columns over thirty feet tall, delineating the inner space. As we approached it the girls ran up the stairs and over to Lincoln's seated figure. They certainly didn't appreciate the solemnity of the moment or severity of Lincoln's facial expression. The only issue they were concerned with was how to climb up the statue to sit in his lap. They were bitterly disappointed when I explained that this would not be possible.

By then everyone was getting hungry and I suggested that on the way home we stop for dinner at O'Donnell's, one of the more famous seafood places and according to some of the officers at the Institute, the latest rage in seafood restaurants in Bethesda. It had opened only the year before as the second location, the original being in the District. It was run by the same owners who had opened the original restaurant during the Great Depression. I have to admit that I was trying to impress our parents by showing them that I knew of a fancy, high-class restaurant. From the Mall, I found my way to Wisconsin Avenue and took it north to Bethesda. I hadn't eaten at O'Donnell's before but knew its location on Wisconsin Avenue in Bethesda. The restaurant and its food were fabulous.

Our parents, while impressed by the restaurant, were somewhat ambivalent towards its menu. Having arrived fairly recently from central

Europe where they had survived the Second World War, their culinary experiences hadn't included many seafood dishes or American style preparations. I had learned to very much enjoy shrimp and wanted my father to taste them. When I tried to explain them to him and said they were shell fish, it became clear that they would not pass muster with him. He liked regular fish, however, so I employed a little deception by telling him that the restaurant prepared small fish sautéed in butter. I knew that he liked regular fish and that he liked butter!

Once he tasted the sautéed shrimp he loved it, saying it was the best fish he had ever tasted He even requested that mother learn how to prepare this dish. For years to come, whenever we took our parents to a seafood restaurant, I would see the waiter beforehand and tell him to offer us a special dish of "sautéed small fish". My father would always order it although I was certain that if I had told him they were shellfish he would never have eaten them.

The holidays passed and my parents returned to New York. The weather turned rainy and chilly and the trees began to lose their leaves. I was busier than ever with all three projects moving at a rapid pace. The machine shop staff had managed to mount a thermistor inside the bore of a 24-gauge hypodermic needle and was in the process of designing the electronic circuitry and measuring devices for the "thermistor-needle". They also were helping to redesign a water bath that would maintain the water temperature with great precision. All of this was in preparation for the experiments dealing with the effects of heat on the testes.

I soon learned that Chief Dixon (Bill) had tremendous connections, not only at the Institute but also throughout a large segment of the Naval Medical Corps because he had served at various Naval Stations at one time or another. This was a stroke of luck for me. As time went by, we began to function like a well-oiled machine. Bill supervised the laboratory staff and was intimately involved with the project dealing with the effects of heat. Jimmy plugged along with the TEM project, and John was helping each of us where necessary. The TEM project had progressed sufficiently that I had to train Jimmy to conduct microscopic evaluation of the tissues and analyze the data. I had hopes that we would have adequate data to demonstrate the specificity of TEM's effect on the testes by the winter of 1957 and be able to submit a paper for presentation at the 1957 annual spring meetings of one of the scientific societies.

During December 1956, I spent considerable time in Connie's laboratory fascinated with his metabolic studies using different tissues as models. At this time, the focus in testicular research had been slowly but steadily moving from complex microscopic and cytochemical studies of the germinal epithelium to studies looking at various changes in the metabolic pathways and the effects of hormones and various other substances on it.

Connie was focusing on studies of oxygen consumption using the then famous Warburg Apparatus, a large and complex contraption. Since Connie looked at various types of tissue, I suggested that we use the apparatus to look at the metabolic behavior of testicular tissue. When preliminary results from the pilot experiments became available I was flabbergasted. They were essentially opposite of what I had predicted on theoretical basis. Even Connie was shocked since he had fully agreed with my original thinking. "This needs confirmation and some thought," he announced and proceeded to outline additional experiments. His friend Marshall Nirenberg, who was visiting the laboratory that morning, also weighed in, suggesting even bolder experiments. Marshall worked at NIH as a postdoctoral fellow. I was impressed and happy to see his interest in my work and pointed out that we were approaching the holiday season and should probably defer thinking about a new series of experiments until after the first of the year. Everyone quickly agreed.

We had the first heavy snow early in December. The roads in the neighborhood were very slick. However, the Highway Department cleaned the main roads and I had no major problems driving to work. The girls were having a great time sledding on the new snow in front of our house with the Weigle boys. The street sloped slightly, particularly in front of their house. This provided excellent conditions for sledding and they were busy with that most of the day.

Since my arrival at the Institute, the novelty of service in the Navy and drive to initiate a research program had totally consumed my energy. I hadn't even considered taking time off for leisure activities. The first snowfall, however, reminded me that we should probably arrange a ski trip. Seeing the girls sledding was very seductive and on the spur of the moment we decided to take some time off between Christmas and the New Year for a ski trip. I had to inquire at the Institute concerning the number of days I had available and how to go about arranging the furlough.

We left early in the morning on Christmas Day and planned to return on January 1. On a day that was clear and dry we headed to the Crystal Lodge in North Conway, New Hampshire. We planned to ski at Cranmore Mountain, seat of the ski school headed by Hannes Schneider, the famous Austrian ski instructor frequently called the "father of modern alpine skiing". In fact he had introduced America to the Alberg method of skiing. Pauline was five and Inette was only three but I felt that both should start their ski careers. North Conway would be the perfect place to initiate them to the fun of skiing. I had my own skis, but Ania and the girls had to rent theirs so the first day was spent primarily investigating the lodge and the ski area, renting the skis and trying out the lifts.

At that time skiers were transported up the hills in little cars riding on very elaborate platforms with cogwheels that pulled them up the hill. We had to take our skis off, get on the platform and from there quickly get into a little moving car. There was a beginners hill at the foot of the lift and we decided that this would be where we would begin to teach the girls. In the afternoon with the sun shining warmly on the sparkling white slope, we strapped the skis to their boots and started teaching them how to climb up the hill. It began as great fun, but soon it became drudgery for the girls. They were still very young; they wanted to have fun but lacked the discipline necessary to sustain this exertion and still had to overcome their initial fears. I realized that it would take a great deal of patience not to discourage them during this early stage of the learning process.

The weather was perfect, although a bit cold. We were wind and sun burned but happy and invigorated. The girls had made definite progress on their skiing skills and Ania significantly improved her technique. We decided to drive all the way back to Rockville without stopping. Luckily, we were able to drive most of the way from New England to New York on the recently opened Adirondack Northway. Then the New Jersey Turnpike, a superhighway, took us almost to Philadelphia, a short distance from Rockville. The fourteen-hour trip was quite grueling; however, Ania and I alternated driving and the girls behaved like little angels. Two tasty meals in restaurants along the way, where they felt like young ladies, worked miracles at getting their cooperation and maintaining their good mood during the long trip.

The new rear exploded like a bombshell. Dr. Vollmer called me to his office and wanted to learn the details of my research and plans for the future. I was petrified. Did I do something wrong? Was the direction of research wrong? Was the progress inadequate? Apparently, this was not it. He was actually rather pleased, particularly after I gave him the details on my collaborative research with Dr. Van Liew and told him about our plans to submit a scientific paper for presentation at the Spring Meetings of the Federated Societies. He was overjoyed to hear about my discussions with Connie concerning our collaboration on studies of carbohydrate metabolism in the testes. He agreed that the general direction of research on the reproductive system physiology was moving away from morphology into the area of metabolism, and agreed that studies on the involvement of carbohydrate pathways in the process of spermatogenesis would be quite appropriate at that time. He also agreed that a new approach to the study of spermatogenesis using the new quantitative cytometric concepts and methods offered novel research avenues. After the first round of discussions, I was pleased, but not entirely clear as to where the discussion was going. When he suggested that we should meet again the next day my anxiety level shot sky high. I couldn't fathom what he had on his mind nor could I wait for the next day.

That night I slept poorly. Up to then, I thought that I'd slowly but steadily been carving a niche for myself in this fabulous adventure, the explosive growth of biomedical knowledge. The initial discussion with Dr. Vollmer, however, placed a damper on my hopes. Why? I couldn't wait for morning to continue my discussions with him.

I woke up in a cold sweat from an uneasy slumber and recalled that I was supposed to spend the entire day with Connie. We were to put the final touches on the experimental design for the initial studies dealing with carbohydrate metabolism in testicular tissue, and I was to learn the use of the Warburg apparatus. I had never used one before and it was still a mysterious piece of equipment to me. I couldn't postpone this meeting since Connie had prepared the apparatus for the procedure, which was a complex and time-consuming effort. On the other hand, I dreaded asking Dr. Vollmer to postpone our meeting. I had no choice, however, so at nine o'clock I marched down the hall to Dr. Vollmer's office. Opening the door with trepidation, I tried to formulate a petition in my head to ask for a postponement of our meeting when, seeing my crestfallen face, he started laughing, "I know, I know, Connie talked to me last night on the way home and told me about today's schedule. No problem, we'll talk tomorrow." I felt as if a heavy weight had been lifted off my chest. I had not wanted to offend my Chief and his management of the situation struck me as very magnanimous; I couldn't thank him enough.

That day Connie and I agreed upon the final details of the experimental protocol and his technician was teaching me how to use the Warburg apparatus. We finished before the end of the day and on the way out, I stopped by Jack Christian's Population Dynamics Division. His laboratories were located in the animal facility which was a large three-story building attached to the main building of the Institute by a covered passageway. In addition to his labs, there were several other research facilities and a general animal facility in that building.

Jack's laboratories occupied several huge rooms housing ingeniously constructed cages that permitted him to conduct research on several established "free growing" populations of mice. These studies involved experimental manipulations of the populations and physiologic as well as pathologic investigations. His studies clearly overlapped the field of reproductive biology so we had a great deal in common. The primary reason for stopping in his office at that time was to inquire whether he had any ideas about what could have been behind Dr. Vollmer's mysterious meetings with me. However, he had very little to offer by way of clarification and I went home still in the dark concerning this mystery.

The next day I couldn't wait to see Dr. Vollmer again. Apparently, he was also eager to see me because the minute I walked in, Jimmy was waiting for me to say that Dr. Vollmer was expecting me in his office. The first few minutes were spent exchanging in pleasantries when he suddenly commented, "I hear that yesterday you spent a lot of time in Connie's laboratories and made quite an effort to learn how to use the Warburg apparatus ." I turned crimson to the roots of my hair and stammered haltingly, "Yes, we are planning to collaborate on studies of carbohydrate metabolism in testicular tissue. I hadn't mentioned this to you before because it became a reality only this week." He smiled in his characteristic way, barely opening his mouth. I actually didn't know how to act and what to say. Probably he should have been apprised of my preliminary discussions with Connie earlier in the game. Before I collected my thoughts, he interjected, "That's great; you are really developing a credible research program. Is there anything else I need to know?"

> Yes, Chief Petty Officer Dixon has been extremely effective in helping me to devise a new tool for the measurements of intra-testicular temperatures in experimental animals. The tool is a thermistor mounted in a small hypodermic needle that will measure temperatures in the interior of the testicles. Bill has friends in the electronic shop and when I explained the problem to him, he and his friends designed and fabricated this "needle-thermistor". He did a tremendous job and I'm very grateful to him. Now we will be able to truly measure intra testicular temperatures and study the effects of elevated temperatures in animal testicles and later hopefully in humans.

Dr. Vollmer was shaking his head affirmatively while looking at me intently. After I finished he got up, walked to the window and started gazing out. Finally, he turned around and said quickly, "I have two things to tell you. You'll be surprised, but listen to what I have to say." He was obviously uncomfortable and I could barely hear his words as he said:

> When I decided to have you join me here at the Endocrine Section I was looking forward to at least two years of great collaborative research. However, in the interim, an offer came to me that I could not resist. I'll be leaving in six weeks.

I was listening but again I could not believe my ears. It was déjà vu! I thought I was back at the Portsmouth Naval Hospital listening to Dr. Cottrell. Should I call it luck, or was it a curse? Was this a good opportunity or unnecessary meddling with my attempts to establish a research program? I thought back over the past and found a series of events that had thrown me unexpectedly into very favorable situations that had worked out well for me. Was this just another piece of good luck in a chain of miraculous happenings? These thoughts were churning in my mind at lightening speed and I was definitely not prepared for what I heard next.

Dr. Vollmer looked at me with a firm gaze and, as if having arrived at a decision, quickly returned to his chair behind the desk and continuing to look at me slowly and deliberately said:

> I made a recommendation to the Commanding Officer of the NMRI that you be appointed Chief of the Endocrine Section upon my departure. He accepted my recommendation and you will shortly receive the appropriate appointment documents.

This was not a temporary, interim appointment like the one at the Portsmouth Naval Hospital. This was my first real, serious professional promotion. I opened my mouth in attempt to say something when he raised his hand, saying, "Let me finish. There's a lot more that you must hear; however first I need to ask you a question. Are you familiar with the, the National Institutes of Health (NIH)?" By now I was shell shocked, bewildered, and somewhat confused. I was quite familiar with NIH through W.O. He was connected to NIH and had been the recipient of one of its earliest research grants, awarded for his research on male reproduction. My response to Dr. Vollmer's inquiry was a simple, "Yes". He looked at me somewhat surprised, raised an eyebrow and asked, "What do you know?"

While I'd been in Iowa working on my degree and conducting research, I was daily in the company of young investigators whose conversations frequently strayed to the NIH. They had all hoped to obtain NIH grants, a critical pursuit among the medical school faculty. I had become interested in the methods and the avenues for obtaining research funding, and also particularly interested in the role of government versus private sources of funding. NIH was at the center of these issues. I was brimming with information on this topic and looking for an opportunity to talk about it. I started slowly:

> Well, the NIH is an agency of the United States Department

of Health that actually grew out of a one-room laboratory (called the Laboratory of Hygiene) created in 1887 at the Marine Hospital Service, the predecessor of the US Public Health Service. Initially the laboratory dealt with research related to microbiology and infectious diseases. Gradually the areas of research expanded to physiology, biochemistry, pathology, etc.. The Marine Hospital Service was later reorganized and renamed the 'Public Health and Marine Hospital Service' (PH-MHS, and later just MHS).

The Laboratory of Hygiene became the Hygienic Laboratory toward the end of the century and subsequently, a convoluted history of Congressional acts and reorganizations of the Service led to a revision of the MHS Service Act and the Laboratory of Hygiene became the National Institute of Health. By the end of WWII, the Public Health Service Act was passed and the successful grant program of the National Cancer Institute was expanded to the NIH and its budget began to soar. It has become the primary agency of the United States Government dealing with biomedical and health-related research. Some of the research is conducted within the NIH campus itself, the 'Intramural Research', while the majority is 'Extramural Research' conducted outside the NIH.

Finally I stopped, realizing that perhaps I shouldn't have delivered so long a speech. Dr. Vollmer looked at me with disbelief on his face, and finally exclaimed, "Where did you acquire this bag of fancy "trivia"? My face again turned red as I realized that I may have been bragging a bit. He only laughed, "Are you familiar with the 'Study Section' program at the NIH?" By now, I was getting confused and upset wasn't sure how to react. I was superficially familiar with this program. NIH awarded extramural research grants based on the recommendations provided by members of these 'study sections'. However, by now there was so much damage and confusion to my psyche I concluded that it would be better for me to listen rather then talk.

Well, I see that you are familiar with some aspects of NIH and the Study Sections. This should make the job of explaining these details easier. As you probably know the Study Sections were created by NIH to provide groups of specialists in various areas of biomedical sciences to review and evaluate applications for financial support of research projects proposed by investigators. Members of these Study Sections are selected from institutions throughout the country by a special NIH committee. I am the representative of the Navy to the Endocrine Study Section. Since I am leaving the Institute, I have to find a substitute to complete my term, which lasts through the end of 1958. I'm requesting that the Navy Medical Corps recommend you for my position on the Study Section. Shortly I'll be seeing Dr. Shannon, the recently appointed Director of NIH, on unrelated business, and will mention to him my recommendation.

My head was swimming; I needed to think through these issues privately, calmly, and thoroughly. This one-two punch was a bit too much for me. I got up, tersely thanked Dr. Vollmer, asked if I could see him again soon and left without hearing his response.

For the next several days, I actually avoided Dr. Vollmer and felt lucky that he didn't come to the laboratory to see me. I had to take stock of all the irons I had in the fire and find a way to gracefully decline the offers he had made during our meeting. A list of all my research projects, proposed, initiated and fully active, shocked me. The expression, "spreading yourself too thin" was not just a colloquialism to me any more. Indeed, I realized that I was spread very thin. Adding to it the responsibility of a supervisory position and membership on a NIH Study Section seemed an almost impossible task.

This entire scenario instilled an icy fear in me but then I started thinking about the past. This situation certainly didn't compare in its severity with my experiences in Europe during the war. The pressure was also not as intense as my experiences during medical school or internship. Slowly it dawned on me that actually I should be happy. An extensive research program, this time totally under my direction, was underway, an unbelievable offer for a professional advancement had been made and in addition, I had been given an opportunity to join one of the most prestigious medical research consulting groups in the Nation.

Dr. Vollmer was in his office when I called. "Come over now," I could hear his even, low voice at the other end of the line, "let's talk it over". When I walked into his office he was putting on his coat, "I thought," he said, "that we should have our talk over a cup of coffee. Get your coat and let's go over to the Officers' Club." The Officers' Club was a beautiful building on the Medical Center grounds, a short walk from the Institute. It had a very elegant restaurant, a ballroom and various meeting rooms.

A couple of months back I had joined the Officers Toastmasters International that met weekly at the Officers Club. The Toastmasters were a great bunch of officers, some very young and some who were already retired. This eclectic group would get together weekly to practice public speaking. For me, with my deficits in the English language, this opportunity was a Godsend. Also I had occasionally brought Ania to the restaurant for a fancy dinner to celebrate an important occasion. Thus, I was quite familiar with the club and surprised that Dr. Vollmer suggested having our meeting there.

After we placed our orders, I looked up questioningly and he smiled and said, "Emil, I wish you would call me Irwin. We've known each other long enough". I returned his smile and replied, "Well, I'm not accustomed to calling my superiors by their first names." "But," he interrupted me, "I'm not your superior any more. Yesterday a memo was drafted to you by my Commanding Officer appointing you the Chief of the Endocrine Division. You should get it today or tomorrow, at the latest." The dread I felt when he first proposed the position to me was no longer there. Actually, I felt stimulated and happy. "I'm sorry to see you leave," I said. "I wish you would have stayed. I was looking forward to working under your supervision and am quite certain that I would have enjoyed our interactions. However, under the circumstances I can only say, thank you, and promise to do my best." Here Irwin interrupted me:

> Yes, but we still have more than a week prior to my departure. I'd like to spend some time with you talking about the Division and its research; this may be of help to you in supervising it. In addition, I would like to talk to you

about the Endocrine Study Section at NIH. I've received a communication from them that you have been appointed as my replacement. Within the next several days, you should get the formal letter of appointment.

The waiter came over to our table waiting patiently until Irwin finished his sentence to ask whether we wished to order anything else. "Yes," exclaimed Irwin, "how about an appetizer and a glass of wine. I'd love a nice crab salad. Emil, you must be familiar with the Chesapeake Bay crabs - they are the best in the country!" Actually, I was not familiar with Chesapeake Bay crabs but was happy to try this delicacy. "Certainly," I agreed with Irwin, "let's try some."

After a glass of wine and some of the delicious crabmeat, my tongue found considerable freedom. I inundated Irwin with questions about the Study Section and he answered them all patiently and enlarged on some of the issues. "Remember," he said:

> You'll be in the company of some of the top scientists in the nation. Some have very strong opinions and the discussions become very lively at times. You will have the opportunity to meet people like Dr. Wilhelmi, the man who isolated and purified the growth hormone from the pituitary gland, Dr. Albert who purified human gonadotrophins from the urine, Drs. Dorfman and Eik Nes, the gurus of steroid biochemistry and steroid hormone biosynthesis, as well as a number of other equally remarkable luminaries.

While he was talking, my head began swimming again. I was not sure whether this was due to the second glass of wine or the narration. The longer I listened, the more convinced I became that as a member of the Study Section, I would be functioning in a rarified atmosphere. The Study Section, most likely, would be much too sophisticated for my level of development in the sciences. As my self-confidence continued to shrink, I could hear Irwin trying to build it up.

> I've talked to you on number of occasions about science and you have a good grasp of the literature in the area of reproductive endocrinology. Your criticism of ongoing studies has been sound and you have considerable imagination in

designing research protocols. All of these characteristics are requirements for a good Study Section member. What you lack is experience. This is why I would like to advise you to tread the waters carefully.

The Study Section meets quarterly. Actually, the next meeting will be next week and I would like you to join me. It will be my last meeting and I will report and make recommendations on the grant requests assigned to me. This will give you an opportunity to see how the Study Section operates and will give you some insight as to how write the reviews. In a month or so you'll receive copies of the grants assigned to you to review and report on at the subsequent meeting.

I could hear him talking as if from a great distance. The impact and the importance of the appointment to a Study Section was just dawning on me and, I think, the wine and heaping plate of ice cold crabmeat were exerting an influence on me as well.

The following week I saw Irwin almost daily, both before and after the Study Section meeting that I attended with him. My mind was on fire. Between that and the formalities of taking over the Division, there was not much time for anything else. I was very grateful to Bill Dixon and the other two seamen for their ability to continue our work during that week without much input from me. This was the first time in my life that I had assumed executive responsibilities and it was a scary novelty.

Bill continued to be my greatest asset. He knew all the naval regulations and, most importantly, had the uncanny ability to accomplish almost any task or procure almost any thing from the Navy. At least this was my impression. He even had a rare private typewriter on his desk and was able to create documents and fill out forms. I had no personal secretary because secretarial work was done in a typing pool. However, Bill was familiar with all the necessary reports and was able to prepare them on his own typewriter. This was another major advantage for me.

CHAPTER 3
TAKING TO THE WAVES

Winter was slowly easing. The climate in Maryland was much milder than in Detroit and I realized that I actually enjoyed this change. Winter was great when experiencing it on skis in the mountains but driving every day to work on ice and slush was a real chore. Living here was a pleasant respite.

One of my papers had been accepted for presentation at the annual meetings of the Federated Societies so I would soon be giving my first paper since I'd entered the Navy. It dealt with work carried out since I had arrived at the NMRI dealing with the effects of hyaluronidase and its inhibitor on the mechanism of blood absorption from the peritoneal (abdominal) cavity. This study was a preliminary step in investigations concerning the possibility of administering whole blood transfusions via the abdominal cavity on the battlefield. Doing so could circumvent some of the difficulties of using intravenous transfusions in the field where a needle could be easily dislodged from the vein.

At home life had settled into a routine. Other than some advanced evening courses in biochemistry she was taking at NIH, Ania devoted her time to the girls. Occasionally I was needed for some research activity, usually related to the experimental animals or a scheduled watch duty at the Institute but for the most part, weekends were devoted to family enjoyment. We would spend entire days at the various fabulous institutions in the District of Columbia. The National Gallery of Art was good for at least two solid weeks and we could visit the Smithsonian Institutions indefinitely. The girls were remarkably resilient; as long as we stopped occasionally for a hot dogs and Coke they were happy to trudge with us through the galleries and museums for days. These trips would leave lasting impressions on all of us. Pauline went on to earn a degree from the Pennsylvania Academy of Fine Arts and Inette became an avid art collector.

As the spring progressed I discovered a little pond on the grounds of the NNMC full of nice size crappies, which are beautiful fresh water sunfish. There I introduced the girls to fishing and it became a must do activity for them in the coming summer.

At that time two unexpected things happened. First, Jerry Sherman, my classmate in graduate school, called me. Apparently he learned that I had volunteered for the Navy and was stationed at NMRI in Bethesda. Since he was in the Naval Reserve and needed to spend four weeks during the summer on active duty, it occurred to him that he might spend that time doing research with me. I thought it would be fun to have him in the laboratory for a few weeks but couldn't figure out what research project could be accomplished during such a brief period. As I summarized for him the currently active projects in the laboratory, he interrupted me exclaiming, "I have an idea! Currently I'm investigating various methods for freezing mouse semen and using an artificial insemination system to test the fertilization power of semen that has been stored frozen. We could use this artificial insemination system to study the possible direct in-vivo and in-vitro effects of Triethylenelamine (TEM) on the fertility potential of the semen. These would be very quick experiments, providing us with answers in just a few weeks.

This was a good idea. I had been wondering about the possible anti fertility effects of TEM on mature spermatozoa. These experiments would fit perfectly into our research program. It would be a matter of some simple paper work and Jerry would spend this August at NMRI. Bill, of course, knew all the ins and outs of naval bureaucracy and he immediately got the ball rolling.

The second surprise came during a conversation at lunch in the officer's mess hall with Lee Greenbaum, whom I'd met before. While telling me about the results of his latest experiments concerning diving physiology and issues confronting submariners, he mentioned that the following weekend he was launching his sailboat. My ears instantly perked up. He owns a sailboat! Sailing had always been a dream of mine. I was so excited, I rudely interrupted him. "May Ania and I join you this weekend and help with the boat launching?" He started laughing, "If you'd like to come I'll be there by 8:00 AM. I'll draw you a little map that will explain how to get to the dock since the place can be a little confusing."

I couldn't wait for Sunday. Using Lee's detailed directions Ania and I arrived precisely on time at the boat slip in Annapolis where he was waiting for us. The boat, a beautiful nineteen foot Lightening class sloop with a centerboard and a three-horse power outboard motor, was already in a boat slip next to a private house. Lee had leased it from the house owner and when we arrived, he was on the porch of the house talking with the owner, who appeared to be a friend.

Lee easily maneuvered the boat, under power, out of the slip and headed it into the wind to raise the main sail. After setting the course and trimming the main, he raised and trimmed the jib. A mild breeze of about ten knots an hour was just enough to move us easily past the Naval Academy towards the entrance to the Chesapeake Bay. The day was perfect for an introduction to sailing. The waters were calm, the wind was steady, and there were a few white clouds in the blue skies. We sailed in the Bay while other sailboats darted all around us, some of them sporting large and colorful spinnakers which gave the entire area a very festive appearance.

Lee began to teach us the rudiments of sailing. First, in his quiet and steady tone of voice he began to introduce us to the nautical terms. "The paramount two terms on a boat," he began, "are 'Port' and 'Starboard'. 'Port' on a boat means 'to the left', and 'Starboard' means 'to the right', as one faces the boat's 'bow' (front)." Learning nautical terms was very important according to Lee, since these are used when sailing or talking about matters pertaining to sailing. That summer and fall we frequently sailed together and each trip was great fun as well as a major learning experience. Later, the girls nearly always went sailing with us and soon began to enjoy this sport immensely. Summer was flying by at an incredible pace as I tried my best to savor it.

The number of active research projects was overwhelming. If it were not for the excellent performance of the laboratory staff and cooperation of my collaborators, I would not have been able to carry this load. Jerry had arrived in August and we set up the study dealing with the effects of TEM on mouse semen. I was fascinated by this study, not only from its theoretical viewpoint but also from its technical aspects. I had not worked with mice, nor had I ever done this type of procedure, which called for a surgical approach. Semen treated with TEM was surgically inserted directly into the uterus of a female mouse shortly prior to her ovulation. I was happy and interested in learning this new technique and to observe the results of the procedure.

During this brief period of active duty in Bethesda, Jerry talked a great deal about his primary interest, sperm freezing. He had worked for a while at an animal husbandry organization perfecting techniques for freezing the semen of large farm animals using liquid nitrogen. We also talked about the possible application of these techniques for freezing human semen. We agreed that the following summer he would again request active duty at NMRI so we could continue working on this project.

At that time, Ania and I felt exceptionally happy and grateful to our adopted country for all the opportunities it had offered us. In less than ten years we two immigrants, having arrived to a new country not knowing the language, having no money and no connections, had been able to get married and become the happy parents of two lovely daughters. We had also received advanced degrees and in my case, become an officer in the US Navy and chief of a division at a major national research institute. All of this was pretty overwhelming.

In the fall we were invited to the wedding of a first cousin in New York City. Naval officers had an incredibly elegant white summer dress uniform and I decided to show off a little by wearing one with all of its accessories, including a fancy sword, to the wedding. Since I was earning over $5,000 a year in the Navy, we felt very rich and decided to purchase for Ania, what was then a very fashionable, black "trapeze" dress. In this dress, women could only stand since the rigid trapezoidal shape of the skirt made sitting impossible. When we showed up at the wedding reception in our striking outfits, the guests stopped watching the newlyweds to look at us. We became the center of attention at the reception and, while loving it, we felt a bit embarrassed about competing with the bride and groom. Our family couldn't stop complementing us and my naval career was on everyone's lips. We certainly made a big hit. Driving back home to Rockville we felt as if we were gliding through the clouds not in our Oldsmobile but in some magical chariot. We were feeling wonderful and looked forward confidently to a great future in this blessed country.

The following week I spent most of my time in Connie's laboratory. We were faced with a set of very puzzling results that needed confirmation and would most likely require additional experimentation. Reports in the literature had confirmed our laboratory findings; the increase in oxygen consumption of testicular tissue following damage to the germinal epithelium caused by a "noxious agent" is the result of changes in its cellular composition. Our new data, however, suggested that these changes could be due to other causes.

Connie and I had been brainstorming for days trying to decide on the best approach for further investigation of this issue. We even went to the NIH campus to meet with Marshall Nirenberg and pick his brain. At that time Marshall was getting itchy. He didn't wish to pursue any more studies dealing with carbohydrate metabolism, the topic of his PhD thesis. As he put it, "I want to work on a project that might lead to a Nobel Prize," and leaning towards us, pronounced, "I've decided that it will be equally hard to work on Nobel-type research as any other. One just has to figure out what research may lead to a Nobel Prize." We laughed and kept trying to direct his attention to our problems dealing with 'testicular respiration'. He, however, would not be distracted. Little did we know that eleven years later he would share the Nobel Price in Physiology for breaking the genetic code.

My wanderings at the NIH brought me to the Endocrine Section of the Cancer Institute headed by Dr. Roy Hertz, one of the most prominent researchers at NIH. He was known for being a mouse doctor (a scientist running experiments on mice), and he had been the first to admit a patient to the NIH Clinical Center. His ability to combine basic research with clinical medicine was legendary. I was fascinated by his recent observation in mice that folic acid was essential for the synthesis of an enzyme required for growth of the endometrium (lining of the uterus). That had served as the basis for his hypothesis that a synthetic inhibitor of folic acid might, therefore, prevent the proliferation of the endometrium. In fact, he was able to show that administration of a folic acid inhibitor called methotrexate did inhibit the growth of endometrium.

He then took a step characteristic of his way of thinking. He proposed that methotrexate might also inhibit the proliferation of other types of cells, specifically those comprising a very malignant, rapidly growing and at the time, deadly cancer in young women, called choriocarcinoma. This tumor develops in the trophoblastic cells of the placenta, which is part of the uterine lining of pregnant women. In collaboration with one of his postdoctoral fellows, Dr. Min Chiu Li, they tested methotrexate in several patients. Remarkably, the cancer disappeared, even in patients with so called 'canon ball' metastases in the lungs.

This was an early and dramatic demonstration that a malignancy could be cured by an appropriate pharmacological intervention. To me, this was of particular importance. It demonstrated how a finding in basic research, designed to understand a fundamental physiologic process, could evolve into an important therapeutic modality. In fact, this subsequently became the standard treatment for choriocarcinoma and a total cure could be achieved in a majority of cases. This further strengthened my determination to pursue basic scientific research and combine it with potential clinical applications.

Unfortunately, and surprisingly, Hertz and Li's findings were met with considerable skepticism by their peers. Since the drug was tested in very few individuals, many physicians and scientists concluded that the remission of the cancer could have been due to a spontaneous cure rather than to the effect of methotrexate. The medical community was not yet ready to accept the idea that chemotherapy could cure a solid tissue cancer even though it had been used with some success in treating certain forms of leukemia (a blood cancer). Dr. Li, who was the one dealing with the patients from Sloan Kettering Institute, was actually asked at this time to leave NIH.

I was not ready to accept the criticism and disapproval of these findings. The data, both basic and clinical, warranted further investigation in my opinion; it not only warranted but demanded additional studies. Further discussions with Dr. Hertz strengthened my conviction and led to a decision that when I returned to Detroit Receiving Hospital (DRH) for further training, I would repeat this study. Dr. Hertz pointed out that choriocarcinoma is a fairly rare cancer but I was optimistic I would be able to find and recruit patients with this cancer because the DRH was one of the largest emergency hospitals in the nation and the number of patients flowing through it was enormous. I didn't anticipate any resistance to my conducting this type of a study from the staff at DRH and Dr. Hertz promised to provide me with adequate amounts of methotrexate to treat at least six patients.

Discussions with basic investigators and research physicians at the NMRI and NIH continued to strengthen my resolve to pursue a combined basic and clinical approach during my further training and later in practice. I was also advised to apply for a basic science Fellowship from the National Science Foundation (NSF) for two years of additional subspecialty training in Endocrinology after I'd completed the requirements for board certification in Internal Medicine.

An NSF Fellowship would provide several benefits. First, it was a very prestigious Fellowship. Second, it would ensure that the hospital administration would provide me with time and facilities to pursue the research and third, it would provide me with some independent financial support in the form of a stipend. My colleagues at NMRI, who were familiar with the practices of the NSF, reassured me that my chances of winning this award were better than average. They based their opinions on several facts: I had already published a number of scientific papers and had both an M.D. and a Master of Science degree; I had successfully completed the course work and defended a thesis that had subsequently been published in the journal, "Endocrinology", and I had passed the qualifying exams for a PhD. These arguments seemed convincing so that fall I applied for the Fellowship.

While completing my application for the Fellowship, I couldn't help thinking about the pursuit of medicine and science in general. During the preceding several years I had perceived something special in the air concerning medicine. There was an exuberance among the faculty, particularly among the younger professors and students. It felt as if progress in medicine was gaining momentum, as if something was pushing the medical world toward a new age. Now, looking back to these years, there is no doubt in my mind that establishment of the NIH was an important trigger and positive factor in bringing scientific research to the forefront of academic medicine.

In reality, the concept of applying basic knowledge to the development of clinical means of fighting disease had developed relatively recently. Up until the past few centuries it was greatly influenced by popular beliefs, magic and religion. Early efforts to apply a scientific approach to medicine was observational in nature such as herbalism, which developed as people found that certain flowers or herbs had positive effects on certain ailments. Later, during the 14th and 15th centuries, modern science began to replace herbalism and other pre-modern notions such as the Greek "four humors". By the late 1800s it was discovered that many common diseases were not caused by "bad air" but by bacteria, followed closely by the discovery of antibiotics around 1900. An understanding of the role of microbes and the concept of disease prevention by antisepsis and later, immunity and immunizations, helped to discredit early superstitions and usher in an age of of scientific biomedical research (where results can be tested and reproduced). These advances were capped by the discovery of antibacterial compounds like sulfa drugs and antibiotics like penicillin. Later, the discovery of X-rays and the electrocardiogram at the turn of twentieth century ushered in a new diagnostic era, followed by an era of major breakthroughs in our understanding of metabolic diseases and the mechanisms of disease-pathophysiology.

In my opinion, however, a true marriage between the basic sciences and clinical medicine did not occur until the 1940s and the formation of NIH. There, basic science was practiced in tandem with clinical sciences, each benefiting directly and instantly from the other, as illustrated by Dr. Hertz's work. Having spent several years at a great Midwestern medical school and then at an extremely busy emergency hospital helped me greatly to see, understand, and appreciate this science-medicine connection. NIH was not only a center of excellence for biomedical sciences but also an engine that stimulated research in academic institutions via its extramural research program. This program helped create a network of research laboratories at academic institutions throughout the country supported by grants.

Back in the real world, my service in the Navy was moving inexorably towards its completion. The research tempo was increasing since I knew that upon returning to DRH I would have to suspend these projects. The hospital had no facilities for laboratory research, particularly not for research with animals. Furthermore, I would not have the time to pursue these types of investigations.

The research on absorption of whole blood from the peritoneal cavity was progressing extremely well and I was planning to present the conclusions in the spring of 1958 at the meetings of the Federated Societies. The data showed clearly that the transfused red blood cells are removed from the peritoneal cavity by a remarkable mechanism that allows intact red blood cells to pass into lymphatic structures in the diaphragm and from there through the lymphatic vessels into the venous system.

Our study of the effects of heat on the sperm-producing cells in the testes was also progressing well. However, it would not be ready for presentation in the spring. This was also true for the studies on testicular tissue respiration and the effects of TEM.

Prior to my service at NMRI, I thought the most intense physical and intellectual experience I'd had was my internship at DRH. However, it gradually started to dawn on me that this probably wasn't true. From a purely physical viewpoint, the service at DRH was very demanding but overall the experience at NMRI was even more so. I must admit though, that this was not imposed by the administration or the demands of the environment, it was entirely self-imposed.

In addition to being very much involved in my research projects I had, over the past several months, developed a close relationship with Jack Christian and become more intimately involved with his studies on population pressures in natural populations of woodchucks. Jack was a consummate naturalist and one of few ethologists in the scientific community. Naturalists through the centuries had studied various aspects of animal behavior but the modern science of ethology is considered to have arisen as a discrete discipline in the 1920s with the work of Nikolaas Tinbergen and Konrad Lorenz. By definition, ethology utilizes a combination of laboratory and field research and has strong ties with other disciplines, particularly ecology and evolution.

Jack had made arrangements with the research department of the Army allowing him to use a large munitions dump facility in Pennsylvania for his studies. The facility consisted of underground bunkers set up in a precise grid arrangement spread over hundreds of acres of land. Each bunker had a small earthen hill located where the grid lines intersected.

This provided a perfect area for Jack to map his observations concerning the location, movements, and behavior of woodchucks over the entire grid without placing any constraints on the animals being observed. He and/or his graduate students would make scheduled visits to the area in order to note the animals' behavior. Thus, he was able to study the freely growing and interacting animal populations under field rather than laboratory conditions. This study had already provided sufficient information to form hypotheses concerning free growing populations.

Woodchucks normally use underground burrows and with the grid arrangement of the depot, Jack was able to map the locations of the burrows with precision. His first striking observation was that there was a minimum distance between the burrows. Other preliminary data suggested that the phenomenon Jack called "population pressure" occurs when the burrows get closer than the normally accepted distance. This resulted in a variety of negative behavior from hostility to endocrine changes.

In addition to his full time position at NMRI, Jack held an adjunct professorship at the School of Hygiene and Public Health at Johns Hopkins University in Baltimore. He lectured there regularly and supervised a graduate student in ethology, Jim Lloyd. I frequently joined Jack on these trips to attend his lectures and later delivered some lectures myself. This brought me closer to university activities and prompted friendly interaction with some members of the faculty and graduate students, including Jim, whom I recruited many years later to serve on the faculty of my department in Philadelphia.

The NIH Study Section also became a significant segment of my life at the Institute. It provided me with extremely important professional experiences and an opportunity to meet some of the top scientists in my area of research. The meetings were held every three months at the NIH campus, just across Wisconsin Avenue from NMRI. The first meeting was a major revelation and a heady experience for a twenty eight year old. I felt extremely intimidated walking into the conference room. I couldn't visualize myself as part of such an august and erudite group of scientists even though many of the scientists sitting at the long table were familiar to me, having been introduced by W.O. at various scientific meetings. Professor Alfred Wilhelmi, the world-renowned scientist who had purified the human growth hormone, sat at the head of the long table. He got up, walked around the table to the doors where I stood and, after shaking hands with me he turned and said, with a smile on his face, "This is Dr. Steinberger. He is our new Study Section member, replacing Dr. Vollmer for the Navy. He will serve with us until his naval service is completed in August of 1958." With this simple statement, he returned to his seat.

Everyone at the table got up and shook my hand. I noted an empty chair next to Dr. Al Albert, well known for having purified the urinary gonadotrophins, and since I had met him previously, I decided to sit next to him. He greeted me politely but I sensed some coolness in his reaction towards me. A frightening sensation of awe descended over me and reached the pit of my stomach as I looked around the table at the members of the Study Section. The top brains responsible for the most advanced discoveries in various areas of endocrinology sat there; and I was among them. The enormity of the situation dawned on me and demanded that I never open my mouth but sit there with eyes and ears open to absorb and learn all there was to be learned from this group.

Across the table sat the top expert in steroid metabolism, Dr. Ralph Dorfman. He ran the most effective steroid biochemistry research and training unit in the world at the Worcester Foundation for Experimental Biology. This Foundation was a private non-profit research organization established in 1944 in Worcester, Massachusetts by two scientists, Dr. Hudson Hoagland and Dr. Gregory Pincus. This Foundation was the cradle of the world's greatest research in reproductive biology, steroid biochemistry, and gonadotrophin physiology. It is best known for development of the birth control pill by Dr. Pincus and Dr. Min Chueh Chang, one of his associates. Dr. Chang also was the first to pioneer and successfully accomplished in vitro fertilization in experimental animals.

The procedures of the Study Sections were relatively simple. Membership was by invitation with most nominations being provided by the existing Study Section members. The applications would be sorted by topic and assigned to the appropriate Study Section. Then, the Chairman, working with with the Study Section Secretary (a full time employee of the NIH Extramural Grant Program) assigned each grant to two members of the Study Section according to their specific areas of expertise. Each scientist would be assigned two to four applications for

47

detailed study; however, each member would also receive copies of all other applications approximately two months ahead of the meeting. At the meeting, a complete formal review and critique of each application would be provided by the members specifically assigned to that grant application. The application would then be discussed and voted upon by the entire group. The vote, however, was only for a priority score or rank ranging from one to five, the highest being one. The vote was anonymous and the Secretary then calculated the average priority score for each application.

When the Study Section was unable to arrive at a conclusive judgment, particularly when there was a question about whether the applicant's institution provided appropriate facilities in support of the applicant, or the applicant was requesting a relatively large sum of money, a "site visit" of the applicant and his (or her) institution was considered. Two to four members of the Study Section were then selected to visit the applicant's facilities. A site visit usually lasted one day but could be extended to two or even three days if necessary. The visiting scientists then submitted a written report that was presented at the subsequent meeting for reevaluation by the entire group.

Participation in the Study Section tremendously widened my perspective on the flourishing biomedical research in our country and on the mechanisms of support via governmental agencies. I began to appreciate the politics of science or, more importantly, the relative absence of politics per se. This allowed for a moral, ethical, simply decent way of stimulating the increasing desire of young investigators to participate in scientific endeavors.

During my frequent visits to NIH I was impressed by the number of young physicians opting to join the Public Health Service in the hopes of being assigned to NIH as postdoctoral research fellows or simply as Public Health Officers involved with some aspects of research. After talking with some of them it became clear to me that this was not simply a way to avoid the so-called doctors' draft, which had been instituted in 1950 when medical personnel were needed in the military. The Korean War had formally ended and by this time the draft was at its low ebb. Most of those whom I spoke to were genuinely excited about the direction of medicine and its integration with scientific research.

The 1958 spring meetings of the Federated Societies were approaching and I had to work rapidly on the final analysis of the data regarding blood absorption from the abdominal cavity. The primary point of the current research was to demonstrate that hyaluronidase can speed up this process while its inhibitor, hesperidin, slows it down. This system would provide physicians with a simple method to regulate the speed of absorption of the transfused red blood cells from the abdominal cavity. We were particularly happy to learn that several pediatric groups were experimenting with administering blood transfusions to infants via this route. I was also pleased with our presentation because both Bill, my research assistant and Jimmy, the Seaman who was our laboratory technician on this project, had co-authored this paper.

Spring was in the air and life was filled with interesting and diverse activities. The NSF was in contact with me concerning the status of my application for a Research Fellowship and I was in constant contact with Dr. Maddock, Chief of the Endocrine Section at DRH concerning my residency in Internal Medicine and Fellowship in Endocrinology. A great deal depended on the hospital's willingness to take me on for specialty training as a resident physician and successfully securing the Fellowship.

At NMRI my work with Connie on the regulation of testicular carbohydrate metabolism was coming to fruition but I was afraid that we might not have enough time before my departure to secure definitive answers. This did not deter us from pursuing the project with a vengeance. A similar situation existed with respect to the study dealing with the effect of heat on the testes. Here, however, I could see some light at the end of the tunnel. Bill was assisting with this study and we hoped to have all of the experiments completed by May and tissue samples prepared by June. This should give me just enough time for a qualitative assessment of the data and preparation of preliminary data for presentation at a scientific meeting. The quantitative analysis of the tissue preparations would have to be delayed indefinitely.

The TEM project would also need to be put on hold. Preliminary analysis of histological and histochemical preparations of testicular tissues from various experiments convinced me that a quantitative cytological examination of the tissues would be essential to answer some of the questions raised. Over the preceding several years a group from Montréal had published a series of papers demonstrating for the first time and in great detail that formation of spermatozoa in the testes involved several cell divisions that occurred in a precisely timed process, each of which formed different precursor cell types . Therefore, by analyzing this timing one could develop a technique for evaluation of the cellular composition at different stages of spermatogenesis. Such analysis, performed at appropriately selected time intervals after inducing damage by a noxious agent (ionizing radiation, heat, hypoxia or treatment with a chemical agent), could provide information as to which specific cell type was affected by the noxious agent. With this information one might be able to test the hypothesis that different noxious agents target different cell types in the spermatogenic epithelium.

During this time there were lots of activities competing for my leisure time on the weekends. Early that spring I was introduced to the 'herring run'. I hadn't known that Atlantic herring spawn each spring in the fresh water of the upper reaches of the Potomac River. During the spring the river normally floods, forming tiny coves along its course and the herring swim up from the salt waters of the Atlantic to spawn in these coves. To catch herring at this time of the year all it takes is a dipping net and over-the-knee rubber boots. One can scoop up literally buckets of beautiful huge herring in no time.

One Sunday, when the herring run was at its peak according to a newspaper report, Bill and I took off for a herring adventure. We drove to the little town of Potomac and at its outskirts began to investigate the flooded shores of the river. To our delight the little pools of water left by the receding water were full of herring. We actually scooped up several at a time and dropped them into the big metal buckets we had brought with us.

We were back home by early afternoon loaded with herring. Ania had purchased several dozen glass jars and boxes of Morton's salt. We immediately started the business of salting and packing the herring in the jars. Each herring was trimmed, washed, placed into a jar and covered with a layer of salt. We ended up with two dozen jars of herring and proudly placed them in our outdoor storage shed. After a week we examined the jars and decided they looked OK. A week later I decided to open one of the jars to examine the situation again. Since the herring didn't look like it usually did when purchased from a store, I decided that more salt was in order. Thus, we opened all jars, added several tablespoons of salt to each, resealed them, and returned them to the shed. A week later when I opened one to examine the results, to my great disappointment, I experienced a definite, most unpleasant smell. Even our cat walked by the open jars with his tail straight up and nose turned away. This was the end of our herring adventure and we had to dispose of all our beautiful salted Atlantic herring. Later I learned that additives in the Morton's salt which help keep it dry and maintain other desirable characteristics interfered with the process of herring preservation. Only pure crystalline salt should have been used.

I was winding down my research activities and writing reports. I also had to finish the evaluation of the grant application I had been assigned for the last Study Section meeting. This meeting, as it turned out, was an emotional experience. In the nearly two years during which I served as a member of this Study Section I had made a number of friends with whom I enjoyed interacting and hated to say goodbye to. The Chairman actually asked me to serve out my four-year appointment after leaving the Navy. However, I didn't think this would be appropriate since after leaving the Navy I would interrupt my research and return to training mode as a resident and then a postdoctoral fellow. Although the offer was extremely flattering, I couldn't even consider it.

After the herring episode our normal leisure activities picked up again. We spent two weekends visiting the Cherry Blossoms at the Tidal Basin, the beautiful lagoon adjoining the Jefferson Memorial in Washington, DC. We also began sailing with Lee again and I was particularly happy to see that Ania was warming up to it, and the girls, who frequently accompanied us, were more and more drawn to it. I promised myself that as soon as it became possible, I would acquire a sailboat.

In May, I received an urgent call from Jerry Sherman about a three-week summer service at my Laboratory in Bethesda to satisfy his duty in the Reserves. I was pleased to have him join me again even for so brief a period before I had to leave. When the dates were agreed upon, the question of selecting a project came up. I was intrigued by a phenomenon called 'temperature shock' that had been observed during the freezing of bull semen and wondered if he would be interested in investigating this event. He was almost certain that this 'shock' did not occur during the process of freezing human semen with liquid nitrogen and was willing to do the study. We agreed that July 1 would be a good time to begin and I looked forward to having him with us.

This episode with Jerry gave rise to an important thought. At NMRI I had been, for the first time in my life, an independent research investigator with no direct supervisor over me. I could initiate any study I wished with only the agreement of the Institution's Research Committee and approval of the Commanding Officer. Looking back at the past year and a half, I felt that this trust in me had not been misplaced. I had gained a great deal of first hand experience while initiating a number of new studies, many of which had been completed. This experience would, in all likelihood, help launch my research career, particularly after completing an endocrine fellowship at DRH

I was not fully convinced that three additional years of study would make me a better researcher and by now I was almost certain that research, rather than the private practice of medicine, was my calling. Sometimes, however, I wondered whether this thinking was completely appropriate. Perhaps it would be simpler and a more effective way of taking care of my family if I just completed my specialty training and entered a clinical practice. That way, I could earn a higher income and in doing so, be a better family man. I had been involved in research for the past six or seven years and wasn't sure I could or wanted to function outside the research world. On the other hand, the year I spent as a rotating intern at DRH had introduced me to clinical medicine. Time-wise and breath of experience-wise it was probably equivalent to two or even three years of experience in most other hospital settings. During my time there I had learned to truly enjoy the practice of medicine. This was my dilemma and I constantly mulled it over in my head: would it be basic research or clinical medicine? Could I possibly handle both at the same time and succeed?

At last I received word that my NSF Fellowship was approved and I was delighted! So was Bill Maddock in Detroit who had been calling me on the phone weekly. Bob Leach, his right hand man, had also been in touch with me concerning a big welcome party he planned to have for us when we returned to Detroit. Our old friends there were advising us about suitable housing and it was decided that we should live near Eight Mile Road, not far from the expressway going through downtown and close to the Hospital.

I had to wind up my research at NMRI and complete the project with Jerry for his summer reserve duty. As soon as he arrived, we initiated the temperature shock study and it was quite successful. We were able to demonstrate that human semen, did not suffer the same temperature shock as did the bull semen. This made future development of a procedure for freezing human semen much simpler and served as the basis for important collaborative studies conducted with Jerry in the early 1960s.

Our old friend June had found several apartments in Detroit for us to look at and we made the four hundred mile trip by car to look at them over a weekend. We left Friday evening and arrived in Detroit early Saturday morning. By Sunday morning we had rented a beautiful, two-story, two-bedroom brick duplex on Hubble Street, about one block from Eight Mile Road. We were both thrilled to be headed back to Detroit.

CHAPTER 4
RESIDENCY - HONING MY CLINICAL SKILLS

At DRH, a city emergency hospital and a teaching unit for the Wayne State University Medical School, I felt I was returning home. Here, medical students received clinical exposure and residents trained in various specialties. I was thoroughly familiar with this type of hospital, its practices, training procedures and research philosophies as well as the type of medical care they were capable of delivering. The University Hospitals in Iowa City, where I was a medical student, operated under similar conditions and had similar administrative rules and regulations.

Bill Maddock and Bob Leach greeted me with open arms. Bill immediately suggested we visit the Chairman of the Department, Dr. Gordon B. Myers, a nationally recognized cardiologist and researcher, to discuss in my appointments at the hospital and the medical school. I was looking forward to meeting Dr. Myers and learning what exactly I would be doing during for the next three years. My attempt to get a preview of this meeting from Bill, however, was met with only a smile. Shaking his head he said, "You'll learn soon enough."

Dr. Myers was a tall, gaunt man with an anemic smile playing across his lips. He was dressed very properly, sporting a red bow tie and a white coat over an impeccable black suit. When we walked into his office, he came around his desk, shook hands with me and gestured to a red leather chair in front of his desk. At first I felt vulnerable and scared but once he started speaking in his deep, sympathetic and mellow voice, I totally relaxed and began paying attention to what he was saying. As it turned out, he had a lot to say and I was in for another surprise.

> This year you would normally have started as a Resident in the Department of Internal Medicine. But in view of your service with the Navy Medical Corps and at the Portsmouth Naval Hospital, your previous service as a resident at Detroit Receiving Hospital, and your research accomplishments, you will start immediately as a Senior Resident. However, during the two years following that, while you are an NSF Postdoctoral Research Fellow, you will rotate on night duty with the other Senior Residents.

I almost fell off the chair. At this point I realized what this meant; I would perform all the duties of a resident for three years but during the last two years I would also conduct research during the day. This was shaping up to be a tough three years; however, I had been given an incredible opportunity to train in my specialty and at the same time continue my research.

The following weekend Bob threw a party at his house to introduce me to the entire staff of the Division. I met the postdoctoral fellows, Al and John, who immediately became my friends and started telling me all about the Division. They were involved predominantly with clinical management of patients in the Endocrine Division and in the Endocrine and Diabetes Clinics. They also conducted some clinical research. As we were talking, Bob came by and with a mischievous smile on his round, jovial face remarked, "Did you know that Emil requested serving his first rotation on the Endocrine Service?" I looked up at him with a start but he continued unperturbed. "This will give you guys a chance to show him how the hospital works and introduce him to our clinical and research activities." I looked at him somewhat confused, "Yes" I stammered, "that will be great, but I don't remember making this request." Still smiling, Bob responded, "But I did." Now everyone burst out laughing. "This simply means that you should show up at the Division tomorrow at eight o'clock in the morning." As the festivities continued everyone became a little high on wine and midnight arrived much too fast.

In the morning, I took the elevator to the fifth floor and with some trepidation entered the large general endocrine laboratories where hormone bioassays of gonadotrophins (pituitary hormones that stimulate the function of the ovaries and testes) and estrogen (a female sex hormone) were carried out. At that time, hormone measurements where still essentially a research activity. They were done by injecting a sample of the patient's urine into mice once a day for several days, then sacrificing the mice and weighing certain organs (depending on which hormone was being measured). Under rigidly controlled conditions and within a narrow range, the weight of the organ was directly related to the concentration of a specific hormone in the urine injected into the test animal. These tests required about one hour for the injections (which we did daily), and three to four hours to complete the analyses (which we did three times a week).

I walked into the laboratory a little late, having first stopped at the offices of the Internal Medicine Department. The day's activities were already in full swing; John was sacrificing animals in a jar filled with chloroform vapors, Bob was dissecting the animals to remove the appropriate organs and Al weighed the organs and kept the records. As I walked in, Bob said, "Just stand there and watch. If you have any questions, ask."

By noon they were finished with their tasks and I was given the results and told to carry out a statistical analysis on the numbers. This should have been a breeze for me as I had performed this kind of analysis for five years while serving as a graduate and medical student. Al suggested we run down to the cafeteria for a quick lunch. "Since the General Endocrine Clinic will not start until two thirty, you'll be able to begin the calculations before joining us in the clinic. Hopefully there will be enough time after the clinic to complete them." I had cheerfully volunteered to carry out the assay computations. However, I hadn't realized the extent of the work in the clinic or the habits of the staff doctors, fellows and residents attending it.

In the clinic, we saw patients with general endocrine disorders and endocrine disorders of the reproductive system in both men and women. Patients with diabetes were cared for in the General Diabetes Clinic that was held three times a week under the auspices of the General Medicine section. That clinic was attended by residents rotating through general medicine and endocrinology services as well as by the endocrine fellows.

The first hour in the clinic was an eye opener for me for several reasons. First, I hadn't realized that there were so many patients with endocrine disorders. Second, I was dumfounded by the number of patients with endocrine disorders that were considered extremely rare. Third, I was surprised by the number of patients with endocrine disorders of the reproductive system. I also learned that Bob conducted an infertility clinic for both men and women. This clinic met whenever it was necessary to see a patient and could be any day of the week including Saturday and Sunday. It was attended exclusively by Bob, Bill and the endocrine fellows; the general medicine residents were not included.

The endocrine clinic was mind-boggling; I saw dozens of patients with endocrine disorders I had never seen as a medical student. However, what truly stopped me in my tracks was the infertility clinic. Here I realized that the most frequent causes of infertility in these patients were either endocrine disorders or misinterpretations of some fundamental principles of normal reproductive system physiology. But, the greatest shocker of all occurred a year later when, as an Endocrine Fellow, I was attending a general gynecologic clinic under an agreement between the Endocrine Division and the Department of Obstetrics and Gynecology (Ob-Gyn), to provide some endocrine exposure for the Ob-Gyn residents. Although many of women in this clinic suffered with a variety of pelvic or vaginal infections, the majority presented with endocrine disorders that were either addressed inadequately or not addressed at all. All too soon the endocrine rotation was over and I was assigned to the cardiology service.

At this point, my mind became preoccupied with Ania's education, new developments in the Division of Endocrinology, and with the coming year when I would commence the NSF Fellowship. Our home on Hubble Street was quite adequate but it was located at least ten miles from the DRH and Wayne State University Medical School where Ania was hoping to enroll in a PhD program. She had discovered that the Medical School had a strong department of microbiology with an emphasis on virology. In fact, the Department Chairman was a virologist. Unfortunately, our current financial circumstances made Ania's returning to school almost impossible. My income was not sufficient to support both her schooling and our living expenses, especially since we would need to hire full time help to care for our daughters. Although Pauline was already in first grade in public school, Inette was still in preschool and was home by noon every day. For us to be away the entire day at the Hospital and in the Medical School, we needed someone at our house from 7:00 AM to 7:00 PM. After a prolonged discussion, Ania had a brilliant idea and we developed a plan.

When we lived in Detroit two years earlier she had worked for Parke-Davis, a pharmaceutical company. She then reminded me:

> They were very happy with the work I did on developing the first vaccine against the flu virus. I'm almost certain they would be interested in rehiring me and they pay well. We could save most of what I make and accumulate enough money for me to quit my job.

The following day she telephoned her acquaintances at Parke-Davis and, sure enough, they were interested in rehiring her at the research laboratories and offered her a princely (princessly?) salary. Now all we needed was someone to care for the girls while we were away. With the help of old friends we located the ideal person, Mabel. She was a true "southern mammy", both in appearance and personality. Our girls immediately fell in love with her, and vice versa. To this day, they remember her and her banana pudding pies with the greatest affection.

As our personal lives became more settled and I acclimated to my new role as one of the chief medical residents, something unexpected happened. Bill Maddock, having become disillusioned with the politics at the College of Medicine, purchased a truck, loaded up his belongings and moved his family to Alaska. At least this was the explanation given for his sudden departure. At this point Bob was promoted to Chief of the Division. Although this turn of events was completely unexpected and shook me up a bit it didn't have any direct impact on me or on my work. I was much too busy with the internal medicine service to give it much thought.

I was learning internal medicine on the wards at a prodigious clip. During the day I served as a resident on a ward that housed twenty-two patients. There, I was responsible for the ward, two interns and a medical student who had been assigned to me. Rounds were conducted twice a day with the Attending Physician and I was responsible for each patient's clinical status as well as all the fine theoretical details of the medical disorders suffered by each. The latter kept me burning the midnight oil and gave me an enormous theoretical footing in medicine. This proved very useful to me in the years to come. It was the 'duty watch' every third night that put the chief medical resident to the test. Usually we had eight to ten medical residents, including two chief residents on 'night call'. This duty required us to cover both the wards and the emergency room.

The astounding part of the medical residents' duties in the emergency room was its ubiquitous nature. For example, if the ENT (Ear Nose and Throat) residents were suddenly overwhelmed by an unusually high number of patients with acute problems, the medical residents would assist them with ENT procedures. The surgical residents often needed assistance because our hospital handled a great number of trauma and acute surgical emergencies. Thus, during night call we could be called upon to work in many, if not all, of the various medical and surgical specialties. I had an opportunity to learn about various other subspecialties in internal medicine and delighted in trying to learn everything I could. This incredible experience afforded the physicians in training an unusually broad and well-rounded experience. When I left the endocrine service, I missed attending the endocrine and infertility clinics but knew that during the next two years I would spend a great deal of time on investigations in these areas.

My exposure to medicine in the Emergency Room, in addition to providing a remarkably wide spectrum of clinical experiences, provided some additional insight into the evolution of medical care (currently called 'health care') in a government hospital. As chief resident, I was scheduled to rotate through Wayne County General Hospital and the VA (Veterans Administration) Hospital. Between these two hospitals, the DRH (a city hospital), and a year at the University of Iowa Hospital, (a state hospital), I had a pretty good understanding of the type of medicine practiced and the level of health care delivered in government-run medical facilities. My experience in private hospitals, however, was limited. In Iowa City I had had some experience at a Catholic hospital, in Detroit I'd done a brief rotation at the Beaumont Hospital and I had sporadically participated in rounds at the Henry Ford Hospital, the private hospital par excellence in Detroit. These experiences provided me with some food for thought about the delivery of medical care in hospitals and emergency rooms.

At all of these facilities I observed something in the young physicians, both those in training and those already in practice. There was a sense of excitement and anticipation, as well as a belief that the future in which they were so eager to participate was bright. They were dedicated to providing good medical care and many also wished to participate in what was becoming a rapid progression of discoveries and improvements in scientific and clinical medicine. There was genuine interest on the part of many new doctors in becoming researchers so that they could further basic science and apply its advancements directly to clinical care.

In discussing these ideas with "post docs" (Post-Doctoral Research Fellows training in research), both in Bethesda and in Detroit, I realized the significant influence the relatively new NIH was having on all of us. It was experiencing exponential growth, creating the need for a large number of high quality scientists as well as a substantial number of entry-level investigators like these post docs. Soon, an NIH Fellowship became a very prestigious and sought-after position, and the concept of conducting clinical and/or basic research gained considerable popularity. This contributed to an increase in the desirability and number of fellowship positions at medical institutions throughout the country which, in turn, were increasingly supported by Post-Doctoral Research Fellowships granted by institutions such as NIH.

My residency training was moving at break-neck speed. Since night duty only occurred every third night, the physical demands were much lower than those of my internship with its every-other-night schedule. However, I was looking forward to the commencement of my Post-Doctoral Fellowship when night duty would drop to only once a week.

Despite the pressures of residency, I was anxious to initiate the study I had promised Dr. Hertz I would carry out after returning to DRH.

This was the study of the effects of methotrexate on choriocarcinoma. Methotrexate, an anti-metabolite that acted as a folic acid antagonist, was synthesized in late 1940s at Lederle, a major American pharmaceutical laboratory. It had been hoped that the compound would act as an anti-neoplastic substance for the treatment of some forms of cancer and had been approved by the FDA (Food and Drug Administration). Since folic acid had been shown to be essential for stimulating growth of endometrial cells, Dr. Hertz had reasoned that a substance with anti-folic acid activity would interfere with the growth of these cells in the uterus, a hypothesis that was supported by his studies in mice.

In my naiveté, I assumed that the chairman of the Ob-Gyn department at DRH would be happy to help me set up a study of the exciting new "miracle drug" which had already shown such great promise in the treatment of choriocarcinoma. It was a totally new therapeutic modality, the first attempt to cure cancer pharmacologically rather than using the time-honored approach of simply removing it surgically. I made an appointment with the Chairman with great anticipation.

I knew him from prior contacts during my internship and from annual meetings of the American Fertility Society. As I walked into his office, he brusquely gestured for me to take a seat in the chair by his desk. Before I had a chance to open my mouth he looked up at me angrily and spat out, "No! No way. Do you know what choriocarcinoma is?" Was this a rhetorical question on his part? I had hoped that he was cognizant of the fact that I was reasonably well versed in the oncology of this tumor. "Are you aware of the fact that choriocarcinoma is one of the fastest growing, most rapidly spreading cancers and that it is almost always lethal unless extirpated very early, before any spreading has occurred?" I was flabbergasted; obviously, I knew the history and prognosis for this tumor. After all, I came to him after a stint at some of the more prominent research institutions in the country. So, I took a different tack:

"I believe you know Dr. Hertz, and I am certain that you are familiar with his latest publication, which demonstrated remarkably good results in patients with choriocarcinoma who were treated with methotrexate. As a matter of fact I brought you a copy of his paper because I was thinking of running a similar investigation using his protocol. Dr. Hertz feels that we might be justified in placing more patients on this protocol in light of his initial extremely promising results."

Here he interrupted me:

"Oh no, you don't understand. The treatment of choriocarcinoma is surgical in nature, a hysterectomy with whatever additional surgical procedures are necessary. This is the therapy and I will not consider any other, particularly not a theoretical, non-surgical approach. "

At this point, he got up indicating the conversation was at an end. He hadn't even glanced at Dr. Hertz's publication so I decided to leave it on his desk. I was shocked and couldn't think of any appropriate parting statement. On the way out, I recalled an episode during my internship when he had had an unpleasant run-in with one of the students in my intern class, resulting in a very undesirable outcome for the intern. With this in mind I quietly left.

This experience forced me to reevaluate my thinking about some aspects of research in the medical sciences. It forced me to consider what I came to think of as the "turf" issue. I began to realize that people with training and practice in surgery may have different approaches to clinical problems from those who practice non-surgical specialties. I was also disturbed and perplexed to learn that individuals with administrative powers have the capacity to influence research in such a dramatic and negative fashion. I felt a great need to discuss all of this with Bob and the post docs in the Endocrine Division. Unfortunately, over the next few days we were extremely busy on the wards and particularly busy in the Emergency Room at night. This delayed our talk but during that time I was exposed to another situation that gave rise to some new ideas.

One night in the Emergency Room (ER), I treated a young woman who was in hemorrhagic shock due to acute blood loss. She had experienced severe vaginal bleeding and her hemoglobin level and red blood cell count were very low. A resident admitted her to the Ob-Gyn Section. Several days later, I went by to find out what happened to her and learned that she had been diagnosed with choriocarcinoma. She had had an emergency hysterectomy, which stopped the bleeding; however, her prognosis was very poor. The tumor in her uterus had been removed but she already had extensive pulmonary cannon ball metastases. This episode made me wonder again about the limits of a purely surgical approach.

I couldn't wait to see Bob. When finally I got the chance, both of the fellows were also there and all three laughed at my encounter with the Ob-Gyn chairman. Al said "That was to be expected". Bob added:

> As you know I am running an Infertility Clinic in our Endocrine Division and it's been a bone of contention with him. Some of our patients require surgical intervention and once we refer a patient to the Ob-Gyn Department, they are never returned to us. They feel that all disorders of the female reproductive system should be treated by gynecologists, whether they are adequately trained in this area or not.

For me, this was the first time the issue caused by conflicting professional relationships between the two specialties, Ob-Gyn and Endocrinology, had reared its ugly head. I had been under the impression that medicine was practiced with a view toward greatest efficiency and with primary emphasis on the patient's best interests. Here I began to see a serious rift developing between political and economic considerations on the one hand and the best interests of patients with non-surgical, reproductive endocrine disorders on the other.

After expressing my indignation, I was ready to reveal to them the ideas that had occurred to me in the ER while taking care of the patient with choriocarcinoma. First, I summarized the ER encounter and then quickly blurted out my proposal before I lost the temerity essential to proposing my hair-raising plan:

> There is always a group of internal medicine residents in the ER. The senior resident is usually called in to see very serious cases regardless which specialty will ultimately handle and admit the patient to the hospital. What if I review, in detail, the presenting signs and symptoms of choriocarcinoma with all the medical residents on duty that night and ask them to admit these patients to a medical ward. Once the patient has been admitted there, I could take over her care. When the diagnosis has been determined with certainty, we'll offer

these patients a choice between the experimental protocol (treatment with methotrexate) or surgery. Those who elect to have surgery will be referred to Ob-Gyn and we will treat the others with methotrexate.

There was a deafening silence when I stopped talking. Bob and the two post docs looked at each other and all three threw an occasional glance at me. The silence was becoming uncomfortable when I finally stuttered, "Is this idea so horrible?" Suddenly all three of them looked up at me and started laughing; but it was an uncomfortable laugh, they were clearly having difficulty with my idea. "It certainly would be a novel way to handle the impasse we face with Ob-Gyn concerning our turf," said Bob in a quiet and halting voice. "I'll have to see Gordon (Dr. Gordon Myers, the Chairman of the Internal Medicine Department) and run this idea by him. In the meantime, see if you can convince the residents to go along with this idea." This was music to my ears. I could sense a green light in the near future for this idea. In fact, within a week I was given formal permission to commence the study and soon after, we admitted our first patient to a medical ward. She had an advanced case of choriocarcinoma with metastases to the lungs and high human chorionic gonadotrophin (hCG) levels in her urine, a hallmark of this type of cancer. This was quite a surprise as choriocarcinoma is a very rare tumor, so seeing another one so soon was unusual.

I started administering methotrexate immediately after we were certain of the diagnosis and ardently hoped for a positive response. While busy with this study, I received a phone call from W.O. who had been the Director of the Population Council at the Rockefeller Institute in Manhattan for the past several years. During that time I'd been much too busy to analyze the data dealing with experimental work I had initiated or completed as a student in Iowa. It appeared, however, that W.O. was not prepared to let any of it go to waste.

He reminded me of the work we had done evaluating the effect of TEM (the radiomimetic compound) on the testes and fertility of rats. It was seminal work and W.O. suggested that the analysis should be promptly completed, presented at a scientific meeting and then published in a scientific journal. Another graduate student had assisted in this study in Iowa and one of my assistants in the Navy had helped with histological analysis of the tissues. W.O. suggested that I include all those who helped me as co-authors of the presentation and the future paper. He suggested I present the paper at the annual Endocrine Society meetings and submit the paper for publication in "Endocrinology", the most prestigious American journal in the field of endocrinology. This was a big job. I would have to analyze the data, prepare a presentation in time for the annual meeting and write a major paper for submission to a journal that accepted very few papers for publication. However, at that point in my career, the sky was the limit! I was tickled, I was honored and I accepted his suggestion with enthusiasm.

This call reminded me that I also had additional responsibilities to the Navy, where I had had the opportunity to conduct basic research, and to my assistants at NMRI, whose help made the work possible. Specifically, the work dealing with the effects of heat on the testes came to mind as did the tremendous assistance I had received from Bill Dixon. Another call to W.O. for advice was of great help. He agreed that that research should be reported as rapidly as possible, and that I should make Bill a co-author. He also suggested that I submit this paper to the journal "Fertility and Sterility", the official publication of the American Fertility Society.

I was facing a mountain of responsibilities. Obviously, the first and most immediate one was the back-breaking and time consuming residency program. This was followed closely by the wild pace of establishing the methotrexate research project, my first clinical research project. Now the job of data analysis and preparation of papers for presentation, not just for one but two major scientific meetings, had been added to my plate.

Against this backdrop, one evening after dinner Ania presented an additional little issue that needed to be faced. She was happy working at Parke-Davis in flu virus research. The job was intellectually satisfying and well paid but obviously there was something on her mind. The girls were tucked away in their beds and we were sitting on our third hand couch in the living room-bedroom area, talking about little nothings when Ania said: "There is something that keeps coming up in my mind and will not go away." I looked up at her, brushed away a lock of golden hair from her right eye and responded playfully, "It can't be that serious, possibly a little lovemaking will ease the distress?" She sat up straight, saying, "Be serious, I have an idea. Listen to me carefully." With a big grin on my lips I said, "O.K. you have the floor, lets hear the new idea." She was getting inpatient with me and her thoughts literally exploded in an avalanche of words.

> Yesterday at Parke-Davis, while I was having lunch in the cafeteria, I came across a brochure describing a new townhouse development designed by the world renowned architect Ludwig Mies van der Rohe called Lafayette Park. They will be two-story and very contemporary with a great deal of glass, you would really like them. They'll be available by next summer. I'll be getting a substantial raise next month and next year, once you become a Post Doctoral Fellow, your salary will also go up considerably. I think that with a little additional savings we should have enough for a down payment.

Here her voice lost some of its timbre, as if she had lost the courage to continue. I looked at her with a questioning expression on my face, "Go ahead, say what's on your mind," I prodded her. "Well," she said haltingly, "I think that by next summer we should be able to pay for a townhouse and I could also give up my job in order to work toward a PhD full time." I looked at her with disbelieving eyes but after a moment said, "You are correct, as you were talking I went over some numbers in my head and sure enough we should look into this possibility; we may be able to pull it off."

The following week we looked at the Lafayette Park town homes and learned that the price may indeed be within our reach. The only problem was that although the construction had not even begun, demand for the units was very high and we had to decide quickly. So we trotted back to the developer to negotiate the lowest possible down payment and then straight to the bank to get a short-term loan; anything to get sufficient cash for the down payment right away. Ania was elated and so was I. This had been a dream for both of us, to own a home in America. Furthermore, Ania would be able to get her doctorate degree, another dream we had shared for many years. Once we moved, the Medical School and the hospital would be very close to home, making things a lot easier.

Everything was moving at an incredible pace. The only activity proceeding at a normal pace was the girls' development and schooling. Both were growing up beautifully. Pauline was a happy student in the second grade and Inette was in kindergarten. Once we decided to purchase the townhouse at Lafayette Park, we were particularly overjoyed to learn that a small elementary school was to open in the development. Both girls would then be able to attend school within walking distance.

While my attention was temporarily diverted to the issues of home buying and schooling for the girls', the demands of the hospital were unrelenting. The methotrexate project was moving along swiftly and the response of the first patient was nothing short of miraculous. The canon ball metastases in her lungs simply melted away as did the primary tumor in her uterus. It was an unbelievable situation, but when I brought the data to the Chairman of Ob-Gyn, he simply disregarded it. "This can't be," he growled and I couldn't really blame him for this response. Most doctors in the Internal Medicine department expressed similar doubts about this patient's miraculous response. Even I felt a little uncertain. "We must wait to see what happens after several months," I said. However, deep down I felt quite convinced of the validity of this outcome. After all, Drs. Hertz and Li reported similar results in their original study

As this project progressed I was very happy with the way the interns cared for the coriocarcinoma patients. They were very devoted to the project and took superb care of the patients; of which we now had three. The first was still free of the disease and was seen regularly in the outpatient clinic, carefully followed up and regularly tested. We were fortunate that hCG, a hormone secreted by the cancer, was such a superb marker of the disease and would alert us instantly if the tumor reoccurred. The second patient was also responding well to the treatment and the third hadn't yet been treated long enough to allow for any conclusions. We were happy with the results obtained to date and continued our efforts to recruit more patients for the study.

The spring scientific meetings where looming on the horizon. The illustrations for my talk had to be photographed and made into slides for presentation at the American Fertility Society meeting, which was scheduled for April in Atlantic City. This would be a first for me, I had never presented a paper at the Fertility Society; I wasn't even a member.

However, W.O. insisted that this material belonged on the program at this meeting.

It was a major step when Ania and I put down the deposit for the townhouse. We still couldn't fathom the extent of our daring in aspiring to own one of these beautiful, super-contemporary residences. After we had made this commitment, Ania and I sat down one evening after dinner, having tucked the girls in bed, to review our situation over a cup of coffee. We agreed that at that moment it was impossible to know whether this was a daring but reasonable decision or a foolish one. I felt very optimistic however. We had accumulated sufficient cash for the down payment and after I received a raise that fall, we should have adequate income to cover our living expenses and mortgage payment. "Furthermore," and here I ventured to strike an optimistic note, "this is 1959. By 1961 I will have completed my education and will be ready to embark on a career that will hopefully increase our income significantly." Ania eagerly agreed with me, "This is true. I didn't think of it that way, we only have two more years to worry about finances and then, with our frugal approach to expenses, we should have no major financial woes." It was time to celebrate!

April was beautiful in Atlantic City where the AFSS held its annual meetings. It was a small town with the largest and longest boardwalk I had ever seen. Upon arrival I found W.O. in a huge hotel where the meeting was to be held. Anthony was with him and had already checked into an inexpensive motel three blocks inland; about five minutes walk from the boardwalk. He offered to share his room with me and I instantly took him up on this offer, assuring myself of inexpensive accommodations. That day we all attended the scientific sessions and the next day at 11:00 AM I was to present our paper.

The American Fertility Society meetings were mostly clinical in nature and I was a little leery about presenting a paper dealing fundamentally with basic sciences. In my opinion it didn't fit very well into a primarily clinical program. Nevertheless, W.O. felt strongly that the paper was appropriate because it dealt with experimentally induced reversible sterility in male rats, an issue of clear interest to a Fertility Society. Plus, the Board had discussed with him their desire to have more basic research studies presented at their meetings. That afternoon, all of the papers were based on clinical investigations of women with fertility problems and menstrual irregularities. I didn't find any of it very interesting however, nor did I find the papers of much scientific value since they dealt with descriptive clinical issues and not with therapy.

That evening W.O. had a dinner meeting with his colleagues so Anthony and I went to the boardwalk. It was a glorious evening. We walked for miles mingling with throngs of celebrants, mostly guests from neighboring hotels, all of whom were having a wonderful time. Finally we stopped for a bite to eat before returning to our motel so I could organize the slides for my presentation.

The next morning Anthony and I located the meeting room where our session would convene and decided to listen to the papers presented that morning. The room was small; it probably wouldn't hold more than thirty or forty participants. The main lecture room held over three hundred. The meeting organizers apparently did not expect a large audience for a basic science session and they were correct. There were only ten to fifteen participants at any of the presentations. Although most of the papers dealt with patients, they had a more scientific viewpoint and most dealt with laboratory findings in subjects with infertility. When I started my presentation the audience had dwindled to seven people including W.O. and Anthony.

After my talk I responded to a few questions from the audience and sat down. W.O. turned to me smiling and suggested that the three of us have lunch. We went to a little restaurant next to the hotel and after ordering our meals, a heavy silence ensued. W.O. broke it saying, "You were correct. This was the wrong audience for a basic science paper. However, we have to find a way to bring basic sciences to our clinical colleagues." He started laughing and rocking on his chair:

"Emil, you are a clinician as well as a basic scientist so you should understand even better than Anthony or I. You should appreciate the importance of bringing together individuals from the basic and clinical worlds. This is the obvious route to progress in scientific knowledge and the successful evolution of medicine."

This thought resonated deep within me. I don't know why but suddenly I could see the face of the assistant professor of surgery who was my instructor when I was a senior medical student. He was furious when I submitted a write-up on breast cancer management that pointed out some basic science findings. His derisive laughter as he dumped my paper into a garbage can and admonished me to write another one omitting the basic science "nonsense", still rang in my ears. "I want facts," he cried, "Not theory."

The round face of Dr. Flocks, Chairman of the Department of Urology at the University of Iowa, also floated in front of my face. He collaborated with W.O. when I was simultaneously a medical student and a PhD candidate. I was conducting research on rats at the same time I was on his service as a medical student. He used to call me the "rat doctor" and he didn't mean it as a compliment. Everything suddenly clicked for me and I understood clearly W.O.'s appeal to bring basic sciences and clinical sciences together. At that moment I knew what my fundamental purpose would be in my career. I looked at W.O. for a long time and finally said, "Thank you. I understand and I will do my best."

The following morning Anthony had to leave early. My flight didn't depart until 4:00 PM, so W.O. invited me to lunch. As we sat down in the hotel's luxurious dining room (at this stage of my life probably any decent dining room would seem luxurious to me) I could sense that W.O. was trying to make up his mind about something prior to initiating further conversation. Finally he started slowly, even slower than his usual phlegmatic pace:

> I've been struggling to make a serious decision but I have now made it. First, however, I must apologize for bringing this up to you so late in the planning stages. I was asked to organize an international symposium on Physiological Mechanisms Concerned with Conception. This five and a half day conference will be held in West Point, New York in July of this year. It will be the first international symposium of this nature ever conducted.

I listened attentively but could not guess where he was heading. In the meantime, the waiter was hovering over us trying to take our food orders. This gave me a little time to collect my thoughts, but I still drew a total blank. Once the waiter disappeared, he continued:

> The structure of the symposium will be unique. It will be held in the pastoral setting of an old hotel on the banks of the Hudson River near the West Point Military Academy.

The participants will be divided according to their special interests into eight small groups or panels, each consisting of about twelve scientists from far and wide, including India, Japan and Australia. Each panel, led by a Chairman and one or two Co-Chairmen, will be responsible for analyzing the scientific advancements in the areas of reproductive sciences in which they are experts, for example spermatogenesis, oogenesis, ovulation and so on. The members of each panel will be asked to communicate with each other for several months prior to the symposium. During that time, they will be expected to create and discuss an outline of the material they propose to discuss at the Symposium.

During the symposium, panels will meet during the first two and a half days to discuss their material. Over the next three days the Chairman of each panel will present the material to the entire symposium, comprised of all of the panel members plus a large additional group of invited scientists. Each presentation will be open for discussion to all members of the symposium and guests. Subsequently, the Chairmen and where applicable, the Co-Chairmen, will be invited to spend several days at the Population Council of the Rockefeller Institute (later renamed Rockefeller University) in Manhattan. There, with staff assistance, they will write up the findings of the conference for publication under the title: Mechanisms Concerned with Conception."

Here he paused, trying, I think, to let me absorb this information. I was overwhelmed with the concept and scope of the symposium. I was grateful to him for telling me about it and hoped he would afford me the privilege of attending as a guest. Up to now he had been very serious and somber but suddenly a mischievous smile lit up his face and leaning towards me he said, "Charlie Leblond will be the chairman of the panel on 'Spermatogenesis' and Ed Rosen-Runge the co-chairman." I was beginning to digest this fascinating bit of information when, with a twinkle in his eyes, he added, "And you will co-chair with Charles." I wasn't certain I'd heard him correctly and tried to interrupt it but he didn't let me. "This means you will co-chair the panel on spermatogenesis and collaborate in preparing for the general session. After the symposium, you will come to the Population Council where you, Charlie and Ed will write that chapter."

My mind actually wasn't boggled by the Symposium or by the panels not even by the writing of the chapter. I was totally smitten, however, with the idea that I would be working with the two greatest minds in my area of interest - spermatogenesis, its control and its response to injurious agents. Charles P. Leblond was the Chairman of the Department of Anatomy and Histology at McGill University in Montreal. He had made a number of significant discoveries including a recently published paper on the process of spermatogenesis. I had been working with this concept over the past three years and trying to develop a technique that would allow defining, in a specific and quantitative fashion, changes occurring in the seminiferous epithelium of the testes after injury. He and Edward C. Rosen-Runge were the most prominent investigators in the area of testicular morphology in the human testes.

I, a lowly medical resident and postdoctoral fellow, was to co-chair a scientific session at a symposium and co-author a major analytical paper on spermatogenesis?! This was inconceivable to me. I looked at W.O. in disbelief but he shook his head and in his quiet and even voice he said, "Emil, you can do it. Both Charles and Edward are here and I will introduce you to them. They were very pleased when I suggested that you co-chair the session and are looking forward to meeting you. They've read your papers and feel that your input will be very significant."

On the plane flying home from Atlantic City, a million thoughts were racing through my mind. Charles had suggested that we stay in weekly contact and he was going to develop a work schedule for us. I learned that Charles was a very methodical, clear thinking and practical scientist who expected full cooperation from Edward and me. When meeting with us in Atlantic City, he already had an extensive outline of the chapter he had developed with Edward during the preceding few months. They did most of the work dealing with spermatogenesis and expected me to provide the material dealing with the effect of various agents detrimental to testicular function. This was a tall order and I was afraid I couldn't do it, especially as there was very little time. It was already March and the Symposium was to be held in July. Until the end of June I was still a medical resident with a very demanding schedule and hospital duty every third night. However, I was so taken with the idea of attending the Symposium and participating in the preparation of the chapter that the obstacles shrank in significance.

I felt I was riding a huge wave into a new age in medicine and biomedical science. Numerous discoveries had been made during the past few years. We had ushered in the age of antibiotics and hormones and had seen tremendous developments in basic sciences. At the same time, there were the beginnings of an amalgamation of the clinical and scientific. This made me realize that I was witnessing not only a burgeoning of biomedical sciences, but also the unprecedented application of newly gained scientific knowledge to finding solutions to many age old medical questions. What truly shook me was the realization that I was taking part in this miraculous happening.

At the DRH untold numbers of patients were treated during each twenty-four hour period in the emergency facilities and hundreds more were seen in the outpatient clinics. As part of my residency, I was required to go through a three-week rotation in the Department of Internal Medicine at the V.A. Hospital in Allan Park. This was almost a vacation by comparison. Most of the patients were veterans of the Korean War and on the ward to which I was assigned almost all had rheumatic heart disease.

With the availability of penicillin, the standard treatment was a course of high dose penicillin injections followed by maintenance treatment with oral penicillin tablets. Unfortunately, many of the patients were young men, just kids really, who took medical advice lightly and soon after discharge stopped taking their antibiotics. As a result we saw some acute recurrences of the heart disease, frequently presenting with endocarditis or even pericarditis, both of which are serious inflammations of the membranes of the heart. Thus, a substantial number of our admissions were in fact these recurrences. Since most of these young men were in good physical condition, the doctors had very little to do except convince them to take the medication as prescribed.

On this service, the resident physicians had night duty only once a week and there were essentially no procedures to be carried out. I hadn't had such a relaxed schedule for as long as I could remember. It was a bit of good fortune since it gave me extra time to work on the Spermatogenesis chapter for the Symposium. One night I had an idea. During my rotation on the Psychiatric Service in my senior year of medical school, I had had a lengthy indoctrination in the techniques of hypnosis and its possible uses in therapy. I had become quite adept at it in fact. Why couldn't I hypnotize the young men on penicillin therapy and give them a post-hypnotic suggestion to continue taking the medication after being discharged from the hospital? This seemed like an interesting possibility, but first I had to present the idea to my superior.

The chief of internal medicine, after thinking about my idea for a day, gave me the go-ahead. I selected six subjects and spent one hour a day for six days with each man attempting to induce a hypnotic state. The two youngest of the group were very difficult to hypnotize; however, two of the remaining four easily reached the first stage of hypnosis, light hypnotic sleep, during the very first session. The other two went to the second plane, the medium hypnotic state, during which I could make the post-hypnotic suggestion that they continue their penicillin therapy. I didn't attempt to bring them to the third plane, a deep or somnambulistic state because I worried it might be too difficult for me to handle appropriately.

I worked with these patients during my entire stay at the V.A. Hospital and a year later learned that all six patients had completed their therapy as directed by their physician. This was a very gratifying experience and about six months later, I received a package from one of these patients containing a drawing. It was a cartoon depicting me swinging a pocket watch from its chain in front of his face while he hands me a fist full of dollar bills saying, "You know I don't believe in all of this hypnosis mumbo jumbo. By the way, here's the money I owe you." The cartoon was not just funny; it was heart warming. This was the first time a patient had expressed his thanks in such an imaginative way.

Meanwhile, Ania's application to graduate school had been accepted. She would continue working towards her PhD in the Department of Microbiology at Wayne State University Medical School. She would work at the Graduate School of Biomedical Sciences which was located in a modern building just across the street from our new house. She was assigned to the section of viral immunology under the direct supervision of the Departmental Chairman, Dr. Fred Reitz. We were both elated as were our parents and friends. Before she could begin however, she needed to complete her work at Parke-Davis. It was important research on the production of a flu vaccine and it was coming to fruition.

Our future home was nearly complete. We were informed that in early June we would be able to complete the purchase and would be able to move in by July first. We should have been excited and overjoyed about buying our first house but instead we felt scared and depressed. We had calculated that we would be able to pay the monthly payments and have enough money left over for living expenses. Nevertheless, we were very insecure.

The goal of my research during the two years of my NSF fellowship had been to determine whether there is a relationship between carbohydrate metabolism, as expressed by endogenous respiration (oxygen consumption by the tissues), hyaluronidase production, and suppression of sperm production in infertility patients. At least this was the goal I had outlined in my application. The fellowship included a small budget for research equipment and I decided to purchase a Warburg Apparatus for measuring oxygen uptake in respiration. I also had to set up and validate the procedure for measuring levels of hyaluronidase in human seminal fluid. Such a procedure using human semen did not exist and I would have to develop one. With my prior experience in this area I wasn't worried and decided to work on the method after July 1st.

It was time to look into the purchase of the Warburg Apparatus which was a major piece of equipment. I needed to develop a relationship with the purchasing department and make sure that the NSF funds were properly transferred to the University. Once it was procured and delivered to the Endocrine Division, it was placed in a little room that was to be my laboratory. While I was admiring the shiny stainless steel sides of the huge round water bath, a major part of the equipment, my depression and fears disappeared.

In addition, our daily visits to see the almost completed steel and glass structure that was to be our home, gave me a sense of euphoria. Ania's mood also lifted as we came to realize that we had great opportunities and there was nothing to fear. This change in our mood also influenced our girls who began looking forward to living in their new home with great pleasure and excitement. We decided to have a big 4th of July party in our new house and immediately began planning it.

My residency service was becoming a done deal. I only had to put in the long hours for few more weeks. In between my night duty responsibilities I moonlighted as much as possible, trying to earn a little extra money to purchase furniture for our new house. I worked seven days a week and every other night. These extra earnings allowed us to acquire a beautiful living room set and new furniture for the girls' room. We couldn't wait to move to Lafayette Park.

CHAPTER 5

FINAL YEARS OF TRAINING –THE MAKING OF AN ENDOCRINOLOGIST AND A SCIENTIST

On July 1, 1959 I made the transition from resident to research fellow and moved into the tiny laboratory I shared with my beautiful but bulky new Warburg Apparatus. The laboratory also had a wooden bench fastened to one of the walls where I was given space for my paper work and where I was expected to spend most of my time during the next two years.

The reality, however, turned out to be quite different. While I was to conduct some basic research, most of my time was spent attending clinics and learning the skills I would need to become an endocrinologist. My major and most important activity was taking care of patients with endocrine disorders, which I did when attending specialty clinics that included general endocrinology, diabetes, thyroid and reproductive endocrinology. In addition, we had general conferences regarding diabetes, infertility and endocrinology, (including reproductive endocrinology). Night call was relatively easy and I worked only two nights a week, but I had also retained one night call a week in a small hospital where I moon-lighted for extra income. This extra money had become essential since Ania was now in graduate school full time.

Looming over all of this was the Conference on Physiologic Mechanisms Concerned with Conception which was coming up in less than a month. It was an unbelievable honor to be co-chairing a panel with Drs. Leblond and Rosen-Runge. I was getting weekly communications dealing with topics to be discussed by the panel and I was to be responsible for the section dealing with factors influencing testicular function. Members of my section included leaders in the field, like Doctor Oakberg of Oak Ridge, Tennessee, an authority on the effects of ionizing radiation on the testes; Doctor Tokuyama from Japan, who had the only good data on the effects of heat on human testes; and W.O, who was to discuss the effects of nitrofurans. I was to present data on the effect of radio-mimetic substances like TEM.

The conference was awesome in its scope and one of the most important endeavors of my career to date. It was presented under the joint auspices of the Population Council and the Planned Parenthood Federation of America. After the meeting, we went to the Population Council in New York City to write the book, which was ultimately published in 1963. It was edited by Dr. Carl Hartman, Chairman of the Biological Research Committee of the Planned Parenthood Federation of America and W.O., who was Medical Director of the Population Council. I was extremely proud to have co-authored the lead chapter in this book with Drs. Leblond and Rosen-Runge.

The year 1959 was racing by. At the beginning of the new school year in September both girls had enrolled in the small, newly opened school in Lafayette Park. This was the first year in grade school for Inette and the third year for Pauline. They both enjoyed the school immensely. It was small and intimate and just a short walk of our house. Since the DRH and the Medical School were also nearby, Ania and I were also able to walk our daily tasks. This gave us considerable scheduling flexibility, but we sill needed a satisfactory arrangement for the girls care after school; coming home to an empty house was not an option. We were again visited by lady luck.

At the same time we moved into our new house, the Busch family moved into a neighboring unit. Dr. Joe Busch was an engineer and his wife Barbara was staying home temporarily to care for their young sons. In no time a warm friendship developed between our two families. When Ania's experiments required many hours of incubation or refrigeration, she would come home in the afternoon to study and do some writing and then return to the laboratory in the evening to finish the experiment. On the days when she couldn't get home by early afternoon, our neighbors took care of the girls who, fortunately, greatly enjoyed playing with their sons.

My work at the hospital was sliding into an easy routine. I became mesmerized by the work in the various clinics conducted in the Endocrine Division. It must have acquired a tremendous reputation because patients were referred to us from many hospitals in Detroit and its environs. Some of the referred cases presented very rare endocrine disorders; but even those were a common occurrence in our clinic, I had never seen so many patients with rare disorders. The variety and number of patients provided tremendous training opportunities for the clinical fellows.

The clinics became the major focus of my interest. I was learning at an incredible rate about the bewildering variety of endocrine diseases and soon realized that reproductive-endocrine diseases in both men and women were of particular interest to me. Looking back, it became clear why: the reproductive-endocrine system disorders were the closest to my general interest in the biochemical mechanisms that control gonadal functions.

Infertility was often looked upon by the general population (and often by physicians) as a "female" disorder. However, several contemporary scientists demonstrated the pivotal role of the male partner. Of particular importance in this respect was the work of John MacLeod at New York University, who demonstrated the close relationship between the number of spermatozoa in the man's seminal fluid, their morphologic and physiologic normalcy; and the occurrence of pregnancy. Also, W.O.'s studies had demonstrated that maturational defects often occur in the process leading to formation of mature spermatozoa in human testes.

The staff at the Reproductive System Disorders-Infertility Clinic was comprised of endocrine fellows, professors at the medical school, and private physicians who volunteered their time. These doctors were endocrinologists in private practice with different viewpoints, attitudes, and experiences. I learned a great deal from them about the politics of private practice, dealing with private patients and the nuts and bolts of medical care in that setting.

I was familiar with state hospitals since I had trained at a state university and had received my clinical training in a state hospital. I witnessed the tremendous volume of free care provided by the state at Iowa University Hospital and admired the high-quality of medical care provided essentially free of charge to welfare patients at DRH. I also learned about the free care provided at Wayne County Hospital and the V.A. Hospital. I found the medical care in these institutions to be of the highest caliber although the physical environment, while adequate, was not luxurious. However, I was interested in learning more about various aspect of medical care delivery in the private sector. Dr. Sandberg, one of the stellar private practitioners, was particularly helpful in explaining the intricacies and politics of health care delivery to private, non-welfare patients.

I was impressed by the fact that many private physicians donated an extraordinary amount of their professional time to various government institutions; they provided free medical care to patients, and free instruction to medical students and postgraduate physicians in various stages of their professional training. Dr. Sandberg explained some of the changes in the way medical care was delivered and paid for:

> Many private patients paid their physician directly for office visits or house calls. However, a significant number had a prepaid health plan, like Blue Cross / Blue Shield, that paid for a large proportion of hospitalization costs and a portion of the physician's fee during hospitalization. The direct payment for physician care was an accepted fact by most of the population, similar to the necessity of paying for groceries, clothing, cars, etc. They were considered to be essential expenses of living. Most physicians made concessions for patients who had difficulty paying the bills. Some reduced the price of a visit or a medical procedure, accepted delayed payments and, in some instances, even cancelled the charges. However, when surgery or hospitalization was essential, the financial situation became more complex. While surgeons were willing to discount the cost of surgery for needy patients, and/or allow the patient to pay in installments, the hospital bills usually had to be paid in full and within a reasonable period of time. At

this point, a relatively new phenomenon, health insurance, entered the medical care arena.

Here, Dr. Sandberg emphasized that in order to understand the encroachment of the prepaid form of medicine upon the structure of medical practice I had to look back to the early 20th century. Now quite animated, he continued his exposition:

> Around that time, diagnostic technology and therapeutic modalities had matured just to the point where they made a real difference, and surgical and other interventional technology was experiencing major expansion. Prior to WWI most diagnostic and therapeutic procedures could be performed and administered at doctors' offices, even at patients' homes. Thus, medical expenses were relatively low. After WWI, medical practice and the delivery of medical care began to change radically. There was a significant change in the demographic picture of the U.S. as our population shifted from rural areas to urban centers. At the same time, there was a quickening in the advances in medical knowledge, the quality of medical schools and a growth of medical technology that engendered stricter professional standards for the medical profession.
>
> Many advances were stimulated by an earlier study underwritten shortly after the turn of the twentieth century by the Carnegie Foundation for the Advancement of Teaching. This monumental study was conducted by a prominent medical educator, Dr. Abraham Flexner. He surveyed the state of medical education in both the U.S. and Canada and issued, in 1910, the famous Flexner Report that served as a basis for the reorganization and modernization of medical schools and medical education. He formally recognized the role of scientific progress in the evolution of medical knowledge and technology, and the crucial effects of science on medical education and practice.
>
> These advances encouraged the public to view medicine as science, and stimulated hospitals to provide scientifically

based medical care. This caused an increase in the cost of health care delivery. By the 1920s and 1930s these increased costs stimulated the creation of various forms of prepaid hospital services introduced by both individual hospitals and commercial groups. Eventually, the American Hospital Association (AHA) combined them under the name Blue Cross.

I was barely able to interrupt his torrent of information. It was all new to me. In medical school, we were not educated about the philosophy, structure or politics of health care delivery. Plus, the brutal demands of training and the constant state of exhaustion caused by round-the-clock duties were not conducive to inquiries into the theoretical or political aspects of medicine. Since graduating from medical school I'd had only an occasional whiff of the financial aspects of medical practice. Therefore, I was eager to hear the rest of the story from Dr. Sandberg. At that moment I had to leave in order to attend to some duties on the wards but I made him promise to continue this lecture in the near future.

Ania was very happy to be a graduate student of Dr. Fred Reitz at Wayne State University. Her project dealt with cellular immunity to the vaccinia virus and related to her work at Park-Davis. Her research progressed at break-neck speed and she was working around the clock, often going to the laboratory in the middle of the night to transfer samples from the incubator to the refrigerator or to complete some other brief task. She was hoping to earn her doctorate in record time. I was very happy for her and hoped she would complete all her degree requirements at the same time I finished my post-doctoral fellowship.

Suddenly, disaster struck! I was called by the principal of the girls' school to come immediately because of a medical emergency; Pauline had been involved in an accident. Although it only took ten minutes for me to get there, it seemed like an eternity. Pauline was lying on a couch in the principal's office holding her right eye. She was surprisingly calm and composed, "He shot a bobby pin into my eye" she whispered. I looked and indeed there was a bobby pin protruding from the center of her eye, partially embedded in her eyeball.

I immediately carried her to the car and drove to the Will's Eye Hospital. The bobby pin was removed from her eye in the operating room and I was given the prognosis by the operating surgeon; "At best, it will heal completely and the sight in her right eye will not be adversely affected. At worst, however, she may lose the right eye and possibly develop problems with her left eye as well." She was to remain in the hospital for at least one week.

Ania and I were devastated. Returning home late in the afternoon, we found Inette home crying. She was also very angry. "The teachers don't pay attention when some of the boys use rubber bands to shoot bobby pins at other kids, particularly girls" she told us still sobbing. Apparently, Pauline had complained to the teacher on several occasions but to no avail. I was too concerned about Pauline's eye to act upon my disappointment with the teacher's lack of supervision by confronting her at this time.

We visited Pauline in the hospital daily, sometimes two or three times a day, and watched with great satisfaction as she steadily recovered. For the first few days she was essentially immobilized in bed, but as time went on, she was permitted to sit up in bed and ultimately walk for short distances. After a week, the ophthalmologist pronounced her essentially out of danger and discharged her from the hospital with the understanding that she was to stay in bed for one more week. He felt the only complication she might still face would be the formation of a cataract in the lens of the eye later in life. In fact, in her forties she did begin to develop a small cataract in that eye.

It was now the summer of 1960 and I was enjoying myself immensely. I was working day and night, seeing patients, doing research, working in the laboratory, analyzing data from earlier experiments conducted in the Navy and at NMRI, helping Ania with her final push towards her degree, and taking the girls boating and fishing. I was chronically exhausted but very happy.

In the spring, Jerry Sherman and I presented a paper at the Federated Societies on research we had done on the effects of TEM on the reproductive capacity of mouse spermatozoa. Another paper, dealing with the effects of hyaluronidase and hesperidin on the absorption of red blood cells from the abdominal cavity of rats, was published in the journal, "Proceedings of Experimental Biology and Medicine". I was overjoyed!

Winter arrived and the girls wanted to go skiing, as did Ania and I. We decided to go skiing over Christmas vacation to the Boyne Mountains in Northern Michigan. This was a memorable trip as it was here that the girls truly caught 'ski fever'. Although they had been introduced to skiing in New England, it was during this trip that they truly learned to appreciate the beauty of winter in the mountains and the exhilaration of skiing. Both Ania and I had always been ardent skiers and the girls took to this sport with enthusiasm. It was almost impossible to corral them into the car for the trip back home.

I was busy at work juggling my various responsibilities but with considerable difficulty. Everything was a priority. While busy with ongoing research, clinical responsibilities, and attempts to learn as much clinical endocrinology as possible, I still had to go over the mountains of data generated during my stint at NMRI. One area of data analysis that I had totally neglected, was work done with Henry Wagner, a biochemist who had served two years in the Navy following his graduation from the University of Michigan at Ann Arbor.

During our time in the navy we had obtained very interesting data on the effects of ionizing radiation on the oxygen uptake of testicular tissue. This deserved publication in an important scientific journal and W.O, who was fully aware of our work, strongly encouraged me to complete the analysis and have the paper published in the journal "Endocrinology." After his naval service Henry had been appointed to the faculty of Vanderbilt University. He and I were in frequent contact by mail but I wanted to visit him. However, Vanderbilt was a day's drive away in Nashville and I just didn't have the time so the U.S. mail would have to suffice.

The Reproductive Endocrinology Clinic that dealt with infertility problems had become my favorite. At times I preferred spending time there to working in the laboratory, even though the latter had always been my first love. This recent surge in my interest in clinical aspects of reproductive endocrinology created several problems in my planning for the immediate future. In a little less than one year I would have to decide on a permanent position.

Up to that point I had been certain that basic research would be my career path; that my full time appointment would be at a medical school in a basic science department such as anatomy or physiology. I also thought that with additional specialty training, I would be able to spend a few hours a week at a reproductive endocrinology clinic. Discussion of this issue with Bob, however, was not comforting. He confirmed what I had surmised by then; there were very few clinical endocrine units in medical schools that dealt with human reproductive biology. Most knowledge of reproductive biology was derived from studies in basic science departments or animal husbandry schools. Human clinical endocrinology was pursued in very few places, one being DRH (as a part of Wayne State University Medical School). Human infertility issues were addressed in a few Ob-Gyn departments but there the primary approach was surgical, such as removing blockages of the fallopian tubes (which conduct the eggs from the ovaries to the uterus). I realized that in order to practice reproductive endocrinology I would have to find a medical school with a unit like the one at DRH, and this was a rarity. I began to appreciate the extent of my dilemma.

However, it was difficult for me to abandon the idea of combining basic and clinic pursuits. It had formed over many years and had been fed by teachers in basic science departments and by the few clinicians associated with unconventional clinical endocrine units. I began spending enormous amounts of time talking about this issue with members of our Division and those of the Ob-Gyn department whom I had befriended over the previous two years. The more I thought about it, the more depressed I became. Some silly and odd thoughts began to cross my mind. One even dealt with the possibility of joining a department of Ob-Gyn, conducting basic research in reproductive endocrinology, and seeing patients in their infertility clinics. However, that would preclude me from seeing and studying male patients. To try and do so would have created huge political issues with the Department of Urology, which considered male reproductive system disorders part of their turf.

I realized that the problem could not be solved on a theoretical basis. More information was essential; the type of information Dr. Sandberg was discussing with me. Obviously, some supplemental reading to glean factual information would also be essential. The next time I saw Dr. Sandberg, I begged him to tell me more about the evolution of medicine. He was very happy to do so and suggested we meet the following week in the hospital cafeteria for supper. We could talk there as long as we wished, since it remained open the entire night.

The following Tuesday, in the late afternoon, just I as was finishing up with a patient in the clinic, Dr. Sandberg called, "How about dinner tonight, can you make it?" I was off duty that evening so, after a quick call to Ania, I ran down to the cafeteria in the basement of the hospital and spied Dr. Sandberg instantly.

He was sitting near the far wall at a table with a tray full of plates in front of him. "Have a seat," he said, inviting me to sit down. I was starving and for the first few minutes he didn't hear much from me except the sounds of my chewing. Finally, I caught my breath and asked, "Last time you finished by telling me about the creation of Blue Cross. What happened next?" Dr. Sandberg leaned against the back of his chair and began with a smile on his face:

> Formation of the first prepaid health care organization was probably an essential step in the delivery of hospital care to the general population. It was probably a step in the right direction, although initially it was self-serving for the surgeons. This is because it was taken in response to a strong lobbying effort by surgeons who sensed that increasing hospital costs constituted a threat to their surgical practices and thus their incomes. Considerable and progressive increases in hospitalization costs had resulted in a corresponding increase in the difficulty the general public was having in paying for hospitalization. Since office surgery was only a tiny portion of their practice, it was essential to the surgeons that they be able to perform surgery in a hospital. Therefore, while prepaid plans covering hospitalization was a great benefit to patients, they also had a direct and beneficial affect on the surgeons' incomes.

Dr. Sandberg was obviously deeply concerned with these issues. I tried to interrupt the torrent of his words to ask some of the questions that kept coming up in my mind as he spoke. However, he was unstoppable and continued with great gusto. I slouched in my seat listening with great interest as he went on full of excitement:

> Shortly after prepaid coverage of hospital bills by Blue Cross became a reality, physicians became concerned about coverage of their services rendered in the hospitals. The

American Medical Association (AMA) entered the fray, and by the late 1930s was encouraging both state and local medical societies to develop prepaid plans to cover physician costs, particularly surgeons' fees. Shortly after the end of WWII various prepaid plans, originally organized by physicians groups, were coordinated into the Blue Shield plans. These plans, similar to Blue Cross, were primarily for coverage of large bills; physician's bills for care during hospitalization, and especially the large costs of surgical services. Both Blue Cross and Blue Shield became very attractive to businesses and corporations since they were exempt from both taxes and insurance regulations.

During WWII, prepaid health insurance gained a much stronger footing in the United States. By 1942, Henry Kaiser had offered tens of thousands of workers employed in his shipyards and automotive plants prepaid health care. This was a very shrewd move on his part and was later copied by other giants of industry, the first being General Motors.

The prepaid plan was particularly attractive during the war and the period immediately following the war when government-imposed price controls included a cap on wages. Health care benefits were not included in the wage-cap regulations so the companies were able to offer medical benefits in place of raises. These plans were so successful that Kaiser began offering Kaiser Health Plan Insurance to the general public. While Kaiser, having had extensive experience with health insurance, was confident in promoting its plan, other insurance companies were extremely leery. They weren't convinced the vital statistics tables were reliable predictors of population health. However, the insurance companies soon realized that by insuring the heavy industries they would be covering mostly young and relatively healthy individuals. This drew into the health insurance field a group of commercial insurance companies. As a result, prepaid health insurance became a popular benefit in most large industries, particularly the automobile industry.

I was mesmerized by Dr. Sandberg's summary of the evolution of these private systems for covering the costs of health care. At the same time I was disappointed to realize that this issue was not discussed to any extent in medical school or during subsequent training. I also realized that during our clinical training neither my colleagues nor I had paid any attention to these issues.

This stimulated me to look at information in the medical literature on this topic. I learned that, indeed, during the war years, heavy industry in tandem with a variety of new government regulations placed the private health care industry at the forefront of the United States industrial and health policies. The result was a remarkable growth in health care insurance coverage. In 1940, just before the onset of WWII, only ten percent of Americans were covered by private healthcare insurance plans. By the end of the war (1945), the number of insured had risen to twenty percent. This number more than doubled to forty-five percent by 1950 and reached almost sixty percent in 1955!

This was a startling revelation. I could feel the excitement in the air. Things were moving fast on all fronts. The medical world was unfolding its powerful capabilities for improving the health of mankind, and I felt proud to be even a minuscule part of it. The decade of the 1950s was full of illustrations of this trend: organ transplantation was introduced; Drs. Kendall, Hench and Reichstein won the Nobel Prize in 1950 for isolating the adrenal hormones and demonstrating their anti-arthritic capacities; Dr. Theiler then won it in 1951 for the development of a yellow fever vaccine; and Dr. Salk in 1952 for the polio vaccine. This was followed in 1953 by Watson and Crick's discovery of the structure of DNA, the molecule that encodes the secrets of life.

During the same time, research in other fields of science such as applied physics was also burgeoning and in 1959 the microchip was invented. If we fast-forward a few decades, this led the way to the development of home computers that in turn, were essential to the rapid progress of the science leading to microchip implants.

On July 13, 1960, the Democratic Convention nominated John F. Kennedy, a young, liberal and brilliant candidate to run for president. His candidacy was greatly applauded by most of the young, progressive intellectuals in the country, including many budding scientists, who felt that he would support and advance their ideals. At the same time clouds began to form on the horizon as a series of soul wrenching events gripped and ultimately divided our country. These events had had their inception much earlier.

By the late nineteenth century, the French had formally established a number of colonial holdings in Indochina. Following decades of skirmishes with various resistance groups, they became engaged in a serious fight with communist insurgents. In 1954, the French were summarily defeated at Dien Bien Phu in Vietnam, one of their colonial holdings on the Indochina Peninsula. After they surrender, the Geneva Conference of that year ended France's colonial presence in Vietnam and partitioned the country into North and South with the South becoming the Republic of Vietnam.

President Eisenhower, who had helped the French evacuate Vietnam after their ignominious defeat, began assisting South Vietnam with military and economic aid and sending military advisors. This ultimately included sending 'specialists' to provided 'technical assistance' to the Vietnamese armed forces who had been fighting the communists of the north for five or six years. I wondered and worried whether this might not suck our country into an endless military quagmire. After all this was the continuation of the centuries old Indochina wars with the added contemporary flavor variant of communism.

The Republican presidential candidate and current vice president, Mr. Richard M. Nixon, would probably follow President Eisenhower's policies with respect to Vietnam. John Kennedy, however, could possibly change this course of military involvement. Thus, my colleagues and I were observing the presidential political arena with great interest, convinced that it would have a profound affect on our lives and on the direction of biomedical research in this country. All of these considerations seriously weighed on my own thinking about what to do next.

The second year of my fellowship was in full swing. My research was progressing slowly because no matter how hard I tried to spend more time in the laboratory, my clinical responsibilities and paper writing seriously competed for time. In addition, I was getting more and more interested and involved in clinical problems dealing with reproductive system disorders. Bob, whose primary focus was the Reproductive Disorders Clinic, (which was formally open during the week and informally on the weekends), was happy to see my developing interest. We saw patients seven days a week in the Clinic not because new patients were admitted but because patients who needed a follow up of their ovulatory process needed to be examined every day.

My thinking was crystallizing and I was concluding that I would have to seek an academic position rather than enter the private practice of endocrinology. However, the position I sought was quite unique; it would have to allow me an opportunity to conduct basic research in animals coupled with basic research utilizing clinical material, and a certain amount of clinical practice involving patients with reproductive disorders. This was indeed a mouthful. Bob's Division at DRH met the clinical portion of my proposed requirements but it lacked the facility to conduct basic research with laboratory animals and this was unlikely to change.

I didn't know where to look, but was not discouraged. I felt there must be a place where all of these activities could be done simultaneously. I strongly believed this was the best way to assure the evolution of knowledge and, ultimately, its application to the clinical management of reproductive disorders. Allowing a surgical specialty to be the exclusive manager of non-surgical reproductive system disorders struck me as inviable from a practical, theoretical and academic viewpoint. It would be like having a cardiac (or any other) surgeon act as the sole manager of patients with heart failure no matter what the cause. A surgeon is trained differently, focuses on different techniques and approaches to treatment and is generally much too busy with surgical concerns to deal effectively with non-surgical therapies. I was becoming totally committed to the development of a medical specialty dealing with non-surgical aspects of reproductive system disorders.

Several good friends suggested that I talk to Dr. Romney, Chairman of the Department of Ob-Gyn at Albert Einstein College of Medicine in New York City. He apparently had expressed some interest in the theoretical aspects of reproductive sciences, particularly in the involvement of the Ob-Gyn community in basic research, and thus, might be sympathetic to my ideas. I called my old graduate school colleague, Dr. Shelly Segal, who worked at the Population Council with W.O. and asked him for his opinion. He was very positive, stating that Dr. Romney was a very influential academician, a seemingly good Chairman, and very involved with issues dealing with teaching, research and the politics of the turf battle in reproductive medicine. He also felt that Dr. Romney might have some practical advice concerning my career after completion of my fellowship. Shelly suggested that I consult with W.O. before meeting with Dr. Romney and even invited me to stay with him during my visit to New York.

Time was running short; I had to complete analysis of the data collected at NMRI with Connie Wagner. Upon completing his naval service Connie went to NIH to work at the Section on Enzymes in the Laboratory of Cellular Physiology. Neither of us had had the time or money to travel so we did our work by mail. I promised to complete the statistical analysis and he would go over the literature and write the introduction and discussion of the paper. In this way, the paper for presentation at the Endocrine Congress got under way. I returned to the routine of taking care of patients both on the wards and in the clinic.

There was a bit of excitement one day when a patient I had treated in the clinic for infertility became pregnant. This was my first success in treating an infertility patient and everyone in the Division congratulated me while I pretended that I wasn't entirely certain why. The patient was a thirty five year old woman, who had been married for fifteen years and had been trying to become pregnant for the past ten. The pregnancy was an extremely important episode in her life and after almost a year of treating her, I began to appreciate the tremendous psycho-emotional impacts of infertility.

Although my schedule was filled with hospital responsibilities, laboratory work, clinical research, preparation of scientific presentations, and concerns about my professional future, time had to be carved out for skiing. Both girls had by now developed a great love for the sport. To further stimulate their interest, we decided to buy a pair of skis for each of them. The skis, in light of our precarious financial situation, were second hand and slightly beaten up, but they loved them and couldn't wait to try them out. After juggling my schedule and getting permission from the girl's school for their time off, we left for what was a long holiday to us, Thursday evening to Monday evening. It was the middle of February and the skiing conditions were perfect. We again made a reservation at the Boyne Falls Lodge, where we had stayed the previous winter, and arrived there late Thursday night tired but very excited.

The following morning, after a mountain of pancakes and heaps of scrambled eggs, we took off for the ski area. The girls proudly carried their own skis, laughing and jostling each other. Ania carried her skis on her shoulder and was playing with them like a little girl herself. I felt proud and happy walking behind them. Ania looked so cute and the girls, in my eyes, had grown already into young ladies. Pauline was already nine years old and Inette, seven. Watching all three of them, I realized that Inette was catching up in height with Pauline. However, there was no time for contemplation as the girls, obviously bitten by the ski bug, were running to get started. I promised myself that I would spend most of my time on the beginners slope with them and Ania, like a good sport stayed with us. This time it was much easier since the girls were not babies anymore. They could hold on to the rope tow to be pulled up the hill and they understood the snow-plow technique for slowing down in the descent.

The second day was particularly successful since I was able to teach them how to initiate a turn. They were so enamored by their newly discovered ability to turn, that when late afternoon arrived they refused to quit. We couldn't get them off the hill until the rope tow stopped functioning for the evening. Monday afternoon they refused to get off the hill for the trip home. "One more run" they cried, with big smiles and frost colored red cheeks. I could not have been prouder as a father.

Upon returning to the hospital, a telephone message was awaiting me. Dr. Romney's office had called to make an appointment and I immediately returned the call. The secretary was very nice, cordial in fact, as she offered a number of open appointment dates. I thought a Monday would be best so that I could travel to New York on Sunday and return on Monday evening, losing only one workday.

Waiting for the appointment with Dr. Romney was torture. I was extremely ambivalent about this entire venture and my colleagues at DRH were very doubtful about the possibility of a career for me in an Ob-Gyn Department. Nevertheless, I felt compelled to give this opportunity a chance. I contacted W.O., told him the date of my visit with Dr. Romney, and asked if he could see me the same day. Since my appointment was at one o'clock he suggested we meet that morning for an early lunch so I would have adequate time to get to Dr. Romney's office.

Finally the day arrived; I landed in New York City and headed to Shelly's apartment. He received me warmly and mentioned that W.O. was expecting me at the Population Council first thing in the morning. We spent the evening discussing Shelly's activities at the Population Council and later the conversation switched to Dr. Romney and the possibility of my working there. I was pleased to learn that Shelly was engaged not only in theoretical and political aspects of contraception and population control, but that he also had a laboratory were he could conduct research dealing with contraception. He was very involved with a cadre of foreign postdoctoral fellows who came to train in his laboratories.

The following morning I rode with Shelly to the Population Council. It was located on the beautiful and spacious grounds of the Rockefeller Institute in one of its classic grey stone buildings. The inside looked very much like any university facility with laboratories, offices and lecture rooms. W.O.'s office was a large, airy and bright room on the first floor. When I walked in he instantly got up from behind the desk and hugged me. "It is good to see you!" he exclaimed. We talked about the scientific papers to be written and data analyses to be completed on our previous research projects. However, I was impatient and couldn't wait to hear his opinion about the wisdom of joining an Ob-Gyn department, specifically Dr. Romney's.

W.O. was very complimentary with respect to Dr. Romney and his department; however, I was unable to get a clear sense of his feelings about my getting involved in Ob-Gyn, which was a new area for me. The best I could get was a tepid, "That would be an interesting and probably useful experience". By eleven o'clock, he suggested that we go for a quick bite to eat since time was running short. The Albert Einstein College of Medicine was located in the Bronx, nearly an hour away by subway. During lunch, W.O. brought up a different possibility for me to consider. He knew an endocrinologist who was interested in the reproductive aspects of endocrinology. His name was Dr. Bill Perloff and according to W.O. he had done some very interesting and credible work in the areas of male infertility and polycystic ovarian disease of the female. He was the Chief of Endocrinology at Temple University School of Medicine in Philadelphia, but was in the process of moving full time to the Korman Research Laboratories of the Albert Einstein Medical Center (AEMC), an affiliate of Temple University School of Medicine. W.O felt strongly that I should visit him.

Having lived in New York for a couple of years in the late 1940s, and subsequently visited on many occasions, I was familiar with the subway system. My trip to the Bronx was easy, but as I sat down in the subway for this journey, many thoughts began to scurry across my mind. Did I really want to get involved with additional training? Gynecology was simply an area of surgery limited to the female reproductive tract. I had already decided against pursuing a surgical specialization in medical school because I didn't want to be a surgeon. And since I didn't want to deliver babies, obstetrics was not my area of interest either.

While contemplating these issues, thoughts of going into Urology kept on nagging at me. My major interest, at least my research interest was focused on the male reproductive system, thus Urology seemed more logical. However, it was also primarily a surgical specialty. No, I thought, I spent years of training in the specialty of Internal Medicine with a subspecialty in Endocrinology, why should I look for more years of training? Well, the answer was actually simple. My primary interest was in studying and managing the disorders of the reproductive systems in both males and females, particularly the endocrine or non-surgical disorders of these systems. Most endocrinologists either did not deal with the endocrine aspects of reproductive system disorders, or limited it to involvement of other endocrine systems, such as disorders of the thyroid gland.

When an endocrinologist diagnosed a surgical disease of the thyroid gland such as a nodule, he would refer the patient to a surgeon. However, in cases of endocrine disorders of the female reproductive system, women would usually think first of seeing a gynecologist (a surgeon) first, not an endocrinologist. As a rule gynecologists would try to manage these disorders exclusively using surgery, seldom referring the non-surgical patients to endocrinologists. I realized that I was facing a dilemma in my area of interest and possibly a political quagmire, in additional to scholastic, scientific and clinical issues. Mercifully, the train was arriving at my destination and I had to terminate these disturbing thoughts, at least temporarily.

Dr. Romney was a pleasant, fatherly, rather short, middle aged man. After waiting in his secretary's office for almost an hour, I was ushered into a beautifully appointed office with a massive desk and a huge picture window. In a pleasant voice with a typical northeastern accent, he began to interrogate me. He was obviously very familiar with my past and my background, and knew W.O. well. He assessed the situation at a glance and right away made a proposition that no one with a modicum of common sense would reject.

He clearly understood my research interests and addressed them directly by offering a novel scenario. First, he pointed out that he had been recruiting a number of young new faculty members. He was moving toward a research-oriented faculty; a phenomenon that had gained favor in medical schools in the late forties, and continued into the 1960s. He also clearly recognized the pivotal role of endocrinology in research dealing with reproductive system disorders and with the clinical practice of both obstetrics and gynecology. He visualized the need for formally trained endocrinologists on his faculty to provide the best training in Ob-Gyn. However, he went a step further in his thinking, expressing the idea that individuals like me, with training in internal medicine and endocrinology, should also obtain clinical training in obstetrics and gynecologic surgery, not only to command equivalent financial remuneration but also to acquire the skills and appreciation for Ob-Gyn.

This was a tall order. I quickly did the arithmetic in my mind; four years of college, four years of medical school, one year of internship, three years of internal medicine residency and two years of fellowship added up to fourteen years of academic training. A student starting at the age of eighteen wouldn't be finished with training in endocrinology until the age of thirty two. Adding another four years of training in Ob-Gyn would make one thirty six years old when the training was complete. This was too tall an order for me and probably for any budding academician! However, Dr. Romney dangled a large carrot in order to sweeten his offer. He came around the desk, placed one hand on me shoulder, bent towards me and said in a low voice:

Emil, this is a special opportunity for both of us and for

the field of Ob-Gyn. I'd like to offer you a dual position in the department, you would be an assistant professor of Ob-Gyn, with a full salary, and at the same time, you would be appointed as a special resident in Ob-Gyn for two years. During this time, your responsibility would be only to learn the skills necessary to pass the Board exams in Ob-Gyn. I'm confident that with your past medical-endocrine training and two years of training in my department you would be eligible for the exams. Upon completion of the Ob-Gyn training you would be appointed an associate professor and given free reign to establish a research program.

At this point, he straightened out and walked around the desk back to his chair.

The flight back to Detroit was rough, both emotionally and physically. The plane was a monstrous four-engine Lockheed turboprop Electra with seating for almost one hundred passengers. It was probably the most technologically advanced aircraft of the day. Despite its size and advanced engineering, however, it was mercilessly buffeted by headwinds and occasionally it would fall several hundred feet into an air hole. My thoughts were also being buffeted and falling into holes. I couldn't wait to see Ania and discuss this new situation with her. Would I be able to face another two years as a resident?

After lengthy discussions first with Ania and then with the members of the endocrine section, I called W.O. He was adamant that before making any decision, I should see Bill Perloff in Philadelphia. "Actually," he reiterated, "Bill has the only department in the country closely resembling what you have in mind. It's called the 'Division of Endocrinology and Human Reproduction'. Why don't you visit him in the spring after the meeting in Atlantic City?"

My duties on night call and my extra work in a private hospital occupied most of my time. Unfortunately the fellowship research suffered greatly since, in addition to my various clinical duties and performing new experiments, I still had to complete the data analysis from my previous research with W.O. He was pushing hard to document all of this work for presentation at various scientific meetings as well as for publication. I suddenly realized that I already had twenty-one published titles to my name and I was still in training. This realization stopped me dead in my tracks and a decision began to crystallize in my mind. Why should I consider any further clinical training. Why not begin with an independent position, possibly the one with Dr. Perloff in Philadelphia, rather than consider a complex semi-training position with Dr.Romney. This thinking made me very anxious, I couldn't wait to meet Dr. Perloff and learn about his organization at AEMC.

A call to W.O. was in order. He provided further important and helpful information about Dr. Perloff and offered to contact him about me. He suggested I call Bill the following week for an appointment after the Atlantic City meetings. It occurred to me that while in Philadelphia, I should also be contacting Dr. Charles Czarny, a well-known urologist who had been the first to describe the use of biopsies in the diagnosis of testicular disorders. He too was a good friend of W.O.'s and I hoped to learn more from him about the climate for reproductive biology in Philadelphia. The more I thought about Philadelphia and a possible position there, the more excited I got. When I called Dr. Perloff to see about visiting him he was very cordial; apparently, W.O. had already called him and he was looking forward to our meeting that spring.

Ania's work toward her doctorate degree was still progressing with unbelievable speed. Everyone in the Department loved her. She apparently could do no wrong and her grades were always outstanding. She had completed all of the experiments for her dissertation and was writing up the material for her doctoral thesis. Here I became very useful to her. Despite the crazy load I was carrying, I found time to type a draft of her dissertation on my old Swiss Corona portable typewriter. That way she could easily make corrections prior to submitting the manuscript to a professional typist to produce the final copy.

CHAPTER 6
WHICH PATH TO TAKE?

My mind kept returning to the same question; what direction should I take for my first independent professional position? In the final analysis, the question boiled down to two possibilities: one, whether I wanted to be involved almost exclusively in basic scientific research and two, whether I wanted to include clinical experience and clinical research in my work. This was an extremely difficult, almost impossible, decision for me to make. I could feel the enormous amounts of energy around me in the growing areas of medicine, science and research as new graduates crowded into them. Many were devouring research fellowship, both intra- and extramural, from institutions like NIH, NSF and the Rockefeller Institute. Those going into private practice did so with very idealistic goals about how best to serve the medical and biomedical communities. Despite this enthusiastic and, to a great degree, altruistic attitude, at least among some in this community, the national delivery of health care was still based primarily on the principles of private practice and the capitalistic principles of a competitive economy.

A little over ten years earlier, Great Britain had introduced a national health service, a tax-supported, government-managed health care system that provided free and, apparently, reasonable medical care to all its citizens. A number of other countries also enjoyed various types of nation-wide health care systems at that time. In fact, Germany was probably the first country in the world to address the issue of free nationwide medical care for its low-income population as far back as the nineteenth century.

Ruminations over these issues sent me scurrying to the library in order to obtain more information. I was particularly interested in learning more about Germany's medical care programs. In Germany prior to World War II, my parents, both of whom were dentists, had dealt professionally with the Techniker Krankenkasse (which translates to Sickness Fund), the government supervised medical care system and the largest health insurer in Germany to this day. Later when my family moved to Poland, a part of their practice also involved patients covered by the Kasa Chorych (the Health Fund), a segment of the Polish health care system.

Perusal of a few sources in the library made it clear that Statutory Health Insurance (SHI), the mandatory health insurance in Germany introduced by Otto von Bismarck in 1883, had a long and complex history. The system had been evolving for decades and going through various phases of struggle between practicing physicians, the Krankenkasse, various insurance entities, the government, labor unions and employers, all of whom had parochial, political, professional and fiscal interests in this enterprise.

Although the insurance premiums were primarily derived from funds provided by the employers and employees, they were guaranteed by the national government, providing a solid backing for the insured. The medical care provider was paid using a variety of financial arrangements but primarily on a fee-for-service basis, especially when medical care was delivered by a physician in his or her office. The key to the success of this program was its tripod arrangement: the employer, the employee, and the government. This program provided free medical care to the portion of the population below a certain income level.

Slowly I began to understand the enormous challenges faced by this country in its attempt to use the principles of free enterprise to provide adequate medical care for the entire population regardless of economic status. The Europeans had clearly opted for more socialist-leaning systems.

I observed the interplay between private hospitals like Detroit's Ford Hospital and government supported hospitals like the University of Iowa State Hospitals. Also, I considered the county hospitals like the

Wayne County Hospital, the city hospitals like Detroit Receiving and federally supported hospitals like the Veterans Administration Hospital in Dearborn, Michigan. My experiences at each of the government-operated hospital had been very positive. The level of medical care delivered in these hospitals was enviable, although definitely lacking in niceties. Despite the lack of luxurious facilities the care delivered to the "welfare" patients was generally good; to me it seemed more than adequate. The physicians' salaries were paid by various government agencies and though they were considerably lower than the earnings in private practice I felt they too were rather adequate.

These considerations were important to me since I was in the process of seeking my own place in the medical profession. A purely private practice had never attracted me. I was essentially committed to finding an arrangement that would permit extensive involvement in research as well.

The time for another trip to the East Coast was approaching swiftly and I made an appointment to see Dr. Perloff. The bus trip from Atlantic City to Philadelphia seemed to drag on forever since I was very anxious and impatient. After checking into the hotel, I called Dr. Perloff who was very cordial and offered to pick me up at the hotel. I waited for him in the lobby and within half an hour spotted him as he came through the revolving doors. I had never seen him but W.O. described him to me over the phone in detail. He was a slim man of medium height with a handsome face and a full head of graying hair. He walked into the lobby with the energetic stride of a young man and must have recognized me instantly because he walked directly towards me with an extended hand, "You must be Emil," he said in a low and pleasant tone of voice. When I nodded he took me by my arm and directed me to a black Cadillac parked in front of the hotel. Two hotel attendants jumped to open the doors door for Bill and me. They seemed very familiar with Bill and his Cadillac.

It took us less than fifteen minutes to reach the sprawling grounds of the Albert Einstein Medical Center in North Philadelphia. We arrived at a super modern red brick, glass and steel three-story building with a big sign in front reading 'Korman Research Building.' Broad stone steps brought us to a terrace leading into a lobby on the second floor of the building. Bill took me to the Director's office located just off the lobby. Sam Ajl, the Director, had a rough hewn face, abrupt manners and a big smile. He shook my hand and only said, "We'll see you later". Leading me out of the office, Bill said "Our Division is on this floor. We'll go there now."

As we walked across the floor a pleasant, somewhat rotund looking man came out of one of the doors. "Hello, Al let me introduce Emil Steinberger to you" and, turning towards me said, "This is Dr. Al Kaplan, Chief of the Division of Microbiology". Dr. Kaplan shook my hand vigorously and in a friendly voice greeted me, "Welcome to Albert Einstein. Bill mentioned that you would be visiting. When you finish with him, come and visit a while with me". I thanked him and we went on.

We spent the rest of the day talking, looking, planning and discussing the various possibilities. Bill had just left his position as Chief of Endocrinology at Temple University, and was in the process of organizing, recruiting and building his 'Division of Endocrinology and Human Reproduction' at AEMC. He had brought a steroid biochemist with him, Dr. Jacobson, who was in the process of setting up his steroid biochemistry laboratory. The Division had been assigned a large portion of the second floor of the Korman Building but so far only Bill's clinical offices and the steroid lab had been completed. The rest was waiting until additional staff was recruited so that interior facilities could be built according to their needs.

I had been aware of the vibrant energy surrounding the explosion of biomedical research, and that of the scientists and physicians taking part in it. It was causing exponential growth in biomedical knowledge and the ability to diagnose and treat illnesses. As Bill took me through the Korman Research Laboratories, introducing me to various scientists, and later showing me the rest of the AEMC, including the hospital buildings, outpatient departments and the various ancillary facilities, I was getting more and more excited. This began to look like a place I would truly enjoy! The day was coming to an end when Bill suggested that I return to the hotel for a brief rest before he picked me up for dinner.

Punctually at 7:00, the Cadillac pulled up in front of the hotel and Bill was behind the wheel motioning to me to get in:

We'll go to my apartment and pick up my wife. I didn't

get a chance to go home after dropping you off here earlier because my meeting at Temple ran over time. Anyway, I'd like to show you my place and maybe we can have a drink at home before going to the restaurant. We used to have a big house in the suburbs but about two years ago we moved to a high rise building in Chestnut Hill.

I learned later that Chestnut Hill was one of the most elegant, affluent and historical communities in Philadelphia. It was originally part of a German township that officially became part of the Philadelphia back in 1854.

Bill and his wife lived on the fifth floor of the building; their children were married and living on their own. When I walked into the apartment I couldn't catch my breath. I had never seen an apartment furnished so tastefully, the furniture was stunning. It had been hand-crafted by an artist who'd used incredible imagination to bring out the natural qualities of the wood while wrapping it in a modern esthetic. Some pieces were carved of hand rubbed walnut, others included a combination of wood and sculpted metal. Bill noticed my fascination with the furniture and explained, with obvious pride and pleasure:

> The furniture was created by two artists, Phillip Powell and Paul Evans. They have a shop in New Hope, an artists' colony about an hour's drive northeast of Philadelphia. Powell works with wood and Evans is a genius with metal. Usually they work together, collaborating on their creations. They have been hailed nationally for their imaginative designs.

I was smitten. I had never seen anything as lovely and unusual until I met his wife; she surpassed it with her elegant beauty. We dined in one of the most popular seafood restaurants in Philadelphia, the original Bookbinders, and Bill was a most gracious host. He suggested for our main dish the Maryland soft shell crabs, a delicacy I had never tasted. Mrs. Perloff was unobtrusive but kind and considerate to me during dinner. Bill, on the other hand, very gently but insistently tried to drag out of me my plans for the immediate future, particularly with respect to my research objectives. He was clearly trying to learn how I might fit into his overall plans for the division. As we dined and discussed research and clinical practice as well as the possible directions of his division, I recalled the many discussions I had had with Ania concerning our future.

Ania was trained as a microbiologist and immuno-virologist and was planning to join a department of microbiology at a medical school, preferably the same one that I would decide to join. During her research she had became intimately involved and very adept at tissue and organ culture techniques. We fantasized how this experience might fit into a research program involving reproductive and endocrine biology that might combine our skills and scientific interests. We never reached any serious conclusions concerning the feasibility of such a formal collaboration, although frequently joked about a scientist called the "viral reproductive biologist".

As I listened to Bill's expansive ideas for a broad approach to reproductive biology and endocrinology using techniques from basic and clinical sciences; and drawing from disciplines as diverse as psychology, psychiatry, electron microscopy, biochemistry and population biology, an idea suddenly flashed into my brain. "Bill," I asked him, "If I joined your Division, how would you react to the possibility of my wife Ania joining me as a collaborator in an entirely new direction in my research, the application of tissue and cell culture to problems of the endocrine and reproductive system. Ania is getting her PhD in virology this spring and we have discussed just such an application on several occasions and felt it might be a novel and feasible approach."

He looked at me with his soft, dark eyes for an indefinable period before exclaiming, "That's a brilliant idea!" He startled me with this response since I actually was musing aloud rather than making a direct recommendation. I immediately wished that I could take it back since I hadn't even discussed this possibility with Ania. She was a virologist who had already contributed significantly to this area of science; she might not be interested in changing her research to reproductive biology. It was an unrelated field of endeavor. However, under the circumstances, and with the opportunities suggested by Bill, the idea quickly became an exciting opportunity. The transformation of my thinking must have been facilitated by the continuous flow of excellent wine and Bill's optimism and enthusiasm. I knew that there would be a lot to talk about when I returned to Detroit. I also knew that the opportunity at AEMC should be considered very seriously.

We didn't have enough time to get into any details about the potential positions, specifically concerning rank, salary, spaces, budget, clinical arrangements, etc. so we decided to pursue these issues over the phone and in letters.

However, these were not minor details but important considerations. Therefore, it soon became clear that a second trip to Philadelphia for a face-to-face discussion of these issues would be essential. First, however, Ania and I needed to reach a clear understanding concerning our collaborative work. Her position at Einstein, the direction of our collaborative research, and the availability of facilities to carry out the research would have to be discussed. In addition, I would have to clarify the balance of my clinical practice and basic science research. While Ania agreed to join in research dealing with endocrinology and reproductive biology, the type of studies we would conduct had to be crystallized.

I told Ania that before we could take another step concerning our possible positions in Philadelphia, we would have to outline a research project emphasizing the advantages of using tissue culture approaches for resolving questions in male reproductive biology and endocrinology. The proposal would need to be written in a style that could be submitted as a grant proposal to NIH. There it would be probably evaluated by the Endocrinology Study Section. In that case, my prior tenure on that study section would prove invaluable; I knew the review process in detail and I had a number of friends there who could help me structure the grant.

I suggested to Ania that we draft a research grant proposing to investigate hormonal requirements for spermatogenesis utilizing in vitro (test tube) techniques and have her be the co−principal investigator. She was reluctant at first to take on this additional responsibility as she was still completing her dissertation and preparing for a comprehensive PhD exam. However, I promised to take primary responsibility for writing the grant proposal and let her assume a mainly advisory role until she completed the requirements for her doctorate. I also felt strongly that she should come to Philadelphia with me to discuss our potential positions and administrative responsibilities at AEMC and the Temple

University Medical School. I felt the final decision should be made jointly and that Bill should meet Ania before offering her a position. A visit to Philadelphia over a long weekend would have to suffice.

I was very happy with the idea of having Ania with me to help with the negotiations. She had a strong background in sciences and, having held responsible positions at a major state diagnostic laboratory in Iowa City, and later a senior position in a major pharmaceutical company, she knew a lot about the commercial and practical aspects of running a research unit. I was confident that Bill would recognize and appreciate these assets and, indeed, Ania was a big hit with both Bill and the administrators. Bill couldn't take his eyes off her and kept saying, "She's not only beautiful but what a bright mind and a great personality!" I was swelling with pride. After meeting with the chiefs of other divisions, it became clear to me that this was going to be a very dynamic institution filled with young, enthusiastic and bright researchers, all willing to work hard to achieve their dreams.

Both the research and clinical facilities for Bill's Division still needed to be finished. If we accepted the positions, our grant request would have to include a budget for this purpose. This did not frighten me though, Bill expressed faith in me and I was confident that I wouldn't disappoint him. As our negotiations progressed, I could see that Ania was getting more and more excited about the prospect of working at AEMC. I knew that the first year or two would be difficult for her as she would need to learn more about endocrinology and reproductive biology. However, knowing her scientific abilities, her broad training in scientific methods, as well as her other intellectual resources, I had no doubt in her ability to accomplish these goals.

We decided to accept the positions and together with Bill began planning the design of our laboratory facilities, and of the unit as a whole. The task ahead was of gargantuan proportions. In view of the upcoming meetings of the Endocrinology Study Section, I would need to submit my grant application within two weeks. If the requested financial support was approved, we could receive the research funds almost immediately after assuming the positions in Philadelphia. This would be record time for both the institution and for us. However, accomplishing it would require working day and night for the next two weeks to finish the grant application, getting almost instant approval of it by the Albert Einstein administration, and having someone from Philadelphia make a trip to Washington D.C. to insure that the application was delivered to NIH on time.

Prior to our move to Philadelphia there were many other arrangements to be completed and I anticipated one or two more trips would be essential before the final move. The details of developing my department were overwhelming and Bill wanted my input regarding the development of the entire division and the recruitment of appropriate personnel. He had several ideas in his mind. He had recently met a basic scientist, Dr. Harold Persky, who made a name for himself in the 1940's by purifying several respiratory enzymes. He later switched to investigation of some basic questions in psychiatry as they related to endocrinology. He expressed an interest in joining a multidisciplinary endocrine-reproductive group and Bill was very excited about this possibility. At that moment , however, I was so wrapped up in my own issues and wondering if I'd done the correct thing in influencing Ania to redirect her research focus from microbiology to endocrinology, that Bill's excitement about recruiting Dr. Persky went over my head.

While the immediate issues related to establishment of the new department occupied most of my attention, the issues of starting a clinical practice kept nagging at me. After lengthy discussions with Bill, we decided to develop a relatively small clinical arm in the division. The practice would be run like a private office but the fees would be very reasonable and flow back into the division's budget. The clinicians, like the rest of the staff, would receive a salary. Superficially this arrangement appeared simple and fair; however, subsequent changes in reimbursement modes for medical care complicated it. At that time, these issues also seemed relatively insignificant because neither Bill nor I thought the income from or impact of our clinical practice would be significant.

I hadn't yet seen the clouds gathering over the practice of medicine. We were still completely immersed in the old style of medical practice in the United States. That meant, in general terms, that the federal government supported some facilities designed for special populations as for example the Veterans Administration Hospitals, Public Health Service Hospitals, and Mental Health Hospitals. The state governments supported hospitals for charity patients, such as county and city hospitals and at both for-profit and nonprofit private hospitals free care was provided to welfare patients. Nursing and other auxiliary care in these facilities was supported by the hospitals and physician care was provided by voluntary medical staff. This was the environment for physicians entering medical ranks in the late 1940s, 1950s and early 1960s.

My years of training were finally coming to an end and I was about to enter the "real world". For me this transition was so gradual it was almost imperceptible. Other than some increased responsibilities and a higher salary, I was fundamentally continuing in the same vein. Plus, I was very much looking forward to working with Ania. For her however, the first couple of years were going to be pretty difficult while she completed the transition from being a microbiologist-virologist to a reproductive biologist-endocrinologist. She was also probably wondering whether the decision to change fields was appropriate. I think I was so elated with my new position and the prospect of working together that I tended to disregard these concerns.

On my next trip to Philadelphia, I stopped in New York to see W.O. He was busy developing research laboratories at the Population Council. The place was vibrant with post doctoral fellows from all over the world, particularly India where the Council, in collaboration with the Ford Foundation, very actively promoted the development of research in reproductive sciences, specifically in contraception. I also had a chance to see Shelly Segal and to thank him again for putting me in up at his place during my recent trip to New York to meet Dr. Romney. Both W.O. and Shelly felt that I'd made the right decision in accepting the position with Bill Perloff rather than swerving towards Ob-Gyn. They promised to help me develop my unit in Philadelphia and suggested that as soon as I was settled and got the research started, we should consider accepting an Indian postdoctoral research fellow for training. That was an exciting idea and I looked forward to having a research trainee in my laboratory.

My next visit with Bill consisted of a kaleidoscope of meetings, introductions and a great deal of paper work dealing with setting up the laboratories and formalizing my appointment at Temple University Medical School. Despite my ability to work long hours I was exhausted. It must have been the tension and stress of dealing with issues that were so close to my heart and making the decisions about my independent career. First, in order of importance, were the administrative issues. I left the clinical issues entirely in Bill's hands, at least for the time being. Next were the plans for Ania's tissue culture facilities, both laboratories and housing for the experimental animals. While we were able to outline these facilities on paper, funds had to be secured to begin construction at the Korman Research Laboratories.

On the last day of my visit I spent a considerable amount of time with the Director of the Korman Research Laboratories, Dr. Sam Ajl. He was a rather young but widely recognized scientist in the field of biochemistry. He impressed me as an experienced administrator and had a friendly but tough demeanor. We found we had a great deal of common ground in our views regarding research and biomedical institutions. He reiterated what Bill had said to me earlier, that AEMC was committed to research, as exemplified by the development of these laboratories.

I was particularly impressed when at one point in our discussion he turned to me and said with a serous look on his face, "I'd like to paraphrase a sentence from the inaugural address of our President, John Kennedy, 'Don't ask what the field of biomedicine can do for you, ask what you can do for it.'" Later Bill told me that Sam had been positively impressed by me as I had been with him. I had developed an instant liking for him and was surprised to learn that some members of the laboratory and some of his colleagues had expressed misgivings concerning his personality and the abrasiveness he showed at times. We enjoyed a close collegial relationship and I always admired his abilities and his forthrightness.

I made one more visit to Philadelphia prior to the family move and insisted again that Ania come with me. This time we not only had to deal with professional issues but also had to decide on suitable housing. Bill recommended that we get a loan and buy a large house right off the bat but I felt we should rent first and look for a house only after selling the one in Detroit. I didn't want to obligate us financially prior to knowing how much we would be able to get for the Detroit house. Bill laughed, "You don't need to worry," he kept saying, "you'll be a physician in practice and any bank will be happy to lend you whatever money you might need. If you have any problems, I'm certain that my bank will give you a loan." Although I trusted Bill's judgment, we were conservative by nature and couldn't go along with his reasoning. So Ania and I decided we would rent first.

We needed only a two bedroom apartment close to the Medical Center and Sam Ajl recommended a real estate agent who showed us a number of possible rentals. Within two days we found a row house (now it would be called a townhouse) on Andrews Avenue, across from a small National Cemetery. I couldn't resist a little wisecrack, "At least on that side of the street we'll have very quiet neighbors". The house was only ten or fifteen minutes driving time from AEMC, near Stanton Avenue at the intersection with North Broad Street. We were exhausted but happy and couldn't wait to get back to Detroit to tell our daughters about their new home.

The huge van with our belongings eased its way to the front of our new home in Philadelphia. After parking it with some difficulty, the driver got out of the cab and, casting furtive glances at the cemetery, inquired in an unsteady voice, "You sure this is the correct address?" After an affirmative answer, he motioned to the two assistants in the van and begin unloading. The move from Detroit went smoothly, nothing got lost or broken and the furniture fit perfectly into the new surroundings.

I couldn't wait to get to work. After all, this was my first real job and also my first serious professional collaboration with my wife. In the past we had studied together and helped each other in school but we had never been formal collaborators. I had no doubt that we would work well together and looked forward to it with a great deal of pleasure. At the same time though, I did wonder and worry about how it would all work out.

The major initial chore of settling into a new home was accomplished rapidly but there were some other issues that needed to be addressed. First and foremost we needed a good arrangement for taking care of the girls. Ultimately, we settled on a schedule involving us taking them to school in the morning and having a house keeper home with them after school until we returned from work. We owned only one car and didn't feel the need for a second one since Ania and I went to work together.

I still had not heard from NIH regarding my two grant applications; it would be a disaster if they weren't funded. The construction of our laboratories and initiation of our proposed research projects would be seriously delayed. Bill tried hard to allay my anxiety. He noted that once our clinical activities developed fully they should generate sufficient funds to allow us to initiate construction of the labs even without NIH grants. However, I was becoming more and more anxious and trying to figure out different ways to support our research. It became clear that we needed to develop laboratory facilities that could provide the latest technical advances, and develop new tests that would be useful in the diagnostic evaluation of our patients.

Dr. Jacobson's steroid biochemistry lab was already completed and was isolating, purifying and quantifying various 17-ketosteroids, the ultimate metabolites of the male sex hormone testosterone. The production and metabolism of testosterone in women with hirsutism (excessive hair growth) was his long-standing research interest. He was one of the first investigators to suggest that these women produce excessive amounts of male sex hormone and that treatment aimed at lowering the levels of testosterone would ameliorate the hirsutism.

This work had greatly impressed me. At that time, we were still unable to directly measure the level of testosterone in the blood. We could only make inferences based on the concentrations of its metabolites (the 17-ketosteroids), in urine. Dr. Jacobson's results suggested that measuring these substances in the urine would be helpful in diagnosing and managing patients with diseases that produced elevated levels of testosterone. Unfortunately, the prohibitive cost of these tests made it difficult to use them routinely. Patients simply couldn't afford them.

I was beginning to consider the possibility of having our laboratories perform this kind of testing to generate some additional income. While we were looking for additional sources of revenue, however, two thin envelopes arrived containing simple letters from NIH and our problems were solved. Both of our grants had been approved at the requested financial levels for three years. These funds would cover the costs of conducting the two research projects, constructing the laboratories and purchasing all the necessary equipment. I grabbed Ania and we ran with the letters to Bills office to share the good news. He was elated. "Well," he announced, beaming, "Let's get moving!"

CHAPTER 7
ON MY OWN

We returned from a spring skiing trip to New England just in time for me to take off for the 1967 annual meeting of the Society of American Anatomists. This year the Male Reproduction Club was having its annual meeting in conjunction with the anatomists. I met with Charles Leblond on the first day of the meeting to discuss the Club agenda. This gave me an opportunity to suggest the possibility of changing the name to the "W.O. Nelson Male Reproduction Club" in honor of my mentor and friend. Charles was very enthusiastic about it and suggested that I bring it up to the club membership during my opening statements. He fully supported my suggestion and it was embraced by all the other members as well.

The American Anatomists meeting was just the beginning of a string of scientific meetings and symposia I was to attend that year. These, among other things, seriously cut into my research and clinical time. The secret for managing within such limited time was to quickly learn how to delegate. I was blessed with excellent collaborators and associates who allowed me to begin successfully delegating; that's the only way I was able to keep my head above water most of the time.

Later that year a group of scientists interested in reproductive biology inaugurated a new Society for the Study of Reproduction (SSR). The first meeting was to be held in the form of a symposium at Vanderbilt University in Nashville, Tennessee. Since I was on the organizing committee, I had to attend, present a paper and participate in many of the organizational activities. We elected Dr. Philip Dziuck, a highly capable and renowned reproductive biologist, as the first president of this new society.

Upon returning from Nashville, I found a letter from NIH on my desk. It was from the Secretary of the Reproductive Biology Study Section inviting me to serve as a member. When I had served on the Endocrinology Study Section during my naval service, I was completing Dr Volmer's tenure. Now, however, I had been selected on the basis of my scientific contributions. I was shocked. I hadn't thought about or realized the extent of my research, especially since I had been an independent researcher for only six years. The secretary of the Study Section suggested in his letter that if I accepted the invitation, I could attend the next quarterly meeting to be held in Bethesda that May. I was elated, scared, and very insecure but I accepted.

This invitation was not to be the end of my surprises that year. Another letter arrived from Harvard Medical School inviting me to deliver the annual Distinguished Lecture in Reproductive Biology later that year in the famous and stately Ether Dome Auditorium. It was a great honor and a wonderful experience.

The three and a half day Study Section meeting in May 1967 was a delight. A number of the scientists in the group were old friends and acquaintances. That gave me an opportunity to broaden my contacts with them and learn more about their way of thinking about issues in the sciences. I also had a chance to meet and spend time with scientists whom I didn't know well. Serving on the Study Section gave me an unparalleled chance to work with top steroid biochemists like Drs. Seymour Lieberman, Ralph Dorfman, Chris Eik-Nes, and Ken Savard. I also had the chance to meet Dr. Darrell Ward, an outstanding protein chemist from Houston, Texas who contributed enormously to the discovery of the structure of pituitary gonadotrophins. We became good friends and as it turned out, he would have an enormous influence on my future career.

I returned from the meeting exhausted and Ania also needed a break from the laboratory so we decided to inaugurate the sailing season by launching our first sailboat, the EPIA (an acronym for our first names: Emil, Pauline, Inette and Anna). After getting the boat in the water and cleaning her up that weekend, we even had time to take a short sail. The following weekend was Memorial Day so we decided to take her for an overnight sail to Turkey Point. The girls had several parties planned over the weekend and opted to skip this trip. Our dear and reliable live-in help would keep an eye on them. We were planning to anchor off shore at Elk Neck State Park and stay on the boat overnight. We couldn't wait!

This was our second overnight trip on the boat, the first being a trip the previous year to Betterton, Maryland to meet with our original sailing friend and mentor, Lee. During that trip, however, we had spent the night in a marina tied up to a dock. This year would be very different because we would be on our own and anchored off shore in a park.

When we arrived at our marina, we ran impatiently to the dock. Our beautiful EPIA I was tied up to a buoy and moving in a small ark in response to a light breeze. The marina attendant took us out to the boat in his dinghy and we felt ready for the adventure. Rigging our little sloop didn't take much time and soon we raised the mainsail and were under way. I then steered the boat into the wind so Ania could raise the jib. The wind was blowing from the southeast and our course was almost due south, almost directly into the wind. Thus, we were forced to tack a great deal. This substantially delayed our arrival but gave us excellent practice tacking our new boat. It was certainly easier and nicer to sail this Celebrity racing class sloop than to our first little dingy, called the Peanut, where we constantly worried about being hit by the low flying boom.

We arrived at Elk Neck State Park late in the afternoon and found a small cove where we anchored. I tied a long line to a tree on shore which allowed me to pull the boat closer to the bank to disembark. The cooler with food and drinks was dragged ashore to a picnic table and we were in heaven. As the day began to wane, we decided to return to the boat and prepare for the night. We positioned our sleeping bags on either side of the centerboard housing. Then we put a tarp over the boom and tied it to the sides of the cockpit creating a tent over the two sleeping bags. It had been a fun but tiring day for both of us so after applying generous amounts of mosquito repellant, we fell fast asleep.

Was it a dream? Was I having a nightmare? We were sailing in open waters; wind was buffeting the boat, waves were braking over the cockpit, thunder was booming, and lightning was streaking across the horizon. Ultimately the boat capsized and I found myself in the water. At that moment I suddenly woke up and realized that Ania and I were half submerged in water, floating in our sleeping bags as our boat slowly filled with water. It was pouring rain and sheets of water were coming into the cockpit through the edges of the tarp. A squall was pummeling our boat and it was dancing on the anchor line, partly restricted by the line fastening it to the tree. Lightening was still zigzagging across the sky but the rain began to subside. To my surprise and amazement, Ania was sleeping through all of this excitement. I woke her up and urged her to get out of the soggy sleeping bag and help me bail the water out of the boat. The squall soon passed but we spent the rest of the night cold and wet.

We took off for the return sail just as the sun began rising over the horizon and the sail back to our marina felt like a dream. We were on a broad reach, the fastest and most comfortable point of sail with about ten knots of wind blowing off the southwest quarter. The day was glorious; the sky was deep blue with not a cloud in sight. The sun had turned hot and everything began to dry out. I was extremely happy sailing in these perfect weather conditions but I could see that Ania was not overjoyed. She didn't say anything but clearly had something on her mind.

It wasn't until we were settled in the car for the drive home that she started talking. It wasn't a complaint but rather a rumination on the experience we'd had the previous night. She was reassuring me that she enjoyed the beautiful sail back to the marina, however, the lack of adequate sleeping facilities on the boat did put a crimp in our ability to cruise for longer then one day. In soft voice she added, "A cabin on the boat would be great". This obviously would require a larger boat. She didn't realize that her dissatisfaction with our current boat was actually music to my ears. By that time I'd been strongly bitten by the sailing bug and, like so many other sailors, was already dreaming about a bigger boat. I pretended that sailing the EPIA was ideal and that we should learn to rough it since there was really no need for us to own a larger boat. However, I happily made a mental note of her comments.

Returning to work on Tuesday the office was a mad house. Not only was it a short week but Keith Smith had completed his fellowship and left us. During his tenure he had spent about twenty percent of his time seeing patients. Now that he was gone, we had to take up the slack. My time was becoming seriously strained because the institution of a human sperm bank and addition of various other treatments had significantly increased our fertility practice.

The pharmaceutical industry had provided us with a new therapeutic compound, Clomid (Clomiphene Citrate) to initiate a study on its efficacy in women with clinical signs of elevated testosterone levels and difficulty ovulating and becoming pregnant. This synthetic anti-estrogen with limited estrogenic activity, had been investigated for several years as a possible female contraceptive. Serendipitously it had been observed that when administered at a certain time in the cycle, it seemed to induce ovulation in women with ovulatory problems. Our practice was ideally suited for this research since many of our patients suffered from ovarian disorders associated with lack of ovulation and infertility.

We had demonstrated that a gonadotropin surge during the menstrual cycle was most likely responsible for stimulating ovulation and we had the necessary technology for measuring these surges. Furthermore, we had recently received a supply of a highly experimental preparation of partly purified human gonadotropin hormones called Pergonal. We were to study its ability to induce ovulation in patients who had previously failed to ovulate spontaneously, as well as any resulting pregnancies. This combination of studies should prove helpful in obtaining the desired information and I couldn't wait to begin the studies.

That summer our fourth of July had turned into a long weekend of parties with some guests coming from New York, including Ania's parents, cousins and some of our friends. My parents now lived in Philadelphia, not far from our house, as did our friends, Henry and Lilly Altschuler, and coworkers, the Perskys and Fichers. Our girls particularly enjoyed the dinners, barbecues and celebrations. By now they were both very charming young ladies. Pauline was sixteen and was proudly introducing her boyfriend to every one present. Inette, just over fourteen, was busy acting like an experienced hostess and enjoying the attention lavished on her by friends and relatives. This year's celebration was the largest and most memorable in our family's history.

After the long holiday weekend both Ania and I plunged back into our research world. We had recently acquired two postdoctoral fellows, Dr. Tjioe from Indonesia and Dr. Sud from India. Dr. Tjioe was to work with me on human spermatogenesis and the effects of decreased blood supply to the testes, while Dr. Sud was going to investigate the effects of certain chemicals on spermatogenesis in rats. Dr. Chowdhury, also from India, worked on the effects of heat on the testes and Dr. Miguel Ficher had developed sophisticated techniques to investigate the synthesis of testosterone in the testes of both experimental animals and humans.

Despite our frenzied research activities, I had other issues on my mind. One had to do with our boat and Ania's comments after our overnight outing and the memorable rainstorm. We started looking for a new, more rainproof boat and I thought it should be a boat with a fixed keel as opposed to the centerboard of the Celebrity. Our search focused on the Eastern Shore of Maryland because of our time constraints. I still hoped to do some serious cruising that year and it was clear that Ania would not put up with the primitive arrangements we had on the Celebrity. We needed a boat that would accommodate brief periods of living aboard. Our relatively limited finances (I did not like to buy items on credit) and sailing experience suggested we look for a small boat with a cabin.

During our search we were exposed to a new world. It included boat dealers, boat designers (naval architects), and boat builders, both "blue bloods" and average builders. The field was complex and bewildering. There were the Tartans, the C&C's the Columbia boats, the California Boat Company building the very fast and comfortable 'Cal' boats, etc. Our good friend, Lee Greenbaum, sailed a beautiful twenty seven-foot Columbia. Some of the best boats were built by the Bristol Boat Company of Rhode Island. Their boats were considered among the high end in design, construction, seaworthiness, and certainly price!

I received a recommendation from a boat yard supervisor in Oxford, Maryland, a small fishing and boating town on the Eastern Shore. He told me that a very nifty, almost new twenty-four footer, built in Bristol, Rhode Island was coming on the market soon. It was to be handled by John Holmes, a yacht broker at Egg Harbor Marina in Georgetown, which was also on the Eastern Shore. I called Mr. Holmes for further information and was told that the boat was there and would soon be hauled out of the water for bottom painting. If we went that weekend we could inspect her. She would then be launched and we would be able to take her out for a sail. I was delighted and Ania and I went the next Saturday afternoon.

The drive from Philadelphia to the marina took about two hours. Once we reached the Eastern Shore and crossed the Bohemia River we turned off into Egg Harbor just before the Sassafras River. As we walked into the harbor office and identified ourselves, a middle aged, flamboyant man with a shock of blond hair jumped off a chair from behind a little desk, took us by our hands and announced cheerfully, "I am certain that you can't wait to see the little gem". Mr. Holmes had an easy way with people. From the moment he greeted us, he literally didn't stop talking. Remarkably, I was actually interested in everything he had to say.

He led us to an area behind the little building that housed his office to a large lot facing the river. The marina had several perpendicular boat docks and there were also a number of boats, primarily sailboats, sitting in cradles on the lot. He led us to the shore where sitting in a cradle was a beautiful boat with a dark blue hull, copper-red keel and white decks and cabin. It looked huge to me. Mr. Holmes, who now insisted that we call him John, bowed and said, "Meet the 'Corsair'". I looked at John, then at the boat, and said, "But I thought I was seeing a 'Bristol 24'?

> Oh yes, John chuckled, that's a common misunderstanding. You are looking at a Sailstar Corsair 24, designed by a much-respected naval architect, Mr. Peter Coble. The boat is built by the Sailstar Boat Company of Bristol, Rhode Island, thus is often referred to as a Bristol 24.

Soon I learned that the Corsair was a fixed-keel sloop, 24 foot 7 inches long with a beam of eight feet and a three and a half foot draft. I quickly climbed up the ladder into the cockpit and was shown the inboard-outboard motor mounted in the lazaret, a compartment aft of the boat's cockpit. The interior of the boat was remarkably roomy; an average height person could stand comfortably in the main cabin. There was a bow cabin with a V-shaped double berth and a head (bathroom). The main cabin housed two bunks, a sink with water tank and a small, two-burner alcohol stove. Aft of the main cabin there was a single "watch-berth".

The boat had fairly attractive lines although I thought her a little stubby. Never the less, she looked solid and seaworthy. The decks were roomy and the running rigging looked new, as did the sails, a main and a working jib. I was amazed that the boat looked and smelled so new. This tiny mystery was quickly resolved by John who explained that the boat "Is being sold by a young man who bought it only last summer as a wedding gift for himself and his new bride. Unfortunately", he continued, "The couple is getting divorced, and he is joining the marines. That's why he needs to sell the almost new boat as rapidly as possible". To my inexperienced eye, everything appeared perfect. I suggested that we get an official survey and take a demonstration sail the following week. The asking price was $4,500 and we happily put down a ten percent deposit.

On the way home Ania was very excited, "This boat," she kept repeating, "Is more than I expected. We could actually live on it, sleep comfortably, prepare meals and use an indoor head". Since the boat was used, many small items that made it more sailing-friendly had already been installed. "I looked at the sails", she continued, "They are like new, especially the mainsail". I was thrilled to see Ania's enthusiasm and interest in the nautical details. She was slowly but steadily becoming an intrepid sailor.

We arranged for the formal boat survey on Monday and would take the boat for a demonstration sail later that week. If all went well, we could return the next weekend, sign the papers, and take possession of our new acquisition. There were, however, two crucial issues still remained to be solved. First, we had to sell our Celebrity. The second was finding a marina for our new boat which was closer to Philadelphia and had better access to the main sailing areas of the bay.

On Monday I called the Evanston Boat Yard in Riverside and asked for Stan. He recalled the details of our boat and remembered who I was. After I told him that I wanted to sell it, he started laughing. "You won't believe this. Last week we had a customer who wanted to purchase a used Celebrity. Since we carry only new ones I'm certain that he'll be interested in yours." Stan also indicated that if I didn't have a broker he would be interested in brokering the boat. I agreed on the condition that he pick the boat up from my marina and take it to their dealership in Riverside. There he could easily show it and take it for demonstration sails on the Delaware River. I also suggested that he move the boat that week so that I could use its mooring at the North East River Marina for my new boat.

The survey of the Corsair was satisfactory, the test sail was superb, and by Wednesday I had signed the contract. Saturday morning we were to pick up our new boat and sail her to North East River. Thursday I got a call from Stan with the news that the buyer had offered $2,000 for our Celebrity and was willing to sign the contract at any time. This was almost unbelievable. I had only paid $1,800 for the boat! I happily accepted the offer and on Friday deposited the check to my account. It appeared to my inexperienced fiscal mind, that in trading for the larger boat I was not losing but was actually gaining. This made me chuckle and shake my head.

Early Saturday morning all four of us drove to Georgetown. The girls were very impatient to see the new boat and John was waiting outside the dealership for us. "The boat is ready any time you are," he announced with a big smile on his face, "I even filled the five gallon gas can for you." As we talked, we walked towards the docks where our new boat, called of course, the EPIA II, was tied up.

As we headed for the boat, an english setter puppy ran out of the open door of the dealership office, and headed for us. The dog looked exactly like Diana, an english setter puppy we had purchased the previous year. She had disappeared on Christmas Eve while playing outdoors and the girls had been heartbroken for months. The dog running towards us even had a black patch over the left eye and ear, just like Diana; it was an uncanny resemblance. When the dog caught up with us the girls let out the loudest double barrel squeal, "Diana!" I looked at the dog again carefully; it couldn't have been Diana. By then she would have been an adult dog. The puppy following us now was only about four months old; about the same size as Diana was when we first got her. "Diana's back!" the girls cried with tears running down their cheeks while they hugged and kissed the dog. They wouldn't even listen when I attempted to explain why this could not be our Diana.

I turned to and John tried to explain the situation to him. In the meantime, the puppy was wagging her tail and jumping on the girls as the trio became instant friends. At this point John explained, "The dog actually belonged to the owner of the Corsair and since he's joining the marines and divorcing his wife, he decided to leave the dog with the dealership. So, if the girls like the dog and would like to have her, we'll will be very pleased to give her to them. We were elated as the five of us sailed the boat happily back to the North East River Marina trailing a beautiful little fiberglass dinghy that had come with the boat. The dinghy turned out to be an absolute necessity whenever we anchored off shore, particularly now that Diana was part of the crew and would have to be taken ashore.

I have to admit that I took an extraordinary amount of time off so that I could sail as much as possible during the remaining few weeks of summer and early fall. We had decided to move the boat to a new basin on the Bohemia River where we could keep it at a dock. This made coming and going much simpler and faster since we didn't have to use a dinghy to get back and forth to the boat.

In a few weeks, the boat would have to be hauled out of the water for the winter and we decided to make two trips prior to that time. First we sailed to Annapolis to meet Lee. We felt like real sailors taking off for a passage that was to take an entire day, some eight to ten hours of sailing. It ended up taking even longer than expected because we were hit by squalls. The wind probably didn't blow more than twenty-five knots but it felt like a hurricane to us. I had been told, during conversations with "old salts", that the appropriate maneuver during these conditions is to head up into the wind, drop the main sail, and try to control the boat with just the jib.

I was about to follow these dicta but had to first get the girls and Diana below deck, hand the tiller over to Ania, and secure the boom, which was swinging wildly over our heads. Ania adroitly steered the boat into the wind which reduced the wild gyrations of the boom and controlled the thrashing of the main sail. This gave me a chance to work my way to the mast and release the main halyard, allowing the sail to slide quickly down the mast. Once the huge sail came down, the boat's wild movements subsided although the sail was still flying around wildly while I attempted to tie it to the boom. This further stabilized the boat and quieted the abominable sounds of lines and sail shackles banging against the metal mast and boom. A relative quiet set in and Ania "manned" the tiller and calmly steered the boat down the Chesapeake Bay. Diana and the girls were below in the cabin looking scared but smiling. The squall had ended as rapidly as it started. In about thirty minutes the skies were clear and we were able to raise the mainsail and fly towards Annapolis.

I was fairly familiar with the Annapolis area and the Statler Hilton Hotel where we planned to stay. It was the only hotel on the water that provided boat slips for guests arriving by water. It was a glorious weekend. Lee came over with his wife and two daughters, four and six years old and they spent the entire weekend with us. We purchased bikini bathing suits for the girls and they changed into them instantly and wore them proudly throughout the visit. Our sail back to the Bohemia River Marina was uneventful; we were rapidly gaining experience and self-confidence in sailing our new floating home.

Our second sailing trip was scheduled to take place three weeks later. We planned to traverse the Chesapeake-Delaware Canal and sail the Delaware Bay to Cape May at the entrance to the Atlantic Ocean. This would give us few miles of ocean sailing and we thought it would be a neat adventure. By then, however, the new school year was under way so we decided to leave the girls at home and make the trip by ourselves.

We left on a clear Friday morning sailing the Elk River to the northwest. As we turned into the Chesapeake-Delaware canal, the weather began to change. The blue sky with just a few fast-moving clouds became threatening and overcast. We sailed the canal under the Chesapeake City Bridge and several other bridges. By the time we reached the entrance to Delaware Bay it had started raining heavily. By mid-afternoon I gave up on the idea of reaching Cape May that day and started looking for a cove where we could anchor. The visibility had deteriorated, but we were lucky enough to find a partly protected body of water off the northern shore with a spit of land separating it from the Delaware Bay. After setting the anchor I sat at the bow for at least twenty minutes watching it and hoping it would hold. It appeared that we were sitting snugly in this little cove.

The motion of the boat became quite tolerable and Ania even volunteered to light the stove and prepare some supper. We were overjoyed with the amenities in the boat's cabin. With the lights on and the little alcohol stove purring, it was quite cozy although outside the weather was deteriorating. I went into the cockpit to select several sights on shore that could be easily spotted, and marked their positions. One hour later I rechecked our position to see if we were dragging the anchor but so far all was well. Ania warmed a can of my favorite bean soup and we had supper while listening to classical music on a portable radio. Then, I made another check of our position... no change. The wind was howling and rain was pelting the decks but we felt relatively secure and decided to rest; soon we were fast asleep.

I woke up suddenly; a glance at my watch revealed that it was a few minutes after midnight; the boat was moving erratically and the wind had intensified. A quick sprint up the cabin ladder into the cockpit confirmed that the boat had turned in a wide arc. However, a check of the landmarks on shore revealed that we were still securely anchored. This helped relieve my increasing anxiety but I woke Ania and suggested that we alternate two-hour watches throughout the night to be sure we weren't dragging the anchor.

When Ania's last watch ended at 7:00 AM she woke me and we reassessed the situation. It was still blowing between fifteen and twenty knots. The Bay waters were choppy and the rain, while having diminished somewhat, was still coming down pretty heavily. The boat had no cover over the cockpit or any other provision to keep out the rain. Thus, if we were to go on we would probably get pretty soaked, even though we wore foul weather gear to help keep us dry. If we tried to wait out the rain we might not make it back to the office on time for work.

Ultimately, we decided to move on but that proved difficult. Our Danforth anchor had dug deeply into the sticky clay bottom and I was having great difficulty getting it out. Just as I was about to dive in and dig it out by hand, another maneuver released it. However, it was so covered with think, hard clay that it took us nearly an hour to get it clean. Once that task was finally completed we engaged the motor and steered the boat north to the mouth of the canal.

Shortly after entering the canal, as we passed under the tall Reedy Point Bridge with its enormous pilings, I began to feel increasing resistance as our engine labored to push us through the canal. We were motoring against a steadily increasing current. A few hundred yards past the bridge our progress slowed to a crawl and then we began to be pushed slowly and steadily backwards towards the bridge pilings. I ran to the bow and threw out the anchor, hoping to stop the boat, but to no avail. The bottom of the canal had been dredged so smooth the anchor couldn't take hold. I was getting panicky. Even with the throttle wide open and the gear in forward, the boat was gaining speed in the opposite direction. The rudder barely steered the boat and I was getting pretty concerned that we could be smashed against the pilings. Finally, in a last ditch effort to avoid disaster, I managed to steer the boat close to shore and throw the anchor into the bushes growing there. It finally took hold and stopped the boat. I felt elated as one major disaster was averted, but what to do next? Clearly the outboard motor was not up to the task of pushing our boat against this strong current. However, at least temporarily, we were safely at the anchor. Feeling more secure, we decided to have some hot coffee.

After we had changed into dry clothes and were finishing a second cup of coffee, we noted that the rain had stopped and the skies had begun to clear. There were many boats motoring up and down the canal so I attempted to flag one down. A small runabout with an older man, obviously a fisherman, in it motored over to us. I explained our predicament only to be met by a deep satisfied laugh:

> There are quite a few underpowered boats like yours that can't stand up to our local currents, and the scoured bottom in the canal won't hold an anchor. However, the good news is that this is a tidal current. The tide will be slack in one hour and then change direction to flow toward the Chesapeake Bay. Then you'll have yourselves a current that will take you back home.

We cheerfully thanked our "savior", sat back and finally relaxed. While waiting for the tide to change we talked. "It appears that whenever we take our boat out for more than a routine sail we encounter difficulties that expose some weakness in it. The glaring problem with the Peanut was the low boom," I said. "Yes, and bumps on our heads when we were hit by it as it went flying over the cockpit", Ania interjected. "And then we got soaked on the Celebrity because there was no cabin". She looked at me with sparkling eyes and jumped in, "Yes, and you used it as an excuse to buy a new boat." "Sure," I responded laughingly, "now I'll use this experience to push for a new boat with a bigger engine."

Ania's ears perked up, "What are you saying?" "Well…, I procrastinated, "Let's have another cup of coffee". This gave me a chance to collect my thoughts.

When we returned to the cockpit to sip more hot coffee, I looked at the waters around the boat. The current was definitely slacking and the skies were slowly turning blue. I began quietly. "We've been sailing now for eight years and this is our third boat. It appears that sailing will be our recreational passion."

"Don't forget skiing!"

"You're right, but one cannot ski in the summertime. Unquestionably our boat is underpowered. I like our little Corsair but I feel strongly that we need a larger boat with a more powerful inboard engine."

Ania didn't say anything. She just smiled said, "I think the current has switched direction and we can move towards the Chesapeake." I started the motor, maneuvered the anchor line to free the anchor from the bushes on shore, and we moved on. It was getting dark by the time we reached the Chesapeake City Bridge. There was a little marina snuggled close to its southern end and we decided to stay there overnight and continue on to the Bohemia River in the morning.

As fall approached, so did the deadline for submission of papers for presentation at the annual meetings of the Endocrine Society to be held the following spring in Miami, Florida. When I brought this up at one of our lunches, Miguel came up with an idea. "Since a number of us will have interesting data worthy of presentation this year, why not go to Miami by car. We could drive three or four cars and make a mini-vacation of it. This way we could take all of our fellows with us at a minimal expense." This was a great idea and the entire group began preparing their papers for presentation at the meeting. Our research had accelerated in several directions, stimulated in part by the development of new methods for looking at hormone synthesis and recent discoveries related to enzymes in the biosynthetic pathways of male sex hormone formation in the testis.

I felt like a bombshell had exploded earlier when I received an invitation to present a major paper at the 1967 Ciba Foundation Colloquia in Great Britain in late fall. This Foundation had been formed by the Swiss pharmaceutical company Ciba Limited in 1949 as a scientific and educational charity. It had been established to promote scientific excellence by sponsoring international scientific meetings and publishing scientific books. At its opening ceremony on June 22, 1949, Lord Beveridge summed up the Foundation's main aim: "To provide a forum where scientists from across the world can meet and exchange information and ideas". A distinct exclusivity had been created by limiting the attendance at each colloquium to twenty-five or thirty invited participants, all of whom were scientists who shared a common area of interest although they had differing backgrounds and skills.

An invitation to participate in a colloquium, particularly for a young investigator, was a major honor. The invitation included a three-day stay, along with some of the other participating scientists, at the famous Ciba House in London. It was a wonderful opportunity for Ania and me not only to participate in this gathering but also to visit the great city of London for the first time. We would also have the opportunity to visit two aunts and a cousin whom I hadn't seen since before the outbreak of WWII in 1939.

I was to present an overview of our work which gave me an opportunity to tie together a number of research projects I had been involved with for the past several years. I elected to feature Ania's experiments in cell and tissue culture systems dealing with testosterone synthesis in Leydig cells (specific cells in the testes responsible for testosterone production) and discuss other pertinent work that shed light on testosterone synthesis in the testes. Thus I could also feature the work of my other associates, Dr. Vilar, an electron microscopist, Dr. Solomon, a steroid biochemist and Dr. Sud, a reproductive physiologist.

With fall approaching, our trip to London loomed large. There was a flurry of last minute activities to complete the slides for the presentation and, on the personal front, making sure that our two daughters were well taken care off during our absence. The day of our departure arrived much too fast.

After changing planes at Kennedy airport in New York, we arrived at the London's Heathrow airport at 9:00 A.M. We were picked up by a uniformed driver and taken by limousine to the Ciba House at 41 Portland Place, apparently a well-known and prestigious address. There, we were met by a medieval-looking butler in a gold embroidered jacket and gray pants. He informed us that we would be meeting Sir Gordon Wolstenholme, Director of the Ciba Foundation, during afternoon tea.

A reception and dinner was scheduled for later that evening and there the scientists could meet each other informally.

The Ciba House was a stately building. The ground floor was occupied by an auditorium were the meetings were held, a long narrow dining room, a library, and a number of small meeting and sitting rooms. It was furnished with beautiful antiques and the floors were covered with magnificent Persian rugs. The living quarters occupied the second and third floors.

I was anxious to contact and visit my relatives and tried to determine when a break from our busy schedule would allow it. The following evening was free so I called my aunt Bronia to inquire whether that would be a good time for our visit. She was very happy to hear my voice and assured me that she, my other aunt, her sister Lola, as well as my first cousin, her son Harry, would all be delighted to see us for dinner at her house. She suggested that Harry pick us up at the Ciba house and I was very much looking forward to seeing my family.

After a short afternoon nap to help our jet lag, we were ready to see some of our old colleagues and make new acquaintances. At the afternoon tea we met a number of British scientists and Sir Gordon Wolstenholme. He was a tall, very handsome gentleman with a low cultured voice who moved among the guests like a sober and benevolent teacher. I was impressed and humbled by the entire experience, still feeling uncertain about whether I deserved to be in this august company. I certainly was pleased to meet some of my old friends: Dr. Dorfman, the famous steroid biochemist who, in addition to lifting steroid biochemistry to its current heights, had written the fundamental textbooks in the field, and Dr. Eik Nes, the tall Norwegian from Salt Lake City, who provided us with details of biosynthetic pathways in steroid producing tissues like the testes. My old friend Charles Leblond was there with his young collaborator, Dr. Yves Clermont, who did most of the work on the kinetics of spermatogenesis. There were also a number of other scientists who I knew from meetings of the NIH Reproductive Biology Study Section.

I was proud to introduce Ania to those who didn't know her. When I explained that she was A. Steinberger, the author of many research papers dealing with hormonal regulation of the germinal epithelium in vitro; it caused a furor. "You mean this little blond, blue eyed beauty is

A. Steinberger, the scientist?" This question was asked frequently and I basked in pride unable to hear enough of the accolades they accorded her.

Dinner was a very formal affair. We had been offered several rounds of delicious sherry before being shepherded into the formal dining room. The seating arrangement assured that each foreign scientist was seated next to at least one British colleague. Soon I realized how important and thoughtful this seating arrangement was.

My name card was to the left of Ania's and to my left sat a British scientist from Birmingham, Dr. Scott. Soon I struck up a conversation with my neighbor and automatically, when reaching for a cigarette, offered him one. He became quite agitated, lowering his head as he leaned towards me and whispered, "No, no, you may not light a cigarette before a toast is offered to the Queen". I froze and then, glancing around the table with embarrassment, realized that Sir Gordon Wolstenholme was standing at the head of the table with a wine glass in his raised right hand. In a crisp British accent he proclaimed "To the Queen!" Everyone around the table stood up and exclaimed "To the Queen!" I don't know what possessed me but once all sat down, I got up again, raised my wine glass and announced in a clear, loud voice, "To President Eisenhower!" Everyone looked at me in astonishment and Ania kicked me under the table. I sat down embarrassed again and Dr. Scott could not stop laughing. He leaned towards me and whispered, "That was great. It should teach them a lesson." I just kept quiet.

After dinner, the participants were invited to a sitting room for an after dinner drink. I walked over to Yves and started talking shop when he interrupted me with the question, "Do you realize how important these Symposia are?" I looked at him, shaking my head while responding, "Probably not. I've never paid much attention to these things." He started laughing:

> You should read up on these matters. These Symposia are probably the most intensive international, cross-disciplinary scientific get-togethers in the world. The participants are selected carefully and are very limited in number. The Chairmen of the sessions are chosen for their ability to stimulate and provoke lively discussion which often produces new and sometimes risky ideas.

The inside information provided by Yves was fascinating to me. If it were not for the fact that I was to deliver a lecture the next day and still wanted to go over my presentation, I would have stayed much longer. However, I must have been very excited because sleep refused to come to me that night. While Ania was sleeping peacefully, I was reviewing my latest data and the list of slides for my talk.

My presentation was met with considerable interest, particularly by the steroid biochemists who worked with intact animals on various perfusion systems. The possibility of using fragment cultures or pure cultures of Leydig cells that normally produce testosterone in the testes, caught their imagination. The discussion after the paper was longer that the forty-five minutes I took to present it. Ania was delighted. This was a real tribute to her research and she knew it.

Cousin Harry was to pick us up at 6:00 o'clock and we were waiting at the hotel entrance when he called to say he couldn't make it. After apologizing he suggested that we take a taxi. Aunt Bronia lived in a red brick row house in a nice section of town and she and Aunt Lola where waiting for us. I hadn't seen Lola for twenty years but easily recognized her. I last saw Bronia when I was about eight years old, however, and didn't recognize her at all. Harry was exactly my age and although I also hadn't seen him since we were eight or nine years old I had no difficulty recognizing him.

It was a bittersweet reunion for a variety of reasons. Many of our immediate family members had perished in the Holocaust. Lola survived Auschwitz but her mother had been murdered in front of her eyes. That horrible trauma had apparently left her emotionally disturbed and I was terribly sad for her. That was the last time I saw either of my aunts. Harry moved to the United States to teach at Princeton University and we saw each other occasionally but never became very close. Some years later, however, I did become close to his son, Gil who lived in California and came to visit us often.

Our entire experience in London and at the colloquium was superb. We saw a number of old friends, made a few new ones, learned a great deal from the deliberations, and showcased our research in front of many top international authorities. We even had a chance to visit the Tower of London, the British Museum and watch the changing of the guards at Buckingham Palace.

Upon our return I gave a summary of the meeting to my group since many of them were co-authors of the paper I had presented. In addition, since this was Ania's first major international meeting, she shared her impressions and ideas about the meeting. Everyone agreed that it had been a great opportunity to present our work in the European arena. Ania and I both felt that attending this type of international meeting was great fun and very important, but definitely not a vacation. We saw relatively little of London and nothing of the rest of the country.

CHAPTER 8

THE OTHER SIDE OF THE WORLD

Winter flew by and the trip to Miami Beach for the 1968 Endocrine Meetings was approaching. Most of the abstracts we had submitted for the program were accepted and we were ready to go. Our entire group could be accommodated in two large cars and we decided to drive the one thousand miles to Miami in two days. We planned to leave by 7:00 in the morning, have quick lunches along the way, and consume our major meals in the evenings.

By noon of the first day, as we were driving through a small town, Miguel flagged me down and said, "Ilda (his wife) suggested that we have lunch in the restaurant we just passed; she thought it looked very nice." We all agreed and went back to find it. Indeed it was a superb looking restaurant with a fabulous menu. I was amazed to find so elegant a restaurant with an extensive menu in such a small community. Looking at the menu and its relatively reasonable prices, Ilda suggested that we have our main meal now and only a small snack that evening. Suffice it to say that at our evening stop we also came across a superb restaurant and had another sumptuous meal. The following day the story repeated itself as we actually ate our way down the East coast and again on the return trip.

The meeting was a huge success. All of our presentations went well and we had a great time. Dr. Keith Smith, our former postdoctoral fellow also attended the meeting and we were thrilled to see him. We had several long talks about his job in Pittsburgh and about the growth of our unit in Philadelphia. Ultimately we discussed the possibility of his joining our unit and he seemed quite interested.

The trip back to Philadelphia went without a hitch with one exception. We stopped in St. Petersburg to visit some tourist sites and also to go to the beach. Dr. Sud, a postdoctoral fellow from India, stayed in the hot June sun for hours. We tried to tell him to be careful but he only laughed, "Look at my dark skin, I won't get sunburned". However, the next morning when we met at breakfast, he was suffering from a severe sunburn. I never understood how he got so sunburned when he did indeed have the dark skin common to people from southern India.

When we returned from Florida our schedules were packed. Although Bill had stayed behind and seen our patients, I was totally behind in my clinical work and in preparing papers for publication. In addition, I had received information from Professor Grobstein regarding a Japanese American Science Exchange Program I had agreed to attend. He wanted a tentative itinerary for my travel in Japan following an initial meeting at the University of Tokyo. He also wanted a brief outline of the talks I planned to give at several universities I was scheduled to visit as a part of the exchange group.

As I was getting back slowly onto an even keel with respect to my various responsibilities, I noted some peculiarities in Bill's behavior. Despite the rapid and successful developments in the clinical and basic research areas of the Division, Bill began to show signs of stress and discontent. I was unable to put my finger on the possible causes for this change. There were medical problems with his wife who apparently had a serious cardiac condition; however, in my opinion, this would not cause the severe symptoms Bill exhibited. I decided to ignore this situation but it only became more acute over the next few months. Finally one morning Bill called the entire staff to the fellows room and without a preamble announced, "I'm leaving for California. My wife is unwell and we have to go." He simply made this statement and left the room.

I immediately went to Sam, the Director of our Institution for advice. He was also shocked by this development but responded by saying, "I won't look for another Chairman to lead your Division. Your group has developed very successfully and I think you should decide among yourself who should be the next Director. I will accept the group's decision."

I called Jack, the Chief of the Department of Population Endocrinology and Harold, the Chief of the Department of Psycho Endocrinology to discuss the issue. Harold suggested that one of the three of us should be Chairman and that all doctoral members of the division should be asked to vote. Jack concurred and suggested that we meet the next afternoon in the fellows room with the entire doctoral staff for a discussion followed by an election, a simple show of hands, for one of the three of us.

After dinner that evening, I sat down with Ania to discuss these events. She was wise and I always valued her opinion greatly. Unfortunately she wasn't very experienced in matters of academic politics. "You are the youngest of the three," she started, looking at me with an uncertain gaze. "Jack is the oldest and probably the one with the greatest scientific recognition. Harold is very bright, energetic and erudite. He has also made some important scientific discoveries. You..." and here she started laughing, "You are you, what can I say...?"

"I think Jack should be the Chairman, he is the most senior scientist in the group and has excellent connections in the scientific and academic communities as well as at the granting agencies. He probably could lead the Division with greater success than Harold."

"But Harold has great connections in the pharmaceutical community, particularly in the large drug houses and an impeccable scientific record. It will be difficult to make the decision tomorrow."

"The discussion among the entire staff tomorrow may shed more light on this issue and clarify the priorities in our minds. I think that either Harold or Jack would make a great Chairman."

"We'll see, tomorrow is another day" Ania concluded.

The morning was very busy with Bill's and my patients to be seen. I realized that after Bill's departure, we would have to recruit an additional clinician very quickly. By 2:00 I was done but there was no time to go to the laboratories. The meeting was starting at 3:00 and I still had to make several phone calls to patients and sign a bunch of papers.

When I entered the fellows room at 3:00 it was buzzing with excitement. It was obvious that the entire group was highly agitated;

some had just learned of Bill's impending departure. The graduate students and postdoctoral fellows were all there as well. I nodded to Jack and Harold to step out into the hall where I asked what we should do with the students and fellows. They shook their heads and in unison responded, "They should not participate in the discussion or voting, and should probably leave the room." I agreed with them and returned to politely ask the students and fellows to step out.

In opening the discussion I stated that in our group Jack and Harold had the most experience and, in my opinion, one of them should be elected Chairman. The ensuing discussion was not very long. There were several opinions voiced supporting either Jack or Harold. However, after a brief discussion Jack got up and in his usual quiet but intense tone of voice said:

> We are an integrated basic science and clinical medicine unit, a relative rarity in our country. Ideally, whoever leads the unit should have credentials in both. I realize that Emil is the youngest; however, he contributed significantly in both of these areas and is gradually becoming recognized by both. Consequently he would be the logical leader of the group, particularly since in my opinion he has shown the ability to lead.

After Jack finished and other faculty members expressed similar opinions, the voting became simply a formality. Right after we finished voting, someone ran to fetch Sam who arrived with the usual big smile on his face and extending his hand to me said, "Congratulation, Chairman. It will be a pleasure to work with you."

I did not expect this issue to be resolved so rapidly and so smoothly. In addition, I didn't think that I would be the one elected. Only later did I learn that Sam had campaigned for me on the basis that I was bringing in the largest number of grants and had the greatest chance of securing even more grant support. Had I known this at the time, I wouldn't have been very happy. I thought I had been elected on the basis of my scientific and clinical qualifications as well for my ability to lead, not for my aptitude at securing funds.

In the midst of this turmoil, I received a call from Keith Smith who wanted to talk more about the possibility of joining our group. It occurred to me that he might not be interested in joining the Department in light of Bill's departure and my ascendency to the Chairmanship. I quickly apprised him of these new developments and learned that he was delighted by the change. He revealed that the one reservation he had had with respect to joining our group had been Bill. Now that Bill was leaving, the position became much more desirable to him. We agreed that he would join us in December as an "Assistant Member," the equivalent of an Assistant Professor.

I was only thirty-six at the time and driving home that evening the reality of what had happened finally dawned on me. Was thirty-six too young to be the chairman of a large academic department? Once again I considered myself to be very fortunate. I had been thrust into leadership positions ever since my graduate school days so taking over the department at this time in my life didn't scare me. What amazed me and also made me very happy was the fact that my associates, particularly my seniors, trusted me to lead them. My mind was in turmoil. There were so many things to do. The trip to Japan was imminent and there were many final touches to be put on the lectures I was to present.

Scientists participating in the Japanese-American Science Exchange Program were to leave for Japan in three weeks time. This was my first trip to Japan and I was very excited. So were Ania and the girls, although they were also a little worried about me. Ania insisted that a scientist visiting Japan should wear a hat. Therefore, we bought a very elegant and expensive grey hat for me to take along.

I hadn't known that the Tokyo airport was in Narita, a considerable distance from the city. It took almost two hours by taxi to reach the New Otani hotel located in the center of Tokyo. It was the newest and fanciest hotel in the city, a skyscraper. It looked rather incongruous in a neighborhood of much smaller and more typical looking Japanese buildings. The room was elegant, although not very large, with a huge plate glass window overlooking the city. I directed the bellman to unpack my luggage but I personally deposited my new hat on a shelf in the closet.

The opening ceremonies of our program were to be held the following day at the University of Tokyo. The huge lecture room, which held at least three hundred people, was full. The program called for each of us to present a fifteen-minute talk on our work which was then followed by a ten-minute question and answer session. I elected to speak about our latest findings dealing with the regulation of pituitary gonadotrophins by gonadal steroids, testosterone and estradiol. Professor Ichiro Kato of the University President's Office opened the Symposium and introduced the Chairman of our group, Professor Cliff Grobstein. Cliff was to present a talk dealing with the mechanism underlying the induction of cellular differentiation.

After an introduction by Dr. Kato, who was very proper but extremely difficult to understand because of his heavy Japanese accent, Cliff walked briskly to the microphone and began his presentation. I couldn't believe my ears; he was speaking in Japanese! I looked around at the audience. Some were smiling, others were turning their heads as if trying to listen more attentively, and still others were simply fidgeting. I was transfixed. When he finished, Dr. Kato walked over to present him with a scroll and began speaking in his heavy accented English. He thanked Professor Grobstein and then, with an inscrutable expression on his face said, "We appreciate you presenting the lecture in Japanese, however, could you please repeat it in English so that all of us can understand it better".

Cliff was momentarily taken aback. He had had his Japanese postdoctoral fellow translate the lecture into Japanese and had spent a great deal of time and effort practicing its delivery. Nevertheless, he took this blow to his ego with good humor and, with a smile on his face, returned to the podium to repeat his lecture in English.

We stayed in Tokyo for another day of lectures. Subsequently each of us had a different itinerary for visiting various universities. John, a member of our group from the University of Chicago and I decided to spend some time visiting popular tourist sites. That evening we decided to sample the nightlife of Tokyo. That meant a visit to the Ginza, the glittering business and entertainment center of Tokyo. I had read a bit about it and knew that the Ginza (meaning silver seat) was named for the Ginza silver coin mint established in the early seventeenth century. I also knew that it had burned down in the nineteenth century and was rebuilt by an English architect named Thomas Waters. He designed the two and three story European-style buildings and had them built in brick to be more fireproof.

I was not prepared for what met our eyes once we got there. This entire section of town comprising many city blocks was covered by neon and other very unusual commercial signage. Although it was already late evening, it felt as if it were midday because of the incredible illumination. The sidewalks were full of people. Many women wore classical Japanese kimonos with obis and some of the younger women had their faces made up. Some of the men, particularly the older ones, wore traditional Japanese jackets and sported thin, hanging mustaches and their long hair was tied back in ponytails.

I was getting dizzy watching the people, cars, lights, oriental clothing, and hearing the sound of such a foreign language, but primarily it was caused by the pressure of the sea of human beings around me. John, who I think was also getting dizzy from the experience, beckoned to me saying, "Let's stop at a restaurant for something to eat." I nodded my head gratefully and added, "Let's go in and ask if they speak English".

As we walked into the first restaurant, we were greeted by two young girls dressed in exquisite kimonos. In response to our question they nodded their heads yes, took us by the hand and led towards the center of the restaurant. There we saw a huge water tank filled with many exotic species of fish and after seating us at a table right next to the fish tank, left gracefully.

Within a minute, two beautiful women who could best be described as looking like dolls, sat down next to us. One spoke a few words of English and soon we learned that they were our "geishas" and would keep us company during the dinner. The name of the girl who spoke some English was Misaki and the other was named Riko. They said that a typical meat dish is sukiyaki and that a popular dish among Americans is tempura. However, they also tried to persuade us to select one of the fish swimming before our eyes in the huge aquarium.

We learned that tempura is lightly battered, deep fried foods such as shrimp or vegetables. Sukiyaki is thinly sliced raw beef and vegetables served with a pot of almost boiling broth in which one would immerse the meat and vegetables. Before they were fully cooked, one fished them out of the broth with chopsticks and ate them. Joe and I tried to taste everything while struggling to master the art of using chopsticks.

Eating with chopsticks was an experience, however, the Geishas were very adroit at assisting us during the frequent disasters caused by our clumsiness. They guided our hands and delicately wiped our mouths with fragrant, beautifully embroidered cotton napkins. This was a funny and embarrassing experience and one which underscored the differences in our cultures.

After dinner and an extensive parting ceremony, the two Geishas led us out of the restaurant bowing constantly. Back in the Ginza the bars, clubs, restaurants and various gambling parlors were mesmerizing. We ended up in a little bar for a drink. As we walked in a young man led us to a small table in the corner and instantly two pretty young girls in kimonos with heavily made up faces joined us. One sat very close to John and started calling him "uncle" while making small talk in broken English. I noticed that John was becoming a little put out by the "uncle" title, feeling aged by it. I explained that because I looked younger than my age, almost young enough to be his son, the girls did it out of respect. After that he graciously agreed to be called uncle.

At 11:30 an almost unbelievable event was played out and being unprepared for it, I was shocked. All of the young ladies suddenly got up, began bowing to the customers and pointing to the exit. A large segment of the men were fairly inebriated and not happy about leaving. The girls, however, began to gently push those who were reluctant to leave with their hands at the small of their backs. We paid our bill and left as well. The street outside was full of inebriated men who were being cajoled by girls in beautiful kimonos to go to the subway stations.

The next day we learned that the last subway train leaves Ginza by midnight and the 'bar girls' were providing a service to their customers by helping them make it onto the last train. This was such an unusual experience, it taught me a great deal about Japanese culture and the charm of this type of simple human concern.

After our last day in Tokyo we were assigned to various universities to lecture and consult. I was assigned to spend a week in Kyoto and about the same amount of time at a marine biological station on a little island on the Kobe bay. I was to travel to Kyoto on the new super-contemporary "bullet train" (Shinkansen) that had been placed in service less than two years before and reached speeds of up to 130 miles an hour (210 kph). From the outside, the train looked like a silver bullet and on the inside the amenities and passenger luxuries were truly remarkable.

The seating arrangements were entirely different from what I had seen anywhere else in the world. Each seat was an upholstered high-back chair that swiveled and reclined. There was also an extension table at each seat to be used when needed. One could swivel into a position that provided an unobstructed view through the huge plate glass windows. There were stewardesses in beautiful kimonos serving food and drink, and I began to think I was in paradise.

I had been given a precise description of my host in Kyoto, Professor Yamamoto, who was to meet me at the Kyoto train station. It would be pretty easy for him to identify me among the arriving passengers based on my western physiognomy. As I exited the train car, a medium sized man in a traditional Japanese jacket, with a wispy mustache and long grayish hair in a ponytail, came over almost instantly. He extended his hand and as I clasped it, he said in a friendly tone, "I am Doctor Yamamoto, Professor of Barology". I didn't pay much attention to his pronunciation of the word Barology, assuming that it was a pronunciation problem and that Professor Yamamoto probably meant biology. This assumption turned out not to be entirely correct.

It was late fall and quite cold in Kyoto. The laboratories of the Kyoto University, the largest educational institution in the city, had cement floors and the occasional wood or coal fired brassier did little to alleviate the chill. This was exacerbated by the custom of taking off one's shoes and walking in socks or thin slippers on the cold cement floors. However, the enthusiasm of the graduate students I met and their eagerness to learn made me forget my ice cold feet. In the afternoon Professor Yamamoto offered to take me back to my hotel to get ready for the evening.

I was staying at Hotel Sumiya, a historical Japanese Inn built in the "sukiya" style of Japanese architecture. It was located close to the Gion Corner, (a famous old Geisha district), the Yasaka Shrine and the famous Buddhist Temple called Kiyomizu.

Professor Yamamoto suggested that I relax at the Inn for three hours when he would return to pick me up. He also mentioned that I might enjoy a traditional bath in the 'common bath' of the Inn. The hotel rooms had nice small private baths but his comments about the 'common bath' and the way he spoke about it piqued my curiosity. I thanked him and at the hotel, asked for directions to this bath. I received directions and was reminded that there would be a white 'bath' kimono in the room.

The common bath was quite an experience. It was a large, glittering heated pool. At various locations around it there were resting mats and large round, barrel-like structures filled with hot water. A number of women in white kimonos with colorful trims could be seen around the facility and I observed that some of the barrel-like tubs were occupied by couples. It soon became clear that the women were helping the men bathe. This site unnerved me but I kept trying to convince myself that this was normal behavior in this culture. It also became clear to me that there were no sexual innuendos in this activity so I thought I could appreciate the natural simplicity of the situation.

Before I had really accepted the idea emotionally and intellectually, however, one of the girls walked over to me and, before I could say anything, led me to the steps outside one of the barrel-like tubs. Gently, ignoring my initial resistance, she started taking off my robe and coaxing me into the tub. The water was hot and there was a round seat on the inside perimeter. I slowly sat down and at this point, the girl took off her kimono, under which she wore some sort of bathing suit, and climbed into the tub.

I was embarrassed but forced myself to be brave and continue with the experience. She soaped and scrubbed me, making me feel like a baby. She tried to engage me in conversation but her English was extremely limited and my Japanese non-existent. Afterwards she led me to another tub with clean water to rinse off the soap and then to the pool where a number of other men were talking to each other or to the women, like the ones who assisted me in the tub. It was a memorable experience indeed.

When I got back to my room it was time to dress for the evening with Professor Yamamoto. First we went to a traditional Japanese restaurant where I tasted a truly outstanding example of sukiyaki. After dinner I learned what Professor Yamamoto meant when he introduced himself at the airport as a professor of "barology". It turned out that he had not mispronounced the word "biology," but meant "barology" as a joke because. It turned out that Professor Yamamoto was considered to be the Japanese version of Dr. Kinsey. Kinsey was the famous American scientist who did pioneering research on human sexual behavior and published two seminal works in this field: "Sexual Behavior in the Human Male (1948) and "Sexual Behavior in the Human Female (1953). Dr. Yamamoto's current research dealt with the sexual behavior of Geishas. He was obtaining his data by interviewing them at the bars and geisha houses were they congregated, hence the term "barology".

After dinner we went to make "bar rounds". He was a well-known figure in the bars and was treated everywhere with extraordinary respect. He showed me his interview techniques and the experimental protocols used for the interviews. Later that week, he familiarized me with the statistical tools used to analyze the data and draw relevant conclusions based on the information obtained from the interviews. Of particular interest to me was his juxtaposition of some of Dr. Kinsey's finding with his own observations.

As we entered the first bar a small man in a very elegant western suit walked over to us and bowed deeply to Professor Yamamoto and then to me. I noted with curiosity that the bow was not a single act but was repeated several times, becoming deeper with each bow. Later I learned that this was a technique used to establish social standing between two individuals, the one bowing deeper being the subordinate.

The gentleman greeting us was Mr. Mizoguchi, the owner of the bar. He lead us to a table in the back of the room, close to a semicircular bar where sat several girls dressed in what to my inexperienced eyes were very beautiful kimonos with high combed smooth black hair and chalky-white make up on their faces. As we sat down, two of the young ladies approached us and apparently asked Professor Yamamoto whether to sit down. He responded with a short sentence whereupon the girls bowed and retreated with beautiful smiles on their faces.

I knew that sake was a traditional drink of Japan. However, I quickly learned that beer was even more popular. Professor Yamamoto asked for two beers, leaned back in his comfortable, softly upholstered, American style chair inviting me to do the same and opened up the conversation:

> Now you are in my research laboratory. I conduct interviews in these types of bars, Geisha Houses and various performance venues. However, before demonstrating my interview technique, I must say few words about Japanese Geishas. You should be aware that that after the American

occupation of Japan, the group of women called Geishas became confused with the time-honored profession of prostitution. In many instances their roles became misinterpreted in a way detrimental to their tradition. I brought you a book written in English. It's rather short but contains relevant historical, philosophical and factual information about Geishas.

In my publications I stress the definition of a Geisha similar to the one found in western sources such as the Encyclopedia Britannica. To paraphrase: Geishas are women who have been engaged for hundreds of years in an occupation devoted to the sophisticated, professional art of entertaining. They were and are highly accomplished performers who spend years in training to acquire proficiency in playing traditional instruments, singing, dancing and knowledge of classic literature. They also must be able to entertain the customers with witty, clever and well-informed conversation. However, they have traditionally been prohibited from engaging in sexual activities for monetary returns. It is also true that Geishas could have a 'patron' with whom they might engage in a variety of interactions and relationships including, under certain circumstances, sexual intimacy. One aspect of such a relationship, however, is clearly understood. A Geisha's intimate relationship is reserved exclusively and permanently for the patron and is not available on a 'fee for service' basis. Thus, Geishas are entirely different from 'bar girls' or prostitutes. It should be noted that patrons are often the wealthiest businessmen and most influential politicians in the community.

After WW II and the occupation of Japan by the US Army, many girls dressed in traditional kimonos and wore traditional face makeup. They worked in the bars as prostitutes, a profession that traditionally was legal in Japan. The GIs didn't understand the difference and called them all Geishas.

I listened to this story with my mouth agape. In my mind, from the limited past reading I'd done dealing with Japan, I also thought Geishas were prostitutes, very high-class, but still prostitutes. As Professor Yamamoto tried to continue I interrupted him with a burning question. "How does one differentiate and recognize one group from the other, particularly since they apparently wear the same or very similar traditional Kimonos and make up?"

Here Professor Yamamoto started laughing, while pulling repeatedly at his long, thin mustache.

> In my study-groups I sub-classify the average 'bar girl' within the general group of prostitutes in order to separate them from both the prostitutes and the true Geishas. There is a definite difference between a 'bar girl' and a 'street walker'. Both will engage in sexual activity for money. However, a bar girl will be more prone to spend time with the customer providing 'supportive conversation' and social assistance, activities much valued by the average Japanese male customer.

I listened to the Professor with great interest, realizing that I had also been confused about the role and function of the Geishas. Furthermore, I was fascinated by his area of research. Dr. Kinsey's work was a topic of many animated discussions during my medical school years since his books were published around that time. The discussions usually dealt with the political implications and the scientific merits of his research. The ethical aspects of conducting this type of research were also vigorously debated. Some faculty and many students questioned the validity of the experimental designs and, in many instances, the validity of the research in this area as well as the utility of the conclusions.

Professor Yamamoto's research moved very actively into areas that would be almost impossible to deal with in our country. My interest in this general topic was limited to the clinical aspect of sexual dysfunction as related to the decrease or absence of testosterone in the human male. The results obtained by Professor Yamamoto were not only interesting but also somewhat surprising. The sex life of Geishas was clearly quite austere, depending very much on having a patron and the complex traditional culture of Japan.

The next morning I lectured medical students on feedback mechanisms in the hormonal control of gonadal growth and function. In the afternoon there was a lengthy seminar with graduate students where I discussed our work dealing with in-vitro experiments directed towards the elucidation of hormonal control of spermatogenesis. This was an area of great interest to the Japanese students, and we barely finished by 6:00 PM. Professor Yamamoto suggested that I get some rest that night as the following day he warned, "We will have a very full day and a long evening". After my experience in the bar with interviews about the sex lives of young girls and their partners I thought was prepared for anything.

The next day as we were leaving the University, Professor Yamamoto said he would pick me up at 7:30 to take me to the Gion Corner for dinner. He appeared precisely on time and suggested we have a some tea first because he wanted to tell me a little about the Gion District of Kyoto. After we sat down on the couches in the reception area and had been served our tea he began his story:

> Since Gion is one of the more important sources of research material for me, I thought I should provide you with some background information. Gion is the classical Geisha District in Kyoto, the one with the greatest history and tradition, and the most renowned in Japan. It was constructed in the middle ages in front of the Yasaka Shrine. By 1712 the teahouses (ochaya) in this area were formally licensed by the government (the Tokugawa Shogunate) permitting Geisha entertainment and the sale of alcoholic beverages like sake.

> Unfortunately, during the early twentieth century the district experienced a general downturn and the number of Geishas declined. However, because Kyoto was not bombed during WWII, none of Gion's beautiful architecture was destroyed. This helped paved the way for its current resurgence. A few years back, the Mayor, with the support of City Hall officials, declared Gion a national preservation district. Thus, it has been able to retain its traditional architecture and has resurrected its artistic richness.

Professor Yamamoto briefly interrupted his exposition and looked up as two Geishas materialized. He said a couple of words and within minutes we had two containers of hot sake in front of us. Curiosity was getting the best of me; "What is being done now in Gion and the Gion Corner?"

> Four areas of entertainment are being pursued: First of all the 'tea ceremony,' second, traditional koto and gagaku court music (traditional music of Japan and frequent accompaniment to dance), third, flower arranging and fourth, dramatic performances. These artistic activities have been carefully organized and arranged to attract tourists and are performed in specially constructed theaters.
>
> In addition, there are small establishments where these various forms of artistic entertainment are offered privately to individuals or small parties. They are exclusive and usually quite expensive. We will attend such a gathering tonight with several of my associates from the University. We will be guests of the establishment where, you might be interested to know, no wives or other female companions are permitted to join us. This activity is restricted to men.

The following day Professor Yamamoto took me to see the ancient city of Nara. He picked me up at 8:00 for the one hour train trip and as we sat down in a comfortable private compartment, he began to tell me about Nara, the first capital of Japan. He explained that the city was remarkable not only because of its historical relevance but also because of its extraordinary number of historical treasures, including beautiful temples and shrines, an extensive archeological site, the Nara Palace, and the famous Kasugayama Primeval Forest.

The city is small and we were able to walk to most of the important sites, each of which Professor Yamamoto described in great detail. He was not only knowledgeable, but also very proud of the heritage and beauty of the sites. We visited numerous shrines and temples but I was most impressed by Todaiji, a group of buildings including one that housed the largest statue of Buddha in Japan. It was called Kondo, or Great Hall, and was the largest wooden building in the world. It housed a forty-five foot tall, bronze, seated Buddha. It was an awesome site, indeed.

By noon my head was swimming with historical information. We continued with a visit to the Kasuga Taisha shrine located at the edge of the Nara Park. It is one of the oldest and most celebrated historical sites in Japan. While it was less impressive than Todaiji, the traditional style of the building had great charm and oriental beauty. The interior was full of hanging bronze lanterns donated by worshipers. The approaches to the shrine were also lined with hundreds more stone lanterns, all of which are apparently lit during the Lantern Festivals in February and August. I could only imagine how beautiful it was when all of them were lit.

As I was admiringly gazing at the shrine, I felt suddenly as if someone had stabbed me in the back with a stick. As I turned around, to my great surprise I was facing the antlers of a deer! Professor Yamamoto was laughing heartily as he explained, "According to legend, the deer were sacred messengers of the gods. They roam the park freely and sometimes even the streets of Nara, under the protection of strict laws." They were about waist high, tame and had beautiful golden beige coats sprinkled with white spots. We saw more of them later in the afternoon and for me these deer were one of the highlights of our trip to Nara.

My last few days in Kyoto were spent lecturing at the University, conversing with the students, visiting laboratories and making 'bar rounds' with Professor Yamamoto.

My next destination was Kobe. As the train pulled into the Kobe railroad station, Dr. Toyoda of the Kobe University Marine Division was waiting for me. After checking me into my hotel, he informed me that I would be spending most of my visit there discussing with students and faculty their research dealing with reproductive biology. Although their interests were in marine organisms, they felt that my experiences with mammalian reproductive biology might provide some new insights and new directions for their research. Also, he added, they would like me to spend a day at the marine biology station located on a little island off shore.

I was picked up by a motor boat and delivered to the marine station within twenty minutes. The entire staff was at the dock to greet me. This visit was more of a "show and tell" by them than a lecture by me. Their experiments on marine animals, I learned, were conducted in a very different fashion than those carried out on warm-blooded mammals. In comparison to our concerns during mammalian surgery, they worried a great deal less about infection while performing surgery on sea life such as lobsters. Everything was done faster and much more simply. It was a very interesting and memorable visit.

Since the island was near a pearl farm I was taken by boat to one of the hundreds of floating spheres used to attach hanging baskets or other devices designed to hold the pearl oysters. One of the baskets was raised to the surface and an oyster was removed. Upon our return the oyster was opened and inside was a beautiful pearl about six millimeters in diameter. It was given to me as a souvenir and I cherished it as a reminder of the warm hospitality I experienced during my visit.

Around 2:00 lunch was served in a small dining area at two long tables with benches that sat eight people. After we sat down at one of the tables, a huge four or five pound live lobster was brought in on a thick wooden board. One of the young men at our table took a long, curved and very sharp knife and cut through the entire length of the wriggling lobster's dorsal shell. Then, with a small, narrow knife he diced the tail meat while the lobster's eyes circled like periscopes. With a mischievous smile on his lips the knife-wielding student turned towards me, handed me two chopsticks, and in near perfect English suggested, "Take some of the meat when the lobster isn't looking." This unusual dining experience, like my entire experience in Japan, was fascinating and memorable.

After returning to Philadelphia, my work as Division Chairman began in earnest. I was responsible not only for my research but, indirectly, for everyone's success. In addition, shortly after coming back from Japan, I had to attend a quarterly Study Section meeting. There were twelve members and for each meeting we had to review between sixty and a hundred applications. Each application was reviewed by two members with the primary reviewer writing a rather lengthy, detailed review while the second reviewer could write an abbreviated one. Both reviewers presented their critique to the entire study section and, after an ensuing discussion, each application was awarded a "priority score" ranging from one and four with four being the lowest. Since there was a finite amount of money in the budget, only a fraction of the submitted grants could be funded. The secretary and staff computed the "cut off" point for funding. Once this was established, the approved grants underwent final deliberation and approval by a Council composed of scientists from the general scientific community and NIH intramural investigators.

There were usually several grant proposals that the study section considered worthy of approval, but had concerns about whether the facility was adequate or some other concern called for an on-site evaluation. For this purpose, "Site visit teams" composed of several study section members were charged with inspecting the applicant's laboratory and his or her institution to examine and clarify specific areas of concern. Each team would then prepare a detailed written report to be discussed at a subsequent meeting.

I was assigned to a team visiting an applicant from the University of Pennsylvania in Philadelphia, and some weeks later, with another from the University of Southern California in Los Angeles. These visits were time consuming; however, they were an essential part of my responsibility as a study section member so I gladly participated. It was also good experience. I not only learned about the work of my colleagues, but also about the universities where they worked.

CHAPTER 9

THE UNEXPECTED CRACK

The 1968 Presidential election campaign was reaching a fever pitch. My interest in politics could be described as tepid at best and I had a mostly middle of the road philosophy. However, I leaned in a liberal direction, leading frequently to my support of Democratic candidates. This was probably a reflection of my cultural background and the influence of my father's democratic attitudes during my childhood. Since President Lyndon Johnson followed many of President Kennedy's ideas, I generally supported him and was particularly pleased with his policies regarding the "great society". He had continued President Kennedy's efforts to pass civil rights legislation that formally outlawed discrimination against minorities and assured their right to vote. I also watched with great interest when his administration enacted the Medicare and Medicaid Bills in 1965 (as Titles XVIII and XIX of the Social Security Act). However, listening to his discussion of these bills on television, I became somewhat disturbed. It wasn't until a week later that I thought about it again and realized that what had caught my attention in his speech was contained in one small moment when the President emphasized that the Medicaid Act would entitle patients to "equal services". To me it seemed that all patients should receive the "best quality" medical care but that is a slightly different notion. It wasn't until a couple of decades later that I realized what it really was that had bothered me, but this was the first tiny crack in my idealistic view of medicine in our country.

The crack began to widen a bit when a new Executive Vice President for Planning at AEMC, Mr. Robert M. Sigmond, was hired. In his prior position he had served as Executive Director of the Hospital Planning Association of Allegheny County. My antenna rose a bit the first time I heard him talk. He called attention to the "Ailing American health care system" and spent considerable time criticizing the primary health care insurance system in our country, Blue Cross and Blue Shield, pointing to its history and referring to its "rise and decline". Then he focused on what he referred to as, "The crisis in today's health system" and the "Failure of the ailing American health system to cure itself". I was shocked since I had been totally unaware of these deficiencies in the system I had so actively participated in. Although, I have to admit that my professional concerns dealt primarily with research. The social and financial details of our medical practice were important but not of paramount interest to me.

Our clinical facility provided care to anyone who needed treatment regardless of their ability to pay for our services. However, we expected those who could afford it to pay a fair fee. We were not attempting to get rich from our clinical fees, only to earn sufficient income to allow us to live reasonably well. Each year we provided three months of free medical care in the outpatient clinics of the endocrine section at the main hospital and three months free attending service at the Internal Medicine Division. These were hospital facilities for patients who had no funds to pay for either hospitalization or physician's fees. I never attempted to determine if the medical care for patients who couldn't afford to pay their bills was socially adequate. I didn't even understand how one determines who falls into the 'welfare' category or ponder the philosophy, sociology or economics of medical care. However, since Mr. Sigmond was so forceful, insistent and abrasive in his presentation, I decided to learn more about him. Most of the information was not difficult to obtain.

He was a graduate of the Philadelphia public school system and the Pennsylvania State College, where he received a Master of Arts degree in 1942. During this relatively brief formal education he could not have studied a great deal about medical economics, hospitals, the practice of medicine and issues of health care delivery. Subsequently, during WWII, he served in a civilian capacity at the War Department and after the war moved into the area of medical economics. He secured a job as a research associate at the Hospital Council of Philadelphia and in 1950, was appointed an Assistant to the Executive Vice President and Medical Director of the AEMC, where he served until 1955. During a leave of absence from 1952 to 1954 he served as Director of Fiscal Studies for the National Commission on Financing of Hospital Care in Chicago.

We discussed Mr. Sigmond's speech at length during lunches in the fellows room. Most of the staff was not particularly concerned; they felt that greater interest among bureaucrats might help bring about positive evolutionary changes in the health care system. I tried to convince them that his ideas and directions may be quite narrow-minded. I believed the existing medical care system had numerous hard-wired, historically proven methods for providing adequate medical care and that "health care" was a different category that was part of the Government's responsibility for public health.

In his address Mr. Sigmond had also enthusiastically described what he called the "new initiatives" of the federal government. These apparently involved lucrative financial support for hospitals that set up clinics for needy citizens that would operate twenty-four hours a day, seven days a week. This part of Mr. Sigmond's speech also made me stop and think. Was he interested in providing the best and most affordable health care for the "needy," or was he trying to promote a system that would be most beneficial to the hospital as a for profit corporation? I was in a quandary.

On the national scene, politics were in the forefront. The election was greatly influenced by the Vietnam war, which had been supported by President Johnson. The antiwar sentiment in the country contributed substantially to his decision not to seek a second term. This resulted in a contest between Hubert H. Humphrey, the Democratic Party nominee, and Richard M. Nixon, Vice President under President Eisenhower in the 1950s. Since my interest in politics was limited, my main concern was the direction Mr. Nixon might take with regard to Medicine and Biomedical Sciences should he win the election. Little did I know of the problems our country was to face during Mr. Nixon's presidency.

Just before the presidential election, I received a communication from NIH inviting me to accept a seat on the Advisory Panel of the Center for Population Studies at the National Institutes of Child Health

& Human Development, a very important and prestigious panel. The NIH had recently established a funding category for support of centers of excellence dealing with the reproductive system. These were to be called "Centers for Population Studies," a title which I thought had probably been selected to take advantage of recent Government and media interest in a new issue, the "population explosion". While the focus of these Centers was on the development of contraceptive techniques, the research had to cover the reproductive systems of both men and women. Directly or indirectly the programs would have to deal with basic reproductive sciences and since I felt that the development of contraceptive technology and basic reproductive sciences were closely related and very important, I gladly accepted the appointment.

December of 1968 was just around the corner. A phone call alerted us that Keith Smith would be arriving from Pittsburgh on the tenth. I was happy to hear this and told him that we would have a party that evening to welcome him, and to come directly to our house when he arrived. I planned on having the entire staff at the party. We rented a thirty foot long red carpet that I placed in front of the house to welcome Keith and his wife Connie. As we were putting the final touches on the party preparations, a phone call brought news of a disaster. Their car had "blown up," on the road, and they were at a car dealership buying a new car. This would to delay their arrival by several hours! When they finally arrived at 11:00 PM, the welcoming party and the red carpet were still there but the party was significantly abbreviated.

The winter of 1968-69 was beautiful. There were lots of sunny days, some snow to make it feel like winter, and several ski trips up north. Both girls were becoming excellent skiers, making me very proud and happy. Ania, as usual, skied steadily and safely. The only problem we encountered was a most surprising and unusual development with Pauline. When the weather turned very cold on the ski slopes, she would develop huge hives. A quick visit to an allergist clarified the cause; she had developed a very rare immunologic disorder, 'Cryoglobulinemia'. She was essentially allergic to cold. This pretty well put an end to her skiing as well as swimming in cold water.

With Keith in the office, our clinical activities expanded considerably and gave me an opportunity to devote more time to basic research. Four years earlier Ania and Keith (during his research fellowship) had done some very interesting work on developing an immunological technique for measuring pregnancy hormones produced by the placenta. So, we embarked on the development of radioimmunoassays for measuring the pituitary gonadotrophins, LH and FSH. This turned out to be very successful, and by the late 1960s we were able to measure these hormones with considerable accuracy. Unfortunately, attempts to develop similar techniques for the measurement of steroid hormones, particularly the male sex hormone testosterone, were not as successful. The entire scientific community dealing with measurement of testosterone levels in the blood was searching for effective techniques. Some laboratories claimed a degree of success using radioactive antibodies to testosterone, but we remained unsuccessful.

This was a stumbling block in our attempts to decipher the etiology and mechanisms related to the development of ovarian cysts, severe bleeding episodes and infertility in women with clinical signs of excessive male sex hormone levels. The clinical signs, such as excessive body hair, facial hair and other stigmata of increased levels of testosterone (clinical 'hyperandrogenism'), while tantalizing, were not quantitative or definite proof of elevated testosterone levels. At this point we were almost certain that these disorders were related directly to elevated testosterone levels. It explained the success of a treatment devised by Bill wherein the adrenal glands, which were responsible for producing the excessive amount of testosterone, were suppressed. However, we would be unable to prove it until effective measurements of blood testosterone became available some years later.

When we were unsuccessful that effort, we directed our attention to developing techniques for characterizing the biosynthetic pathways of testosterone formation in testicular tissue. Here our attack was two pronged. Ania had been successful in developing highly enriched Leydig cell cultures and Miguel Ficher had made remarkable progress in adapting current biochemical technology to look at testosterone's biosynthetic pathway. We now had a way to learn about the synthetic processes dealing with testosterone formation in the developing and adult testes. The first major summary of our findings were to be presented at an annual symposium of the Society for the Study of Reproduction. The paper would summarize several years of research on the mechanisms of testosterone biosynthesis during testicular development and our theories about androgen biosynthetic pathways in the developing testes.

That same year we provided data to support the hypothesis of endocrine control of spermatogenesis in the testes, which had originally been presented by our laboratory in 1967 at the Brooks Lodge Workshop on "Capacitation of Spermatozoa and Endocrine Control of Spermatogenesis". At that workshop, we had demonstrated specific points in spermatogenesis that were under hormonal control. I used my theory of specific cellular response in the germinal epithelium to noxious stimuli, and provided evidence that different cell types in the testes had specific responses to different hormones. This is what enabled both their development and differentiation. The paper was well received and I returned to Philadelphia stimulated and happy.

My positive state of mind continued during a meeting with Paul Wapner, Chief of the Ob-Gyn Department. Although the department was closely related to Temple University School of Medicine, it was separately administered. Bill Perloff, who went on to establish the Division of Endocrinology and Human Development at AEMC, had originally been Chief of Endocrinology at Temple. But his interests were heavily skewed towards the reproductive endocrinology so he found the Department of Ob-Gyn at AEMC under Paul's leadership much more receptive to his ideas. After Paul assumed the Directorship of our Department our interactions were always very easy, pleasant and productive. We referred patients to each others' departments and enjoyed an excellent collaborative spirit. I invited Paul to dinner so we could relax, talk about our interests, and investigate further avenues for collaboration. I suggested a little Italian restaurant on Ogontz Avenue that served superb lobster "fra diavolo".

We began with Scotch on the rocks and some appetizers. Interestingly it was Paul who started telling me how much he and members of his group enjoyed our mutual style of practice.

> You see Emil, we are surgeons, but we also want to be obstetricians. Many of us like to operate, while others prefer to deliver babies but most of us do both. Additionally, some Ob-Gyn doctors like to take care of non-surgical disorders of the reproductive system. Here we create friction with Endocrinologists who feel that the reproductive system is an

integral part of the total endocrine system; it's composed of endocrine glands, and it's controlled by complex feedback mechanisms throughout the rest of the endocrine system.

Gynecologists love surgery, we spend many years training to become proficient in these tasks, and I see no reason for the friction. After all, in most areas of medicine we have two types of doctors taking care of disorders. For example, we have neurologists, who take care of the non-surgical aspects of disorders of the nervous system, and neurosurgeons. Similarly, we have cardiologists or peripheral vascular specialists on one hand, and cardiovascular surgeons for the surgical aspects on the other. We have Nephrologists and Urologists, Gastroenterologists and General Surgeons, Pulmonologists and Thoracic Surgeons, etc., etc. But the Ob-Gyn specialty is particularly resistant to collaboration with Endocrinologists.

I was taken aback by his lucid explanation of an issue I had struggled with for the past ten years; one which I had often discussed with my colleagues practicing gynecological surgery. Before I could respond, the waiter served the fra diavolo and we both became occupied with more immediate pleasures. I was mulling Paul's words over in my mind but was having difficulty accepting these ideas from a Gynecologist.

Paul stopped eating and his face lit up in a smile, "This certainly is 'hot as the devil,'" he commented, "but I really like it; how did you find this place?" "By chance really. I like this type of Italian food and stopped here last year on the way home. It's very close to Curtis Arboretum where I live and ever since that time I've been a steady customer". After few more generalities I could not resist continuing our discussion.

Paul, I'm pleasantly surprised to hear your clear illustration of the surgical versus non-surgical specialties, including your very appropriate examples. Before asking your opinion concerning the views of your colleagues on this issue, I'd like to point out that there is an additional issue that needs to be added to this picture. When a woman is having difficulties becoming pregnant, she automatically sees her "baby doctor," an Ob-Gyn. If he finds a problem, he initiates some form of therapy and if not, and this is relatively rare, he may refer her husband to a Urologist, a Genito-Urinary Surgeon. The latter, in turn, will usually order a semen analysis. If there's an abnormality, he'll then perform a testicular biopsy, (a minor surgical procedure for obtaining a tiny sample of testicular tissue for microscopic study to make a diagnosis); all of this even though there is generally no effective treatment for these disorders.

Here Paul interrupted me, "What do you propose? Should the Ob-Gyn also manage the husband?" I burst out laughing, "No but the Ob-Gyn might refer the husband to an Endocrinologist, who is interested and well trained in disorders of the male reproductive system and work together with them." I liked Paul, I found him to be very logical, concerned about his patients' well being, and willing to cooperate with us. So I didn't pursue the issue further although I had some ideas about what more could be done.

Despite the ever increasing tempo of our professional lives, Ania and I tried hard to maintain a reasonable family and social life. Not only did we have frequent parties with our friends in Philadelphia and friends and relatives from New York, but we also spent many weekends sailing on the Chesapeake Bay. Our experience on the Chesapeake-Delaware canal had spooked us, however, and we began seriously looking for a boat with a more powerful inboard engine and better sleeping facilities. Although Pauline enjoyed a weekend of relaxation on the boat, she was not enthusiastic about sailing. Inette on the other hand took to sailing in a serious way and was becoming a good little sailor. Ania showed great interest and skill in navigating the boat, and particularly enjoyed sailing in fair weather. I enjoyed everything about it and was thrilled when we decided to get a larger boat to be named, following our tradition, the EPIA III.

The hunt for the boat began in earnest. We poured over sailing magazines, visited marinas and boat yards, took demonstration sails, etc., all in the hopes of finding closer our "dream boat". This would a difficult task since the "dream boat" also had to fit within our budget. By now we had sailed three boats and had considerable experience, which made shopping both easier and more difficult. As most sailors can attest, there is always something bigger and better out there.

One Monday after a long weekend sail, I was informed that another meeting was scheduled for the following Friday with our new Executive President for Planning, Mr. Sigmond. He was to apprise us of some of his new ideas for the Medical Center. Since the first meeting had left me with a bad feeling, I was not looking forward to the following Friday. This time, for reasons I could not clearly comprehend, he focused on issues related to basic science research, both at AEMC and at other major medical center that, like ours, was part of a medical school. I was confused by what he had to say, particularly when he turned to economic issues and lashed out against basic research as a financial burden.

The Korman Research Laboratory Building was built using grants, mostly from NIH, an institution of the federal government. Furthermore, its activities, mostly fundamental research, were financed almost entirely through research grants and these grants included a substantial "overhead budget" for use by the parent institution-in our case AEMC. The way I saw it, the research facility provided financial support to the medical center rather than the other way around.

Nevertheless, Mr. Sigmond while speaking mostly about AEMC goals as he saw them, a significant part of the talk was directed towards the financial burden of research activities in the laboratories. He'd spent part of his career in Pittsburgh and was apparently influenced by the coal industry in that area. In the most abrasive part of his talk he used an example he drew from that industry. He explained that managing a coal mine required making difficult economic decisions; if one part of the mine doesn't make as much profit as expected it is closed and the miners are fired, while areas bringing in greater profit are expanded. The same philosophy, he opined, should prevail in managing a major medical center. If the administration does not believe the research directly supports the Medical Center's goals (especially the financial ones), the administration has the duty to limit, or even eliminate such research activities.

I now understood why he had spent so much time defining the goals of AEMC, as he saw them. The "First step in an effective planning process," he rhapsodized, was "selecting our goals," and the first goal was to "…solve the problem of delivering effective, economical health care". He brought up the issue of whether the care should be delivered only to "sick" people, or to the entire community, including "well" people. My ears perked up - was he promoting the idea that hospitals should act as public health institutions? I didn't think so.

When he addressed research activities in Medical Centers like the AEMC, I was appalled.

> Research sponsored by the hospital should focus on the delivery of patient care and evaluations, as opposed to laboratories or animal studies of problems only remotely related to the activities of a busy hospital. The idea that basic research enhances the quality of care and/or the prestige of a hospital will die a slow death, but it will die. Ultimately, research goals will be related to hospital goals and hospitals will become major centers of research solely in the areas of community health and medical care.

I sat transfixed, literally not believing my ears. Having never had a chance to talk to Mr. Sigmond in person, it was unclear to me what he really had in mind. During the question and answer period I decided to take a risk and engage him in a brief public discussion. Since there were very few questions or comments after the talk, I was instantly recognized after raising my hand. "Mr. Sigmond, Please allow me to congratulate you for taking such an active and positive stand in support of hospital-sponsored research dealing specifically with the hospital's goal of delivering medical care to patients from the community. I was somewhat confused, however, about your statements regarding research in 'community health' or 'public health'. I thought this area of research was being actively pursued by other organizations, particularly the City Health Department, the County Health Department, the State Health Department and the Federal Department of Health. Furthermore, I am keenly aware that physicians from our Medical Center and the faculty of Temple University Medical School are involved in research in these public health institutions. Why make a special effort to increase our hospital's participation in the area of public health? After all, doesn't the hospital have its hands full simply delivering high quality, up to date medical care as well as providing training facilities for medical students, interns, residents and postdoctoral fellows?"

He looked at me with his steely cold eyes for what felt like an eternity to me before answering, "In most hospitals today, there is no knowledge of community-based health indices. No particular concern for how well the community is doing. No one is assigned responsibility for knowing and no one seems to care. From an analytic point of view, the hospital is the key to community health, but the hospital does not explicitly set its goals or programs accordingly and therefore falls short of its potential in this area.

The greatest need of hospitals today is the formulation of new concepts for a changing world. This can be achieved only through a new approach to planning. Formerly, we planned for buildings; now the challenge is to plan for change. Fantastic change in health care lies before us. The hospital must tool up to understand, anticipate, and adapt to change, and provide leadership in these changing times."

He had much more to say that afternoon but most of his thoughts were directed towards the same goal, to strengthen the bureaucracy in the hospital, to gain more government grants to provide "community care" and conduct research into the methods of providing "health care" to well people in the community rather than providing "medical care" to the sick ones. He repeatedly expressed his conviction that basic research had no place at AEMC. Much of the audience was in shock.

After the meeting we all gathered in the fellows room to digest this event. Most were dazed and simply didn't know what to say. My initial response was disappointment, anger, and a desire to strike back. This meant we had to leave the institution. I was certain that Sam would call a meeting of the Korman Laboratories research staff in the near future, and that Mr. Sigmond's attitude, ideas, and his ability to implement those ideas would be clarified.

Time moved on, and the calendar turned to 1969. I couldn't devote major attention to the issues posed by Mr. Sigmond because I had more immediate responsibilities. One of them was preparing a paper I was co-authoring with Ania for a major symposium entitled "The Spermatogenic Function of the Testes". In this paper, Ania's in-vitro approaches and my studies in mammals were to be combined to provide our current views of the control of spermatogenesis in the mammalian testes. However, Mr. Sigmond's words kept ringing in my ears, feeding my thoughts of the possible need to relocate the laboratory.

At this stage of my career it only required putting out the word that we would be amenable to offers and, sure enough, calls and letters began to arrive. I also recalled Professor Grobstein's inquiry during our recent trip to Japan concerning my possible interest in a position at the new University of California Medical School in La Jolla just north of San Diego (UCSD). When interest was also expressed by the Medical School at the University of California in San Francisco (UCSF) and by the University of California in Los Angeles (UCLA), a plan began to germinate in my mind. So, one morning while driving with to work I asked Ania, "How would you like to take a two week vacation with the girls and my parents?" She looked at me surprised "A vacation," she repeated, "but two weeks will take all the vacation time we have. How will we be able to take time off for sailing, or in the winter for skiing?"

"Well,…" I said slowly, "my visits to the various schools will involve not only a survey of these places for a possible future move, but also presenting some lectures. What if I could arrange for few lectures during these days to be delivered by you? This way, a part of the trip would become professional business." First she looked at me seriously but then started laughing, "What are you really plotting?" Here I spilled, with a glee in my eyes, my rather complex plan:

> We'll make the trip with my parents and the girls, but devote part of it to visiting various medical schools. We can fly to San Francisco and rent a car large enough to accommodate all six of us. Then we can visit my sister Stella's place in Dublin, only about one or two hours from San Francisco and leave my parents and the girls with her while you and I visit the Medical School in San Francisco. After that we'll all explore California by car and end up in San Diego and visit UCSD Medical School. The entire trip should take about two weeks; it will be a fabulous vacation and a great opportunity to become acquainted with a few schools where we might relocate.

Ania was taken aback a bit by my plan and was thinking intently.

Suddenly she put her arms around my shoulders as I was driving and exclaimed, "That sounds great!" It took almost a month to coordinate our schedules with the different schools but the time for our trip finally arrived. I was full of anticipation---"Golden California!" I had visited some of the big cities in the past, but we had never vacationed there. This trip was sure to be a memorable family experience.

The visit with Stella was a "happening". She had seven children and the youngest, Jimmy, had been only four years old when she divorced her husband a few years earlier. I don't know how she managed to raise this huge family on her own, particularly since her ex-husband hadn't provided any support. However, she seemed quite happy and the kids looked well cared for and healthy. It seemed like a miracle to me.

Our visit to the medical school in San Francisco was interesting but I quickly scratched it off the list. They requested I give a talk on the male reproductive system and explained that they would want me to set up a Division of Male Reproductive Sciences with a strong research arm in the Department of Urology. I, however, had something else in mind. It was summer but the weather in San Francisco that day was foggy, windy and chilly. At this point in my life, sailing had become an important part of my life. If this was summer, how cold was winter? I didn't think I would enjoy sailing the San Francisco Bay in spite of its popularity among sailors; it was much too cold. Anyway, I wasn't excited by the offer so we were ready to continue exploring.

The following day we drove to Yosemite National Park. My parents were elated by the whole experience. Although they were accustomed to seeing beautiful mountains in Europe, Yosemite had a special allure for them. They especially enjoyed sharing the experience with their children and grandchildren despite the fact that we were staying in a tent. We could see the majestic peaks surrounding us, particularly the formidable and beautiful granite mountain called El Capitan. Our two days in Yosemite were spent walking, primarily toward El Capitan, and up to Bridal Veil Falls. We drove through the valley floor to admire the granite walls surrounding it, watched the powerful Yosemite Falls, and visited Half Dome, one of the most grandiose, famous and recognizable formations in the Sierra Nevadas.

The days were filled with great beauty and excitement, but the nights turned out to be part of the adventure as well. Everywhere there were signs, "Beware of Bears" and "Keep Garbage Disposal Facilities Securely Closed to Keep out Bears". Ania, however, was determined to see a bear so she purposely left a bag of garbage next to a securely closed garbage can and stayed up watching for a bear until midnight, but without success. The next morning, feeling very disappointed, she told us about her efforts. I thought it was a foolish and dangerous thing to do and after we had a minor argument about it she promised that not to attempt to lure a bear again.

From Yosemite we drove to Kings Canyon and Sequoia National Parks (which are contiguous). The monumental sequoias are the largest trees and oldest trees in the world and the "General Sherman Tree" is the largest and of them all. As we looked at it we could only admire its quiet grandeur. The tree is 275 feet tall and has a diameter of 36.4 feet, the width of a small house.

After spending the night in the park we headed south, towards the Joshua Tree National Park which is located at the junction of the Sonoran and Mojave deserts. Even before we entered the park, while driving through a forlorn desert, we spotted a most unusual tree; it looked like a combination of a cactus and a palm tree. It turned out to be one of the famous "Joshua" trees. As we entered the formal park area, the surroundings became even more foreboding: desert as far as the eye could see, punctuated by various size Joshua trees, some reaching forty feet in height. The park was also full of other desert formations, primarily cacti, rocks and stones, and the unique rock formations called Inselbergs. These curious formations rose very steeply and abruptly from the desert floor and were scattered randomly throughout the landscape.

By lunch time we had arrived at an oasis in the form of a little Mexican restaurant. Everyone was hungry but also apprehensive about tasting real Mexican food; it was a first for all of us. My parents tried several dishes but didn't like any of them. The girls, on the other hand, loved the tamales, a spicy Mexican dish consisting of chopped meat with spices and corn meal, wrapped in cornhusks and steamed. For Ania everything was too spicy, and I was undecided. It was quite a unique dining experience.

About thirty minutes after leaving the restaurant, I realized I had left my fancy and expensive 35 millimeter camera hanging on the back of my chair at the restaurant. We immediately turned around and headed back to look for it. As I briskly entered the restaurant, the owner came running over to me with a big smile on his face exclaiming, "Senor, you forgot your camera." Soon one of the waiters came out of the back room with my camera in hand. This was such a friendly gesture I tried to give the man a small tip but he firmly refused it, he simply shook my hand with a friendly smile on his face. This reminded me that there are good, honest people everywhere in the world!

Soon we approached the Salton Sea, a huge body of water glistening against the western sun that in turn, reflected brilliantly off its dark blue surface. This "sea" is actually a huge lake that was created by accident at the turn of the century when heavy rainfall and snowmelt caused the Colorado River to overrun head gates that had been created for the Alamo Canal. The floods breached an Imperial Valley dike, causing the water to spill into the Imperial Valley and fill the Salton Basin. Over the course of eighteen months the water submerged the town of Salton and formed a lake sixty kilometers long and twenty kilometers wide. Ultimately it became the Salton Sea National Wildlife Refuge and evolved into a major recreational facility with superb fishing, boating and bird watching.

I was not planning to stop for an afternoon of swimming or boating. Instead I told everyone about a surprise I had planned for them; "We have been invited by a medical school classmate of mine, Dr. Bill Spirtos, to use his vacation house in Palm Springs. His villa is located across the street from Frank Sinatra's compound and, according to Bill, the swimming pool is a refreshing oasis on a hot day." He had sent me the key with instructions to simply move in and stay as long as we wanted. The temperature was over 100 degrees, and we eagerly anticipated a dip in the pool.

We pulled up to a beautiful grey stone cottage with a large front porch shielded from the hot Southern California sun by a multitiered overhang that kept it in deep shade. The interior of the house could be summarized with a single word---lavish. We quickly turned on the air conditioning and began settle in. The house was L-shaped around a pool filled with the clearest, bluest water I'd ever seen. I quickly put on my swim suit and jumped in… and was almost scalded by the water! The sun had heated the water to the point that it was hot rather than refreshingly cool as I had expected. We were terribly disappointed and ultimately decided to stay there only overnight. We would drive on to La Jolla where, in two day's time we had an appointment with Professor Clifford Grobstein at UCSD.

We checked in to the Bahia Resort Hotel on Mission Bay in San Diego. This provided a beautiful vacation spot for my parents and the girls while Ania and I drove to La Jolla to visit Professor Grobstein. The hotel was located by a charming beach on the bay and close to a variety of interesting sites in the city including the famous San Diego Zoological Gardens, Old Town, and Sea World. We felt comfortable that our family would enjoy themselves while we were in La Jolla.

The UCSD Medical School was in its early stages of development and I was looking forward to the visit and possible job offers. I had known Cliff for a number of years and we had recently traveled to Japan for the Japanese American Science Exchange Program. He had joined UCSD a couple of years earlier as professor and chairman of the Biology Department and was instrumental in helping the University build a new Medical School. He had also been recently appointed Dean.

Ania and I were to spend the day visiting the new facilities and meeting with the faculty, particularly those who were most involved with planning the new school. Major parts of the facilities, still under construction, were to accommodate basic sciences. The clinical sciences would temporarily be taught in San Diego, where my guest lecture was to be delivered the next day. The rest of the week we would spend visiting San Diego and its environs, including visits to Tijuana, Mexico and the beaches. I was particularly eager to check out the water temperature since I wasn't eager to relocate to an area were the water would be cold, like the San Francisco Bay or the waters off Los Angeles. I imagined with dread going overboard and finding myself in frigid waters possibly suffering from the complications of cold exposure; that was not for me. This was one of the reasons the offers from UCSF and UCLA had been placed low on our list of options.

Our visit with Cliff was very cordial. He was an urbane and extraordinarily brilliant individual. His office was simple but elegant, and his manner was very personable while commanding respect. His academic and scientific achievements were extremely broad and characterized by remarkable depth and sensitivity. His major contributions dealt with the intracellular matrix, the gelatinous substance interposed between the cells in the body, and on the elucidation of its biochemical composition and its role in the developmental process, particularly during embryonic induction.

During our discussion, it became clear that Cliff's thoughts were focused on reproductive biology and the potential role of the intracellular matrix in the development of gonadal tissue. This explained why he might be interested in having a department of reproductive biology like mine join his basic science facilities. With this in mind we immediately dove into a lively discussion dealing with science, followed by a grand tour of several departments that he proudly showed me.

With the formal responsibilities out of the way, I spent the next two days in La Jolla touring the facilities, meeting with the faculty, and delivering my lecture. A serious discussion dealing with the possibility of transplanting my group from Philadelphia to La Jolla was initiated but there were many factors to be considered. Probably one of the most serious ones was the fact that the clinical facilities were located in San Diego, while the basic science facilities were in La Jolla, some distance away. Our department was a closely knit basic and clinical group, and such geographic separation, even if only temporary, could be disastrous. However, the water temperature would be a decisive factor, and we couldn't wait to visit the beaches. I knew that this would strike others as funny or ridiculous, but Ania and I considered it a serious issue.

We rejoined the family and after testing the waters in Mission Bay, decided they were acceptable, but I was looking forward with impatience to visiting an ocean beach. On Friday we decided to drive over the Mexican border to Tijuana, and on the way back, stop at Imperial Beach south of San Diego. The drive to Tijuana was easy, and the border crossing quick and simple. However, once we crossed into Mexico, we found ourselves in a different world. The girls were fascinated but my parents were sitting in the back seat of the car shaking their heads. It was more that they could assimilate. The colors and the sounds certainly were different from our middle class neighborhood on the East coast. Everything, particularly the houses, were painted in bright primary colors or pastels. Loud Mexican music which seemed to come from every home and store also added to the festive atmosphere. We were admonished not to miss a walk down the Avenida Revolution which begins at Avenida International, the road leading into Mexico from the United States. The throngs of people, the bars, restaurants, dance halls and hotels on the street combined with the vibrant colors and pervasive music were overwhelming. The girls enjoyed the scene so much we had trouble tearing them away from the excitement.

Ultimately everyone became hungry and we randomly selected a Cantina for lunch. The girls had a ball but my parents were not sure whether or not they should eat the food. My father usually enjoyed spicy food but this was not only spicy but also very foreign, so he had trouble navigating through the different exotic flavors. Mother simply refused all of the dishes except for tortilla soup. Ania tasted various dishes while the girls and I also settled on the tortilla soup. The experience was great fun for everyone and we didn't realize how fast the time was sliding by. We still wanted to go to the beach on the way back to San Diego.

It was only a half hour drive and soon we pulled into a parking lot at Imperial Beach. The beautiful white sandy beach was almost deserted with the blue waters of the Pacific lapping peacefully on the sand. It was extremely lovely and unusually quiet with so little surf. The girls and I quickly stripped to our bathing suits and ran laughing into the water. As I dove in, a shock greeted me. This was the most southern stretch of the pacific coast, the day was hot and the sand was burning the soles of my feet, but the water was still very cold. After surfacing I swam for a while trying to warm up but the water still felt like ice.

Returning to the blanket, where everyone had settled while we were in the water, I looked at Ania and shook my head saying, "This area will not do, the water is much too cold. Going overboard in these waters would be very unpleasant". Ania started laughing saying, "I didn't even try". The girls came running out of the water calling, "Freezing cold water! Where are the towels?" The next morning we left for home knowing we hadn't yet found the right destination for our move.

Upon returning from California I was greeted by telephone messages and several letters from various Medical Schools inquiring about whether were truly movable as a department. Apparently, as we suspected, the "grapevine" had worked and we had to decide whether we were really serious about leaving AEMC. Conversations with our colleagues at the Korman Research Laboratories did not provide any hopeful signs. In fact, one of the most powerful Directors, whose group made substantial contributions to science and whose Division was lavishly funded by NIH, thought he might also have to consider relocating.

Mr. Sigmond continued his course of anti-basic research policies and his drive for "Community health initiatives" to be spearheaded by the Medical Center. The clinical chiefs at the Medical Center were still not much concerned however, they thought Mr. Sigmond's ideas could bring more federal funds to the Center, help establish new outpatient clinics, and pay better salaries for young physicians. The clinical staff was also not looking at this issue with any urgency; most were physicians with offices near AEMC. Their well developed private practices were not directly dependent on the Center's politics and would not be affected by the opening of new "night clinics" or other federally funded outpatient services. However, I could see the writing on the wall and continued to consider relocation. This raised many issues that had been of no consequence before then. I had to decide if it would involve just me or whether I should consider the possibility of moving the entire Department. The question was," Who would move?" Clearly, before facing the group with this question, I would have to discuss it in great detail with Ania.

It suddenly dawned on me that Ania and I had almost never discussed our futures at great length. Our minds seemed to work so much in sync that things between us seemed to just happen. Thinking back I realized that I had never even formally proposed to her. Falling in love with her twenty-five years earlier, when we were just sixteen, occurred so innocently and naturally that we didn't even talk about it. We both simply realized that we were in love, a fact that had occurred to me well before I even kissed her. At that time it was 1944, the height of WWII, a time when we and a large segment of population in Alma Ata, were facing starvation and possible death. Our primary concerns were very pragmatic ones but we also had dreams. Uncannily, even our dreams coincided so much that we hadn't needed to talk about them at any length. Ania delighted in fantasizing how she would become a famous scientist like Maria Curie Skladowska, who received two Nobel prizes-in Physics and Chemistry. We were both planning to carry out research in the biomedical sciences but in my fantasy these dreams would come true in the distant Land of Oz - the United States of America.

We felt very fortunate. After the war we had been able to leave the Soviet Union, encourage each other to pursue biomedical studies, and ultimately emigrate to the United States. We had married in the Bronx, New York and ultimately fulfilled the first part of our fantasies by completing our studies and receiving our degrees-a PhD degree in Microbiology for Ania, and an MD for me. During these years, our lives were tough and turbulent but our love was harmonious and steady. Each of us simply performed our duties gladly without asking for special rewards, justifications, or explanations.

A true test of the depth of the love between us came in 1961 when Ania received her PhD and I completed my postgraduate training. We were finally ready to embark on our life's careers and at this juncture, without much discussion, our mutual devotion dictated that we pursue our professional careers together, working in the same department. When I looked for my first academic position, the search always included a position for a PhD associate, my wife. During our initial years of working together, I had helped her retrain from a microbiologist to a reproductive biologist, and initiate grant support for the research. After the first three years, however, she became an independent investigator and a full fledged collaborator. This transformation also occurred naturally and without much discussion. Wasn't this also a function of our deep love and respect for each other? Clearly any possible relocation would have to involve a team of two scientists and collaborators, who also happened to be husband and wife and, if the group chose it, the rest of the department. Again we both agreed on this approach without much discussion. This allowed us to work during the interim period without stress and unnecessary and time-consuming deliberations.

Despite the political turmoil at our institution, intra- and extramural work progressed with few interruptions. My extramural work as a member of the Advisory Panel at the Center for Population Studies was demanding and time consuming. It carried a great deal of responsibility since the Panel was evaluating requests for grants to set up Centers for Population Studies at universities throughout the country. I would need to review several grant proposals; attend the Panel meetings to evaluate and rate the proposals, and participate in site visits to the applying institutions to evaluate them. The competition was fierce and the funds involved were very large.

My other extramural activities involved serving on various scientific committees. I had been elected Chairman of the Membership Committee of the Society for the Study of Reproduction and invited to become a member of the Editorial Board of the scientific journal "Biology and Reproduction". While these appointments raised my standing in the scientific community and were both educational and fun, the time demands were enormous.

The political situation at AEMC, under the influence of Mr. Sigmond, whose ideas of the medical world were at odds with many of the things I believed, and the possibility of moving made the situation particularly difficult. I felt as if I were on a monstrous conveyer, a moving walkway like one sees at airports, with numerous exciting research findings and discoveries moving me forward. But while some people were trying to help me get ahead, I felt as though others were trying to slow me down. One afternoon I met Ilia in the hallway and he suggested we walk over to the cafeteria for a snack. Since I had not seen him for a while, this seemed like a good idea and I gladly accepted his invitation.

As we walked towards the main building, he shot me a side glance and innocently asked in a low tone of voice, "How do you like Sigmond?" Knowing Ilia's predilection for social theories that could possibly be supportive of Sigmond's "Community health care" ravings, I temporized and turned the question around asking "How do you like him?" He didn't respond for a while, finally he said, in an uncertain tone of voice, "I'm not sure. He confuses me. On one hand he expounds liberal concepts with respect to health care but on the other, he acts like an autocrat and is down on basic research and totally insensitive to the role of basic scientists in our society."

I burst out laughing as we walked into the nearly empty hospital cafeteria. We grabbed some food and found a table by the window.

> Did you read the article he published in this year's spring issue of the 'Journal of the Albert Einstein Medical Center'? It's an amazing document. As you know he has no formal medical or biomedical education or background. His first contact with the medical field didn't occur until 1946 when he was hired as a Research Associate at the

Governor's Commission on Hospital Facilities, Standards, and Organizations in Philadelphia. The rest is history.

Ilia looked at me with disbelief in his eyes as I pressed on:

Coming back to Mr. Sigmond's publication, I was amazed and amused by a paragraph in the 'Conclusions' of the article where he states, 'The hospital that is able to formulate sound community-oriented goals is in touch with the health care realities of today, is sensitive to changing forces and is effectively organized to help the community achieve better health. Such a hospital will attract far stronger community support than one which has not been able to achieve a consensus on realistic community health goals.

In other words, in the context of the rest of the article, he is saying that the main role of a hospital should be primarily to provide community "health promotion" services. In most of the article he uses the term "health care," but occasionally he talks about "medical care" and "health care" interchangeably. This caught my attention. I never considered our professional activity to be "health care" delivery. I always thought we provided "medical care" to sick patients. "Health care" to me has always meant the public health activities provided to well people by the Departments of Public Health. This would include a variety of procedures and measures to enhance health and prevent disease, such as vaccinations, purification and fluoridation of water, etc. I never thought of these activities as the responsibility of medical facilities.

Ilia remained silent for a little while, shaking his head. Finally he said, "I never thought about it in that context." We finished our food in silence, then slowly got up and started walking back to the Korman Research Laboratories. At that time I didn't realize how serious, pervasive, misleading and destructive the phrase, "Health care" would ultimately become.

Upon returning from this snack with Ilia, I saw Harold standing in the hall talking to Jack. It occurred to me, with this conversation still ringing in my ears, that now would be a good time to gather the staff of my department and seriously discuss the possibility of relocating to another institution. I suggested that we get together the following day at 3:00 PM. They looked at me questioningly but readily agreed; I then asked our secretary to inform the appropriate staff and join us to keep minutes of the meeting.

As we gathered, I looked around the table with pleasure. It was an admirable group of people and a faculty one could be proud off. It was a true interdisciplinary team. There were psychologists, steroid chemists, morphologists, biologists, electron microscopists, ecologists and clinicians, all seasoned and well-recognized scientists who also interacted well with young and idealistic beginners. I thought of this team as an incredible resource, one that any major biomedical institution would cherish, but that AEMC and Temple were on the verge of losing. Particularly enviable was the close interaction of the clinicians with basic scientists and psychologists. Dr. Harold Persky, a renowned biochemist who had moved into the area of biochemistry of psychology, was having a serious discussion with one of Jack's postdoctoral fellows who had one year earlier received his PhD in ethology, the science dealing with animal behavior.

Everyone was well acquainted with the situation at AEMC and the possibility of leaving. The major questions were when, where and how. I sensed that most of our team wanted to move as a group in order to retain their personal and professional ties. However, there were extenuating individual circumstances. For example Miguel Ficher, the leader of our steroid chemistry team, would have difficulty leaving Philadelphia since his wife Ilda held a professorial position at Hahnemann Medical College, and their three daughters were happily situated in school. She would not be eager to move unless an attractive academic position was available to her at the new location as well. Others would consider a move depending on the destination. But the clear consensus was that we should relocate because the circumstances at AEMC were no longer conducive to our scientific work. We decided to continue our work as usual but carefully consider all offers that might come our way.

Research was moving at an ever increasing tempo and it was a banner year in our lab. Dr. Sud, a junior member of the group originally from India, had discovered a new chemical entity that stopped spermatogenesis at a specific stage of maturation; Dr. Ficher had demonstrated that biosynthetic pathways leading to formation of testosterone undergo a complicated change in maturing testes; and Dr. Tjioe, a postdoctoral fellow from Indonesia, had detailed certain abnormalities caused by diminished blood flow to the testes. A method had been developed to investigate abnormalities in steroid metabolism in human testes utilizing tiny fragments of testicular tissue obtained by biopsy. Dr. Persky and an associate, Dr. Zimmerman, completed construction of an isolation room to study the effects of sensory deprivation on the hormonal equilibrium in humans.

Using her advanced techniques of tissue and cell culture, Ania, working with a number of colleagues, successfully established pure Sertoli cell cultures. This opened new avenues for investigating the function of these cells which play a fundamental role in the maturation of spermatozoa in the testes.

None of this kept us from some weekend sailing and shopping for a new boat. All of our friends at the marina knew about our plans and each had an opinion what boat we should consider. The consensus of opinion favored the Cal 34, a sloop built at the Jack Jensen Marina in California and designed by the famous naval architect, Bill Lapworth. This boat and her big sister the Cal 40, were very comfortable and fast boats; in fact, the Cal 40 was winning in all the racing circuits.

One reason for considering the Cal 34 was the fact that there was one in our marina and her owner, Bob O'Rourke, was a very congenial man. One day when we were at the marina, he found us and offered to show us his boat. As we rowed the dinghy to his boat as it rode on a buoy, she looked very elegant, sitting firmly against a light breeze on the bay. Upon boarding, the first thing that struck me was the wide comfortable cockpit. Below decks one also had a feeling of spaciousness, so rare on sailboats which more often felt cramped and cluttered. There was a double berth in the bow, a salon amidships and two quarter berths in the aft. On a hard beat she "tucked under" and with only a moderate heel quickly developed considerable speed. The modern underbody design, a fin keel and a spade rudder, certainly made a marked difference. Although I was warned that this configuration, coupled with a flat bottom, could make the boat unstable, I felt quite safe on this boat. I was thrilled to have had a chance to examine the boat so closely, to ask Bob's opinions about her design, and to sail her.

The following weekend, on our way home, we stopped for dinner at a lobster restaurant on the Baltimore Pike. There we ran across Karen and Bill, old friends from our Navy days in Bethesda. They were very excited about their recent purchase of a Morgan 34 sloop. According to them, it was a "patrician" among sailboats, the most solidly and dependably built boat of its kind. Bill kept rhapsodizing about the builder-designer, Charlie Morgan and his Morgan Yacht Corporation in St. Petersburg, Florida. This boat, he insisted, was an ocean going vessel, easy to sail, and a beauty! He had piqued my interest and since the dealership was located in Riverside, New Jersey, not far from Philadelphia, I decided to pay them a visit.

Although the boat was often in the forefront of my thoughts, issues at work, particularly the politics, continued to trouble me. It wasn't really politics, but issues of medical ethics, morality, delivery of medical care, and biomedical research that were bothering me. I had some interest in the history, forms of practice and social aspects of medical care, but these were secondary in importance. My primary goals had always been to combine a clinical practice with research in biomedical sciences and to obtain the financial support needed for these activities. I had many concerns with respect to the philosophies and politics of Mr. Sigmond. There were; however, other issues that gnawed at my subconscious and so I decided I needed to understand more about the philosophies and policies underlying the management, and delivery of medical care.

CHAPTER 10
FORCED OUT BY BUREAUCRACY

I was mulling over the history of modern medicine, hoping to come up with an understanding of two new phenomena---negative sentiments regarding basic research and the bureaucratization of medicine. I recalled a lecture given to me during a recent lunch with Harold Persky, the amateur philosopher and historian in our group.

Prior to the 1920s, when medical technology had very little to offer a patient, most medicine and surgery was practiced at home rather than in a hospital, so people enjoyed low cost medical care. With the discovery of antisepsis, immunizations and drugs that cured diseases without seriously damaging the patient, (like Salvarsan for the treatment of syphilis), as well as the development of diagnostic procedures such as X-rays, the effectiveness of medical care soared and the rate of hospitalizations increased substantially. By the 1920s this resulted in significant increases in the costs of medical care and gave rise to medical insurance. This is when the bureaucratization of medicine began.

At this point in history, some of the European countries adapted Otto Von Bismarck's far-sighted medical care policies and began nationalizing some basic medical care. An attempt to pass similar legislation in several states in the US, as proposed by the American Association for Labor Legislation, fell flat on its face. There was no grass-roots demand for health care legislation, and the professions dealing with delivery of medical care felt threatened by the legislation and feared a loss of income. However, the wheels of progress kept on turning.

An interesting study conducted by the state of Illinois in 1919 revealed an unexpected disparity between the lost wages due to illness and the associated cost of medical care. The loss of wages was four times larger than the medical expenditures associated with treating these illnesses. This contributed to the formation of the first non-profit health care insurance company, Blue Cross. For profit health insurance companies began to flourish later, during WWII. I personally feel these were good developments and that ultimately some form of national health insurance program will be developed.

I was not as optimistic about health care issues but at that moment they were not my primary concern. I didn't think health care delivery would become an issue in the near future. I was much more concerned with the medical rather than organizational aspects of medical care. In the preceding several years I had become convinced that we were facing a major problem with delivering appropriate care for non-surgical disorders of both the male and female reproductive systems. There was no specialty dealing with this aspect of medical care. Female reproductive system disorders were addressed by Gynecologists and Urologists (surgical specialists) treated males. With the tremendous explosion of basic and clinical knowledge, the need for specialists to appropriately manage patients with non-surgical conditions had become obvious.

I recalled my earlier conversation with Dr. Wapner when he had pointed out the other areas of medicine where complementary specialties already existed. For example, surgical disorders of the nervous system were managed by a neurosurgeon and non surgical ones by a neurologist. Urologist handle surgery of the urinary system and nephrologists are the non surgical specialists; thoracic surgeons and pulmonologists handle the surgical and non-surgical diseases of the lungs as orthopedic surgeons and rheumatologist handle diseases of the bones and joints and so on. The more I thought about this issue, the more convinced I became that surgical disorders of the reproductive system should be managed by gynecologists and urologists, while the non surgical disorders should be managed by reproductive medicine specialists.

I recalled also numerous discussions I had had with Dr. Samuel

S.C. Yen whom I had met at study section meetings and served with on committees at NIH. Sam was an Ob-Gyn trained in China and later in the United States. He was then Chairman of the Ob-Gyn Department at Case Western University Medical School. Although he was a Gynecologist by training and in practice, he clearly understood the need to unite basic sciences with the clinical practice of Ob-Gyn. However, he felt that urologists should deal with reproductive system disorders in the male. He couldn't see precisely how to manage both partners of an "infertile couple" but had sufficient influence at Case Western University to rename the Ob-Gyn Department the Department of Reproductive Biology.

My question to Sam always was, "How does the Department of Reproductive Biology train medical students in surgery of the reproductive system and supervise surgical specialists?" This discussion always ended in an impasse. Sam was a superb researcher and was interested in bringing basic sciences into a classical, surgically oriented Ob-Gyn department. My discussions with other Ob-Gyn specialists throughout this country and in Europe strengthened my conviction that the time had arrived. We had accumulated sufficient knowledge about non-surgical disorders of both male and female reproductive systems to warrant the creation of a Department of Reproductive Medicine. It would focus on the diagnosis and treatment of these disorders, training students, and conducting research in these areas. Because so many reproductive disorders are endocrine in nature, it seemed natural that individuals trained in endocrinology would be interested in reproductive medicine.

Although I was very preoccupied with research, clinical work and administrative duties, the hot month of August was approaching, and we were very still shopping for a new boat. We visited the Evanston Boat Yard to see a Morgan 34 and it was indeed a beautiful boat. Designed by a well known naval architect, Paul Coble, it was a stream-lined sloop with a keel centerboard that was only 3 ft. with the board up and 7 ft. with it down. This gave it maneuverability in the shallows of the Chesapeake Bay coupled with stability and the ability to point up wind with the board down. It also sported a very good inboard engine, the Atomic 4, that could provide reasonable speed and power. With its 8 ft. beam, the interior of the boat was also very roomy. The port side of the main cabin was occupied by a spacious U-shaped booth designed so the table could be lowered to form a very comfortable double berth. On the starboard side there was a two-burner stove, a sink, and a roomy icebox. Aft of the cabin there were single berths on either side of the compartment that housed the engine. In my opinion this was a very solid, dependable coastal cruiser, though possibly not as fast as the Cal 34.

We decided to purchase it and since we bought our previous boat, the Corsair, from the Evanston Boat Company they knew us and gave us an additional discount. Before taking our new 'ship' to the Chesapeake Bay, we had to arrange for a slip in a marina and after investigating several in the area, decided on the Bohemia River Marina near the entrance to the Chesapeake-Delaware Canal.

We took possession of the boat on a Friday and had a brief christening ceremony to name her EPIA III, which was proudly emblazoned on the transom. We loaded her up with food and other necessities, and on Saturday morning took off with the girls for the Bohemia River Marina. It was a glorious day with temperatures hovering in the upper eighties and a mild to moderate westerly breeze. We sailed south on the Delaware with the river current pushing us along at a good clip. By noon we had sailed past Wilmington, Delaware, and at 4:00 PM turned west into the Chesapeake-Delaware Canal and lowered the sails. We couldn't wait to see how our inboard engine would handle the infamous current. The memories of traversing the canal the previous year were still fresh and not very pleasant. This time however, the experience was quite different. I didn't even have to increase the engine speed. The new engine pushed the boat against the current with ease and I let out a huge sigh of relief. After all, one major reason for acquiring the new boat was to have an inboard engine with sufficient power to prevent the previous calamity.

By 7:00 PM we passed under the Chesapeake City Bridge headed to Chesapeake City, a tiny hamlet with a very nice yacht basin where we stayed for the night. There was a wonderful restaurant in the marina that must have been a gathering place for the locals since it was always full. We were so tired we went to bed right after we'd consumed delicious supper. It was our first night aboard our new boat and I couldn't fall asleep. Quietly I stole up the gangway and sat on deck listening to the music floating over the smooth waters of the canal. The air was still and the temperature had fallen to about seventy degrees. I could hear a frog croaking in a distance and few mosquitoes buzzed in the vicinity. Looking at our new boat made me so happy. I was amazed by my good fortune; I had a loving wife and two wonderful daughters sleeping safely below the decks on this beautiful vessel and it was all ours.

By noon on Sunday we pulled into the Bohemia River Marina and tied up at the main dock. I went up the hill to the marina office to announce our arrival before docking in our designated slip. All was in order, and we slowly motored to the north side of the marina and eased our way into a rather narrow slip. I had dreaded this maneuver the entire morning. Bringing a larger boat (and for me this was indeed a much larger boat) into a narrow slip is always challenging; I felt as though I was trying to thread a needle. However lady luck was with me and I didn't even scratch her. Driving home that afternoon I felt a little guilty for devoting so much time to personal activities. The boat had devoured most of my time on weekends this summer, but I was confident that by working more at night I could catch up.

I was to attend the quarterly meeting of the Advisory Panel for the Center for Population Studies in Bethesda. This Panel was composed of twelve experts in reproductive biology, each with slightly different areas of expertise in order to cover the field broadly. We received all of the applications weeks before the meeting, and each member was the "primary reviewer" for several of them, which entailed preparing a more thorough review to present to the other members. In some instances, the Panel recommended a site visit at the applicant's institution where its leadership (the Dean, relevant Departmental Chairmen and administrative members of the institution) might need to participate. The meetings and the site visits were not only important but also interesting and fun for me. I was usually the youngest member and the opportunity to learn from such renowned senior scientists was wonderful. Studying the applications and listening to the critical assessments of them by fellow panel members was invaluable to me, plus I developed many close friendships.

While flying home from Washington I thought about my life over the past ten years. I had been immensely lucky; I had had a string of successes and good turns. Was it all pure chance? I was fortunate to have a wife who wore so many hats; she was a professional colleague and collaborator, an outstanding housekeeper, prudent financial manager, social director, and awesome lover. Our daughters were delightful shining stars, fun and cheerful, always a part of family activities, seldom giving us any serious cause for concern. My interactions with the faculty in the Division were simple and enjoyable; we worked together for science and never had any altercations. Our common goal was to contribute to science to the best of our abilities and our primary reward for was satisfaction with our achievements and recognition by the scientific community. Personally, I had never expected major financial gains, I was satisfied with a modest but reasonable salary and most of the faculty felt similarly. Was it my influence and example, or had I been just incredibly lucky to form a group of scientists that felt this way about financial remuneration. Whatever it was, my family and my research associates had a common denominator in all of our activities--- work hard and enjoy your work. Correctly or not, I concluded that the love of hard work was probably the driving force in our professional success and general satisfaction with life.

I chased away the reveries of my personal happiness and began to focus on next week's Conference on "The Gonads" organized by Professor McKerns, a biochemist at the University of Florida in Gainesville. I (with Ania as co-author) was to present a paper summarizing much of the research we had conducted during the past decade. The presentation was to be published as a chapter in a book edited by Dr. McKerns. Most of the illustrations for my presentation were ready, but the part dealing with Ania's work still needed some finishing touches.

The office was in turmoil when I returned the next day. While I'd been in Washington, Mr. Sigmond had held another of his "philosophical" meetings where he continued to outline his goals for the AEMC. His ideas had not struck a positive chord with the scientists at the Korman Laboratories; he had reiterated his belief that basic research would be gradually eliminated from the Medical Center and this time the research staff took him seriously.

The chairman of the Division of Microbiology, Dr. Albert Kaplan, was overheard muttering, "There's no point taking this anymore." When I heard this I promptly went to see him. We were good social friends and I knew he would be forthright with me. As I walked into his office he immediately asked when I'd returned from Washington.

"Last night," I responded.

"Well," he said with a derisive smile on his lips, "You should have been here. Sigmond put on another 'performance' and this time I've heard enough. The people at Vanderbilt have been after me for the past year to take over the chairmanship of their Department of Microbiology, and I'll look at their offer more seriously now." I listened to him carefully and commented that Vanderbilt is one of the best schools in the country. He rested his chin in the palm of his left hand and looked at me, "What about you?" I thought for a while and responded with a breezy smile, "We're open to offers, but as you know our case it is somewhat different. We're not a classical medical school department like Microbiology. It will take something special to get us moving."

Al rose briskly saying, "I still have to finish a little job in the laboratory. How about getting together at our house tonight; bring Ania and I'll ask Tamara to prepare one of her fabulous desserts." We frequently visited each other, and our houses were only ten minutes apart. "Sure," I answered, "How about 8:00?" He put his arm on my shoulder as we walked out to the hallway saying, "See you tonight." On the way back to my office I stopped at Ania's laboratory to tell her the plan for that night and she just nodded too busy to look up.

The girls were growing up and rapidly becoming attractive, well-mannered young ladies. Both had boyfriends and were doing well in school. Inette took school in stride, nothing seemed too difficult for her; good grades seemed to come easily. She also excelled in sports, becoming a good skier and an avid sailor. She rarely missed a sailing trip with us and I was beginning to depend on her as a member of the crew. Now that we were sailing a 34-foot boat with 700 square feet of sail to control, her help was greatly appreciated.

Pauline was completely different. She had a more creative mind and developed a serious interest in art, both painting and sculpture. Other subjects in school were of relatively little interest to her. When I questioned her academic advisor about it, the standard response was, "Dr. Steinberger, don't be too concerned, the only thing Pauline needs to know about writing is how to sign her name on the wonderful art she's creating. She is developing into an outstanding artist and this is what she should pursue."

I was shocked by this assessment, which minimized the importance of a general education at Cheltenham High School, one of the top secondary schools in the nation. There was, however, little I could do. Pauline appeared happy with the school and the school was happy with Pauline! The teachers assured me that she was doing adequately in her academic subjects and would be ready to graduate next spring. Indeed, Pauline painted beautifully and was beginning to cast a bronze sculpture that I was very anxious to see.

Ania assured me that Pauline's involvement with her boyfriend was not very serious and would probably pass with no serious consequences. Although the two girls were quite dissimilar in temperament and interest, they got along remarkably well. Our family life, despite heavy professional responsibilities, was remarkably rich and affectionate. Much of the credit for this goes to Ania. She had an easy, warm and loving interaction with the girls, but she also paid attention to fundamental values, imposing fair but firm discipline on them. They often had breakfast together before they departed for school or work and we enjoyed dinner as a family most of the time.

The girls often participated in gatherings with our friends, and sometimes travelled with us to meetings. I felt that this was essential for providing the family with a sense of security and unity. Moreover, exposure to different parts of this country and to other countries, coupled with meeting people with diverse backgrounds, was good for their general education and character development. They also very much enjoyed these experiences. Since we were so busy most of the time, these opportunities for sharing exciting experiences were particularly welcome.

My parents had moved from Florida to Philadelphia a few years earlier and lived only ten minutes away from us. This allowed us to see them frequently and the girls loved to visit and stay with them overnight. I soon learned the reason for this eagerness to visit their grandparents. My mother was spoiling them by giving them breakfast in bed, preparing their favorite foods and showering them with gifts. They would have had a tough time resisting all of that!

October of 1969 was a sad time for us. For quite a few years my father had had serious cardiac problems and had been seeing his physician frequently. One evening, while Ania and I were at a cinema with our friends, he was taken to the hospital suffering from a massive heart attack. His passing had a sobering effect and a strong emotional impact on us all, bringing our small family even closer. After my father passed away, we all tried to spend more time with my mother who now lived alone. However, she eventually moved to California where Stella and her seven children lived. There, she was constantly in the company of her west coast grand children and was happy as a clam.

Since EPIA III had been hauled out of the water at the end of September and was not due to be launched until the following May, weekends during the fall, winter, and spring were spent trying catch up with work. However, the tempo of laboratory and clinical activities never diminished. We were preparing several manuscripts dealing with a new compound that inhibited sperm production in the testes and continuing with research and clinical issues, writing papers, attending conferences and meetings, etc. Our preoccupation with work let us temporarily forget about Mr. Sigmond.

In January of 1970 we had planned to drive to Killington Basin in Vermont for a bit of skiing. It was only about three hundred and fifty miles by car and we anticipated arriving at the lodge by mid afternoon. This would give us plenty of time to settle down, get the lift tickets and acclimate to the area. Unfortunately, during our drive we encountered a violent snowstorm with temperatures dropping below zero. Luckily, soon after the onset of the storm we spotted a rest area with a Howard Johnson's restaurant where we anchored for a couple of hours until the snowstorm subsided. We continued our trip but getting to the lodge at Killington turned into a hair rising experience.

As we got off the Freeway in Albany, the snow began falling heavily. We worked our way to highway 7, which led directly north to Rutland, near the Killington ski area but one we got there we could barely proceed. The car was sliding all over the road despite our new snow tires. The snow was blinding me as it swirled in the headlights and beat against the windshield. It instantly froze on the windshield in spite of the fact that the defroster was operating at full speed. By some miracle, we reached the lodge and slid sideways into a parking spot. We not only survived the trip, but the skis were also still in the rack on top of the car.

The next day we woke up to the most beautiful winter morning. Looking out the windows we saw snow covered mountains crisply etched against a cloudless deep blue sky. The ground surrounding the lodge was sparkling and shimmering in multicolored glory as the sun shown through the minute prisms of fresh powder snow. We couldn't wait to get on the mountain.

As we eagerly rushed out of the lodge a wall of icy air hit us. The temperature was 30 degrees below zero and the air we exhaled formed clouds of little ice crystals. However, nothing could stop us from getting onto the chairlift for a trip to the summit of the mountain, some three thousand feet above. As Ania and I rode the lift together, the panorama of the mountains was crystal clear and magnificent in the still air. The forest beneath us, as we glided over it, was dark green with white swaths of snow-covered trails cutting boldly through it. Although the air was still and the sun was shining, we got gradually colder as we ascended higher onto the mountain. The vapors of our breath were freezing to our faces and Ania began to feel very uncomfortable. As we approached the summit we were greeted by a strong icy wind that took our breath away. We could hardly wait to get off the lift when suddenly it stopped moving. A mechanical malfunction had left us hanging a hundred feet in the air with the wind buffeting us and chilling us to the very marrow of our bones. We tightened our parkas and hoods trying to protect our faces.

We were close to the summit station and thankfully, after about ten minutes the lift began moving again. However, I was apprehensive about disembarking because we were so stiff from the cold. We had to get off the lift and ski instantly away from the chair, which continued moving. Somehow I managed to get off and remain on my feet although the cold had made my body almost totally unresponsive to the dictates of my brain. As Ania jumped off the chair, however, she fell and the chair flew over her just barely clearing her head. After I helped her up we were standing alone at the windswept summit station looking down the steep drop of a "black diamond trail" to a little plateau below. Ania looked at me and shook her head.

"I can't do it, I'm frozen; I can't even move my legs!" I stood there trying to gather my conviction and powers of reasoning. "Please, let me take my skis off and walk down to the plateau below. From there I may be able to ski down."

I knew this would be extremely dangerous; she could easily fall into the very deep powder snow and be unable to move on. The best chance was to ski down.

I suggested that we traverse the steep slope and sideslip where necessary until we got to the bottom. Being, as always, a good sport, she forced herself to move and followed me. It took us almost fifteen minutes to get down and when we finally reached the plateau, we were overheated from the exertion.

Once we'd passed that first drop, the rest of the run down the mountain was sheer pleasure. We were the first to ski on the new powder under the bluest of blue skies, a rare pleasure as there were usually many more skiers. It was perfectly still on the slopes, not a whisper of wind and not another skier in sight. I could only hear the swish of the skis cutting through the virgin surface of the powder snow. All too soon it was time to leave the mountains and drive back to Philadelphia, just as we began to truly enjoy ourselves.

Back at the office, I faced the usual onslaught of activities. The official journal of the Society for the Study of Reproduction, "Reproductive Biology" had appointed me Associate Editor. I had anticipated this appointment for several months, so it wasn't a surprise, but the amount of additional work in entailed, was. Similarly, the Journal of Endocrinology and Metabolism, (the official journal of The American Endocrine Society), notified me that I had been appointed to its editorial board. These responsibilities would add considerably to the reading and writing I would have to do at night. At the same time, my clinical responsibilities kept me on my toes and my responsibilities for clinical teaching were growing. The assistance of Keith Smith, the latest addition to our clinical practice, was invaluable and I was extremely grateful to have him. The rapid growth of our infertility practice and the evolution of new diagnostic and therapeutic modalities in our field had been remarkable.

The introduction of Clomiphene, an anti-estrogen for induction of ovulation, particularly in women with abnormally high levels of male sex hormones, revolutionized the treatment of infertility. The use of gonadotrophins (pituitary gland hormones) to induce ovulation was another major step in treating infertility, and set the stage for the development of in vitro fertilization (IVF) techniques. We were pioneers in these areas of research and they continued to be a major part of our research efforts. This kept me close to clinical medicine and the problems related to it. Our laboratory research supporting the clinical investigations was also progressing well. I was particularly pleased to see the close, friendly, and fruitful interaction we had developed with the Ob-Gyn physicians. Their superb support in diagnosing surgical problems was particularly important to us. They became very proficient at culdoscopy and subsequently with laparascopy. Using a newly developed instrument called a laparoscope, they could view the patient's internal organs and perform surgery without the need for a large abdominal incision. The technique was new but from what I'd seen so far, it looked very promising.

Early in the year I received two important invitations. One was for the Laurentian Hormone Research Conference, an important annual international meeting of endocrinologists, attended strictly by invitation. I was asked to present a paper dealing with our work on the gonads. The other invitation was to present a paper at the meeting of the German Society of Biochemists "Colloquium der Geselschaft fur Biologische Chemie." On top of the papers to be presented at the usual annual meetings and conferences, this was a tall order. Fortunately, I had great collaborators, all of whom participated fully in the preparation and presentation of the papers, as well as in the writing of the manuscripts. All of these activities competed constantly for our time and attention.

Spring brought another milestone; Pauline was graduating from high school. It was a particularly joyous occasion for us since she had also learned of her acceptance to the prestigious Pennsylvania Academy of Fine Arts in Philadelphia. The academy was founded in 1805 as the first art school and museum in the country. It granted a Bachelor of Fine Arts and a Master of Arts degree in conjunction with the University of Pennsylvania. Our biggest surprise was when Pauline asked to rent an apartment in downtown rather than making the lengthy commute from our house in the suburbs. Neither Ania nor I were overjoyed by this request but we conceded. She was eighteen years old and should be sufficiently mature to handle living on her own.

The research staff at Korman Research Laboratories was unusually subdued. Although we talked occasionally about the prospects of leaving, no one was very anxious or overly concerned. The economy was good and the opportunities for positions at other institutions were excellent. A belief that research could conquer all was prevalent throughout the scholarly and industrial worlds. Jobs were plentiful. Mr. Sigmond's political grandstanding hadn't greatly influenced the actions of most faculty members. However, he was gradually implementing his health care management ideas. He organized several twenty four-hour community walk-in clinics, and staffed them with recently licensed foreign physicians. He accomplished this with funds from federal grants established for this type of activity. I wondered how the physicians would feel about this government subsidized free care.

The medical profession, including the staff at our medical center, had always provided a great deal of free care to welfare patients both in outpatient clinics and on hospital wards. I wondered if these new clinics, which handled a large number of Medicaid patients and the growing Medicare population, would cause private physicians to curtail the time they donated to free care. This could also bring an end to the physician input that was the backbone of the welfare health care system. If so, I was convinced it would cost the nation billions of dollars. With the increasing availability of health insurance provided by employers, Medicare paying medical bills for retired individuals, and Medicaid providing medical insurance to the indigent, the free care currently provided by the medical profession might no longer be essential or available.

As I ruminated on this issue, I recalled a troubling experience we had had in our own clinical practice. Mrs. X had been our patient for many years. She was the wife of a retired surgeon who had passed away a few years earlier and since it was our policy to provide free care to physicians and members of their immediate family, she had never been billed. However, after the Medicare Act went into effect, we discussed this issue and determined that it would be appropriate to bill Medicare for the care we provided to this type of patient.

The free care provided to physicians' families was an extension of the centuries-old tradition that physicians don't charge colleagues for medical care. However, if we did not charge Medicare, we would in effect be extending this courtesy to the government, not to a colleague. Previously, Mrs. X, had never received a bill. Under Medicare billing regulations, however, we had to send a copy of the Medicare bill to her with a note saying that Medicare had been billed, and she didn't owe us anything. When she received her copy of the bill, Mrs. X became very annoyed and accused us of defrauding the government, since we had never billed her before! This troubling episode created another 'crack' in my view of the way our health care system was evolving.

Biomedical research continued its explosive growth not only at universities but also at pharmaceutical companies where research had also traditionally been conducted. One of the most successful research programs was conducted at Merck and Co. They had initiated a very active research program in the 1930's, and were now employing an army of basic and clinical investigators. Although most of the fundamental research leading to discoveries of new pharmaceutically active compounds was still done at universities, the pharmaceutical industry led in the development of clinical applications. They also performed the clinical testing required to satisfy the FDA (Food and Drug Administration) requirements for safety and effectiveness. Many new medications were developed in pharmaceutical laboratories and they were in great demand. This in turn provided an incentive for universities to produce more basic scientists.

That year, the science in our division was also flourishing. Jack Christian and his young associate Jim Lloyd, with the assistance of a small army of postdoctoral research fellows, made a number of important observations in population endocrinology and ethology. Their work was based on Jack's original observations of population pressures in woodchucks. He showed that crowding the animals seriously interfered with their ability to reproduce because it caused pathological changes in the ovaries and adrenal glands of the females. Since it was extremely difficult to examine these changes under field conditions, Jack designed laboratory experiments with mice as the experimental subjects. Using huge cages, he started a population with one pair of mice and examined the changes that occurred as the population grew during experimental periods lasting over a year.

The results were mind blowing. As predicted by Jack, when the population grew the interaction among its members increased and produced dramatic changes in fertility patterns. Over time, the population growth rate decreased, then leveled off, and eventually crashed. From an ethological viewpoint this was an important observation and one that brought Jack and Jim a great deal of satisfaction and recognition among their colleagues. I was even more intrigued by the results of endocrine studies and the pathophysiology of this phenomenon. One major surprise, which neither Jack nor Jim fully appreciated, was that in the population-stressed animals the ovaries were polycystic and the adrenal glands were enlarged in the regions that produce testosterone. Keith and I were tremendously excited by this observation. It was essentially the same pattern we had been observing in our human infertility patients: lack of ovulation, enlarged polycystic ovaries, and excessive hair growth (indicative of excess testosterone)! Could this common disorder in women be the result of increased testosterone production caused by stress?

It was mid-summer 1970 and we tried very hard to carve out time to sail our beautiful new boat. However, it was increasingly difficult to take more than a weekend. Since the boat was an ocean-going sloop, I felt that a longer trip was in order. Finally in early September, just a few weeks before we were to haul the boat out of the water for winter, I was able to take off for a couple of weeks. We headed for Annapolis on a Sunday morning and arrived late that afternoon to stay overnight. On the following morning we sailed to Oxford, a beautiful little town on Maryland's Eastern Shore. The passage was uneventful although there was a stiff breeze and the waters were quite rough. We had learned by then that this was not unusual. The Chesapeake waters tended to build up into a nasty little chop even with relatively mild winds. Our new boat, however, handled this with authority and ease; I never even had to shorten the sails.

The approach to Oxford was simple; from the bay we turned into the Tred Avon River, where, near its mouth, we came to a tiny settlement of about a thousand people. During colonial days, Oxford had been a major seaport and the river served as a major shipping lane for the international tobacco trade. After the Civil War it flourished again when oyster harvesting brought another economic boom. By this time, it was known for its beauty, charm and leisure activities like sailing and fishing.

In no time, we were tied up to a dock at one of the marinas where we were given permission to stay overnight. It was a wonderful experience. We got off the boat just as the golden disc of the sun touched the western horizon of the Bay. The waters were calm and there was a mild westerly breeze that kept us cool and comfortable. There was great serenity in the air, and the historical surroundings almost made us speak in whispers. Finally, I broke the spell, "Tonight we're going to splurge." I had been made privy to a local secret; an old-fashioned Inn that prepared the best seafood on the Eastern Shores. It would be expensive but well worth it. The dock master provided us with directions and fortunately it was only a few blocks from the marina.

The Robert Morris Inn looked like all other buildings on that street. It was a two-story clapboard structure with a huge porch running around the entire building. As we approached the entrance, there was a sign to the right of the doorjamb denoting it as "A Historical Inn." That night we had one of the best seafood dinners we had ever eaten. We started with crab cakes, followed by mouth watering sautéed soft shell crabs. Dinner was brought to a delicious conclusion with a fabulous pecan pie, my favorite dessert, and freshly brewed coffee. We couldn't stop talking about the charm of the restaurant and all the delicacies we had consumed.

We spent the following day sailing on the bay in glorious sunshine and mild winds. Ultimately we turned north towards St. Michaels, another historic gem on the Eastern Shore. The highlight for us there was the appropriately named Crab Claw Restaurant. The special that evening was royal sautéed crabmeat that we ordered along with a dozen steamed crabs we planned to eat for breakfast the following morning. It was an unusual dish for us to have first thing in the morning but indeed we were awakened at 7:00 the next morning by a voice on the dock saying, "Sir, your steamed crabs." I ran out to see a young man standing on the wharf with a large paper bag full of hot, freshly steamed crabs. We sailed toward home on a lazy broad reach while cracking crabs and drinking beer. We had never had such an unusual, relaxing and delicious breakfast in our lives!

Our two-week sail came to an end in a flash. Upon my return, I learned to my dismay that Mr. Sigmond had scheduled a meeting with the entire staff of the AEMC for Friday. We all dreaded it. Our work had been progressing successfully and unobtrusively and we carefully avoided discussing any of Mr. Sigmond's philosophies.

At 4:00 PM on Friday, the staff was assembled in the main lecture room when Mr. Sigmond walked over to the lectern, greeted us hastily and moved on breathlessly to the main topic of his talk:

> I thought that you might be interested in the progress made this year in implementing our plans for improving the Center's overall performance. As I have said before, the greatest hurdle facing hospitals today is formulating new concepts for a changing world. This can be achieved only through new approaches to planning. In the past we planned for buildings. Now the challenge is to plan for change. Fantastic change in health care lies before us. The hospital must tool up to understand, anticipate, adapt to these transitions and provide leadership in these changing times.

Fundamentally I agreed with the need for the hospital to respond to the "changing world." However, his speech began to sound like something from "The Peter Principle", a group of "code" words strung together suggesting a profound idea but upon closer scrutiny resolving into nothing but a series of unrelated expressions. As he continued he became even more philosophical and troubling:

"Some may believe that one element of a policy on medical staff appointments is obvious: appointment of the best-qualified physicians available. Unfortunately, the issue can't be resolved that simply. Even assuming that the task of ranking the quality of physicians can be carried out, the fact remains that every hospital cannot limit itself to the best if the needs of all people are to be met. All licensed physicians should have appointments at good hospitals, especially those physicians at the lower end of any scale of quality. Affiliation with a good hospital is the only effective protection the public has against incompetent physicians.

While I anticipated something hair-raising, this was well beyond it. Suddenly I recalled a recently published book called "Atlas Shrugged" by Ayn Rand, about a rabid proponent of pure, idealistic capitalism and an uncompromising free market economy. Words similar to the ones I had just heard from Mr. Sigmond were used in her book to illustrate, in a comic but also tragic light, the insanity of a society run by allegedly "socially conscious" bureaucrats.

Hacking my way through the jungle of Mr. Sigmond words I finally removed the shell of his protective word coating to get to the obscured kernel of truth and I was stunned. He was apparently proposing new concepts in the organizational principles of hospitals: an all-powerful bureaucratic stronghold wherein a non-professional governing staff would be led by a director such as himself. His exposition continued with an admonition to the research staff: "Research carried out at AEMC should be devoted to resolving the health care problems of the community. It should focus on the goals of the hospital and celebrate the staff as a whole rather than the achievement of individuals." At this point I wanted to get up and leave the auditorium, but no one moved a muscle. They all sat stunned. I realized another major crack had appeared in my view of the structure of the American medical care system.

Driving home with Ania that evening I was very quiet. She finally broke the silence saying, "Hey, crack a smile." I obliged and said, "I talked to Sam Ajl today. He said that Sigmond gives a lot of speeches, writes a great deal on the topic of hospital and medical economics, and is a member of various boards and task forces, but we shouldn't be concerned. We brought in the money for the construction of the Korman Laboratories and most of the staff is paid from funds derived from various outside grants. He doesn't really have much power to interfere with our work despite the fact that he is the Executive Vice President.

That afternoon I had called a meeting and the entire complement of our Division gathered in the fellows room. The group was uncharacteristically subdued; Harold was the only one engaged in animated conversation. He was sitting next to Jack, trying to convince him of something. I looked at him and shaking my head said, "It looks like nothing will ever dampen your optimism." "Sigmond is an aberration and he has no real power over us, I would ignore him" he replied. Jack, with a grim expression on his face added, "I agree. Furthermore I think that a visit with some of the Board members may be in order to get him off our backs. The Board is very supportive of basic research and they'll keep him under control." The meeting proceeded in a similar vein. Everyone was optimistic and ready to ignore Sigmond's comments.

After the meeting I trotted over to Sam Ajl's office where his secretary informed me that he was in and could see me. Sam flashed his usual radiant smile, leaned back in his chair, put his feet on the desk and puffed on the thick ever-present cigar in the corner of his mouth. He was a world-renowned scientist and a pioneer in the relatively new field of microbial biochemistry, particularly the discovery and characterization of bacterial toxins. While directing the Korman Research Laboratories he had also chaired the Division of Biochemistry, and was very active in laboratory research. As I walked in, he took the cigar out of his mouth and motioned for me to sit down. "Don't be perturbed by Bob (meaning Robert Sigmond), "that's just his way of talking. There is nothing he can do to our research laboratories. We have the Board solidly behind us." I had suspected as much, but I said, "this is not my idea of a scientific position. I don't think the Medical School would look kindly on a leader who discards basic research as a "socially unconscionable activity." While I talked, I realized that Sam, not being a clinician himself, might not appreciate how wrong it would be to follow Sigmond's suggestion that the Center appoint not just the "best" physicians but "any" physician, even those who aren't adequately trained. I also realized that Sam was not about to open up at this time. He was procrastinating, trying to gloss over the issue. I think he was in a state of denial concerning Mr. Sigmond's ability to implement his philosophies at AEMC.

CHAPTER 11

WHERE SHALL WE GO?

Subsequent to my meeting with Sam, we examined a number of potential offers to move, though still half-heartedly. Ania came with me for some preliminary discussions at Columbia University Medical School in Manhattan. As we were driving back home she joked, "They couldn't drag me to Manhattan unless an obscene salary came with the position; enough for an apartment in Manhattan, a house in suburbia, and a chauffeur". I was more sanguine, "Don't knock it, Colombia University is a good possibility, but I agree that our life-style would be cramped. New York would be far from an ideal place to live, although sailing on Long Island Sound and south to New Jersey could be fun."

The position was fundamentally a professorship and head of a reproductive biology section in one of the school's departments. It was a prestigious position in a very prestigious medical school, but didn't stimulate much excitement in me. I envisioned a great deal of politics and infighting, both of which were foreign and repugnant to me. Ania agreed and, again being the more practical one of us, pointed out that so far none of the places we had visited on either coast had provoked much interest in me. Possibly it was my reluctance to move; I enjoyed working at the Medical Center and was hoping to outlast Mr. Sigmond.

Two chapters of mine had recently been published in the textbook, "Essentials of Clinical Endocrinology," edited by Dr. Schneeberg. Two more chapters appeared in the "Testes", Volume III, edited by Johnson,

Gomez and Van Demark, and a chapter with Ania entitled "Tissue Culture of Male Mammalian Gonads" was published in "In Vitro, Recent Advances in Tissue Culture" edited by Waymouth. I was also pleased to see a chapter of ours appearing in the publication "Recent Progress in Hormone Research," a volume devoted to the proceedings of a prestigious annual international conference of endocrinologists. There were several more chapters written by members of our laboratory published in other scientific volumes. The year had been extraordinarily prolific and we felt good about our accomplishments. I simply could not accept the idea that a bureaucrat could derail scientific activities of this magnitude for purely personal political purposes.

In early December we decided to take off the week between Christmas and the New Year for a skiing vacation with the girls at Arapahoe Basin in Colorado. We planned to arrive at the lodge on December 24, and were working to finalize our reservations. Just before noon on Wednesday of that week, my secretary buzzed me in the office saying that a doctor from Houston was calling. I answered and a voice at the other end of the line announced: "I am Raymond Kaufman, Chairman of the Ob-Gyn department at Baylor College of Medicine in Houston, Texas. We would like to invite you to visit our Department and give a talk on your favorite topic." I couldn't recall ever meeting Dr. Kaufman so I replied cautiously, "Thank you for inviting me but I don't seem to recall meeting you or visiting your institution in the past." He started laughing and replied:

> You are correct, we haven't met. The Chairman of Ob-Gyn at the Medical School in San Antonio visited us last week and suggested that we invite you to give a talk and look at our facilities. He is quite impressed by your research and your integrated approach to teaching the endocrine aspects of the male and the female reproductive systems. I'm certain that our group here in Texas would be very interested in hearing what you have to say.

I was a bit taken aback by this invitation; I had never heard of Baylor College of Medicine or its Ob-Gyn group. However, I had visited Dr. Goldzieher at the Southwest Foundation for Biomedical Research in San Antonio and lectured at the Medical School there. I was intrigued and responded with interest, "Certainly, I'd be pleased to come if we can arrange the visit at a mutually convenient time. I'll need to check my calendar and will to call you within a couple of days." After exchanging a few more pleasantries we hung up.

Shortly after the call, I went to the fellows room where some of the staff were engaged in a lively conversation while wolfing down their lunches. I walked over to a map hanging on the wall opposite the windows where we had marked several cities with little blue pins. Each indicated a possible future relocation. I found Houston, stuck a blue pin into it and turned to my colleagues who were looking at me with questioning eyes. "Well," I drawled, "there was a call from the Chairman of Ob-Gyn at the Baylor College of Medicine in Houston, Texas asking me to visit the place, give a talk and look them over."

Pandemonium broke out. Everyone was talking at the same time and some were laughing loudly. Harold was the loudest, "Did you say Texas? Did you say Houston? Did you say Baylor? Are you sure you not talking about Dallas?" Even Jack who was normally so sedate in his manner, said "Texas? You must be kidding!" Dr. Zimmerman just shook his head; the Chowdhury's listen attentively, while Dr. Sud watched and listened thoughtfully. Dr. Smith didn't say a word, and Dr. Ficher looked perplexed. Ania walked in at this point and looked around puzzled. "What's happening?"

"Why this reaction?" I asked. "It's just an inquiry." Harold looked at me with a big grin on his shining face and asked, "You are not taking this seriously, are you? Texas?" I wasn't certain how to respond to this comment; I felt I was an American through and through. Having spent almost ten years in the Midwest made me feel particularly so, and I had difficulty understanding my colleagues reaction to Texas. True, I knew very little about Texas. The only information I had was gleaned during my one and only lecture in San Antonio. In addition, one of our technicians, Deanna Emerson, was a native Texan and had been admitted to the Medical School in Galveston, sixty miles south of Houston. She talked to me a great deal about Texas. For me it was just another state, but my colleagues' somewhat peculiar reaction stimulated an almost perverse desire to learn more about it.

"I think I'll take Dr. Kaufman up on his invitation, particularly if we can arrange the schedule satisfactorily. We were planning a family ski trip to Colorado on December 24 and I think I could go via Houston. I could fly to Houston first, spend a day there and meet Ania and the girls in Denver." Jack said, "That's a great plan, go for it." Therefore, I called Dr. Kaufman and accepted his invitation.

I didn't know what to expect upon my arrival in Texas. All of my mental images had been conjured up in the distant past when I was a nine or ten-year-old boy living in central Europe before WWII. I had been enthralled by soft cover weeklies that extolled America's "wild west." They detailed the heroic acts and exalted life style of the cowboys, as well as the vicious and cowardly acts of the Indians. I couldn't entirely dispel this image of the wild west from my mind. Somehow, I still expected to see horses tied up in front of the airport waiting for their owners. Consequently, I was somewhat disappointed when I found myself in a beautifully designed, sparkling clean and modern gate area that led to a huge circular structure were all the usual airport facilities and amenities were located. A taxi drove an extensive system of expressways on its way to the Shamrock Hotel, an elegant multistory building in an area that looked almost like a park. Everything was lush and green, and the temperature was in the upper 60s. I had left Philadelphia under grey skies and temperatures in the 30s. What a difference!

Upon registering in the hotel, I was given an envelope with a greeting note from Dr. Kaufman informing me that he would pick me up in the lobby at 8:00 AM. I was waiting anxiously in the lobby five minutes ahead of schedule and at exactly 8:00 I spotted a man, supported by a cane, walking through the entrance. He stopped to look around the lobby and walked, with an obvious limp, directly towards me. He was tall, slim, with blondish hair and a quizzical and friendly smile on his face. As he came closer he asked, "Dr. Steinberger?" Getting up and extending my hand to him I asked, "How did you know?" He responded laughing, "Well, I was given a very precise description."

As we walked towards the exit he said, "The Ob-Gyn Department is located at St. Luke's Episcopal Hospital in the Texas Medical Center. Although it's only a one block or two from here, we'll drive." As we got into the car he asked, "Are you familiar with the Texas Medical Center?" I shook my head no. He continued:

Well, the Center is an interesting phenomenon. In 1930,

exactly 40 years ago, Mr. Monroe Dunaway Anderson, a wealthy local businessman and philanthropist, proposed that an important Medical Center be established with his support near the existing Hermann Hospital. In 1936, he established the MD Anderson Foundation and in 1941, the Texas State Legislature allocated funds to build a cancer hospital in Houston. The MD Anderson Foundation offered matching funds and free land if the State would locate the hospital in Houston, next to Hermann Hospital in the Texas Medical Center (another project funded by the Foundation) and name it after Mr. Anderson. This offer was accepted and the University of Texas MD Anderson Cancer Center was established one year later. Subsequently, in 1943, the Foundation offered Baylor University College, located in Dallas at that time, free land, large construction grants, as well as a grant to cover ten years of operational expenses if the College would move to the Medical Center. That is how Baylor College of Medicine (the name having been changed in 1969 when it became independent of Baylor University) ended up in Houston.

While I had been listening to this interesting history we had arrived at the hospital building. It was an attractive, modern building at least ten stories high with an impressive, tastefully furnished lobby. I was to give my talk first and meet various faculty and hospital officials later that day. The material I had chosen to present in my lecture had to do with defining new concepts in the management of infertility. I was looking forward to a good discussion since I knew that there were a number of gynecologists in Houston who were very interested in infertility.

After laying out the general background and introducing some classic definitions and purposes, I plunged into a new area, one that would later become highly controversial and emotional. I introduced the concept of "couple's infertility," the simultaneous management of both male and female partners of an infertile couple. Why was this "new" and, why did it quickly become a controversial concept? In most cases, only the women would see a doctor, a gynecologist, who generally did not evaluate the male partner. The husband's possible role in contributing to the couple's infertility was generally ignored. Only recently had gynecologists begun to refer the male patients to urologists for evaluation. However, most urologists were either not interested or insufficiently knowledgeable in this area. The evaluation may have consisted of a "sperm count" but it was often performed in a laboratory that didn't even have a technician properly trained in this type of testing, especially since they were so rarely requested. Furthermore, no one with adequate training would have been available to interpret the test results accurately. My thesis was that "infertility" would best be managed by specialists specifically trained to handle both partners, rather than by two specialists from totally different areas of medicine managing each partner separately.

As anticipated, the discussion following my talk was very lively. I enjoyed every moment of it and found it very instructive. This was not only the first time I had articulated this new concept but the data was being presented for the first time to a group of strangers. The gynecologists at our own institution were quite familiar with our concepts and philosophies for clinical management of infertility. The audience in Houston was clearly stimulated, and the discussion soon moved from lively to heated.

Following my lecture, I was taken to an operating room to observe a laparoscopic procedure. This new and exciting technique had initially been used primarily for diagnostic procedures but was now being successfully employed for surgical therapies. The surgeon operating the laparoscope was unquestionably very skillful, and I enjoyed observing his elegant work.

During lunch, we talked about my concept of "reproductive medicine," one that I had trotted out over the past several years at various medical meetings. They were interested in my ideas about how reproductive medicine would impact Ob-Gyn. This was one of my favorite topics and I was glad to elaborate on it, particularly since they seemed so interested. As a result, we didn't finish the lunch, or to be more precise our lively discussion, until 2:30.

Afterwards, Raymond took me to meet the Dean of the Medical School, the famous Dr. Michael DeBakey, a renowned cardiac surgeon with an unusual gift for surgery and a burning interest in research and teaching. He was also an outstanding innovator and inventor who had placed cardiac surgery at the forefront of medicine. As we arrived he seemed to be on his way out, but stopped and shook my hand saying; "You must be Dr. Steinberger." Dr. DeBakey was a rather slight man with a narrow aquiline nose, and deep set burning black eyes. He led us to a couple of easy chairs by a coffee table and gestured for us to sit down. Raymond introduced me in glowing terms and briefly summarized my talk. Dr. DeBakey looked at me with those penetrating eyes, smiling and saying, "Ah, an innovator." I burst out laughing and couldn't resist saying, "You mean a trouble maker?"

As the conversation turned to more serious topics, a secretary interrupted to say, "There is a phone call for you Dr. Steinberger. Would you like to take it here?" Dr. DeBakey suggested I use his office, where I wouldn't be disturbed. "Where is the call from?" I inquired with concern for my family. She responded, "It is a local call." "I don't know anyone in Houston, there's no reason I can't take it right here," I said to Dr. DeBakey as I picked up the receiver. "Hello" I heard in a voice that seemed to me to have a heavy Boston accent with a tinge of Southern drawl. "This is Cheves Smythe, I am the Dean of the new University of Texas Medical School at Houston, and I would like to have dinner with you tonight."

I was totally taken aback since I didn't know a Dr. Smythe, and didn't know that a University of Texas Medical School existed in Houston. I was a guest of the Baylor College of Medicine and was in the office of its Dean! I stood there shocked, with the telephone to my ear and an expression on my face that must have evoked concern on the part of my hosts. I simply did not know how to respond. Ultimately, some common sense prevailed, and I attempted to respond with a degree of civility and in a calm tone of voice. "Thank you but tonight I have a dinner commitment with the faculty members of Baylor College…" The voice at the other end interrupted me saying, "Fine, I'll pick you up tomorrow morning at the Shamrock Hotel for breakfast." I simply hung up, wondering what he had in mind. The remainder of the afternoon was spent visiting outpatient facilities and I was impressed by the clinical offices and the interesting mix of patients.

We had dinner at a fabulous restaurant with true southern elegance and hospitality called "Ye Olde College Inn." It was located only just a few blocks south of the Medical Center on Fannin Street. The largest oysters on the half shell I had ever seen were served by tall, handsome waiters in immaculate black tuxedos. I literally had to cut the oysters in half because they were too large to swallow. This was followed by a fabulous crabmeat salad and then the most fragrant sautéed scallops. Dinner was topped off by a southern desert, the likes of which I had never seen before and one that instantly became my favorite. It was pecan pie baked with bourbon and accompanied by a glass of Southern Comfort; I was in an epicurean paradise.

The day had been filled with solid impressions, and the evening continued with more exciting discussions and fantastic food and drink. When I was finally deposited at the Shamrock Hotel, I collapsed into bed. The ringing of the phone by my bedside finally brought me to consciousness and I slowly realized where I was. Daylight was streaming through the windows and the telephone persistently intruded with its shrill ringing. Finally I reached for it, and a voice at the other end of the line announced, "This is Cheves Smythe; I'm waiting for you in the dining room by the pool." I was still half asleep and totally confused. However, slowly as if from behind a cloud of smoke, I reminded myself of his phone call the day before and, still not entirely awake responded, "I'll be there in few minutes."

I was fully awake by the time I entered the dining room. It was huge, but only a few tables were occupied. A wall of glass separated the dining room from a beautifully landscaped olympic size pool. A man sat at a table near the window facing the entrance, as if looking for someone. When I walked toward him, he got up asking, "Are you Dr. Steinberger?" He was a tall slim, almost gaunt, man with steady grey eyes. He extended his hand and there was an uncertain smile on his face. I nodded my head affirmatively "You are Dr. Smythe?" Instead of answering, he walked back to the table and pulled out a chair for me. I offered my hand to him saying, "This is an unexpected pleasure and a surprise, I wasn't aware that University of Texas had a medical school in Houston. I am only familiar with the schools in Dallas, San Antonio and Galveston." With a half smile he responded, "Oh, yes, we have a school. It's still partly on paper, but the first class of students was admitted last fall. They're farmed out to the three UT medical schools you mentioned but we'll get them back for their clinical years." As he talked, his face became animated and suffused with warmth and a sense of purpose. He was obviously on a mission, and I could sense that he wanted to talk more. As he sat back in his chair making himself more comfortable I couldn't resist asking him, "Please forgive me, but I must ask you first how you learned about me and how did you know that I was visiting Baylor?" He looked at me mockingly and responded:

"Oh that was easy. Dr. Darrell Ward, the head of the department of biochemistry at MD Anderson told me about you, your research and your innovative concepts of teaching medicine. I was intrigued, and when he told me that you would be visiting Baylor, I decided to contact you. I'm glad you asked that question as leads right into what I want to talk to you about."

As we continued our conversation, a waiter hovered over us trying to take our orders. "I'll have some toast and coffee," said Dr. Smythe but I was starving. I went for a full breakfast, as was my habit when traveling, and ordered two fried eggs sunny side up with ham, hash brown potatoes, toast and coffee. While ordering I looked out the window where the sun was reflecting on the blue waters of the pool and against the white and green surroundings. There were several lovely young girls swimming and frolicking in it and it suddenly dawned on me that it was late December and back home the landscape was buried under snow and ice.

Returning to Dr Smythe I asked him to continue. "Coming back to teaching medicine," he stepped right back into his train of thought, "I found your concept of an 'integrated approach' quite compatible with my own ideas. I'm trying to introduce 'systems teaching' in the new medical school, and to organize departments that would integrate basic and clinical teaching." This was music to my ears, and I instantly began marketing my ideas of teaching reproductive medicine and biology as an integrated basic and clinical course.

Cheves wanted me to know a little about the history of the UT Medical School, Houston (UTMSH). It had been established by the Texas state legislature in June 1969 in part because the City of Houston and the State of Texas needed more physicians. One way to accomplish this was to build another new medical school in addition to the existing three. One year before the school was established, on January 1, 1968, an agreement between the Hermann Hospital and UTMSH had been signed agreeing that the medical school could do its clinical teaching at the hospital.

There were many factors for me to consider, and several were particularly compelling. I was somewhat familiar with the Medical-Academic picture in Texas since I had served as secretary of the Liaison Committee on Medical Education, a joint venture of the American Medical Association and the Association of American Medical Colleges. In that connection, I had participated in several site visits to educational institutions in Texas. The thinking in Houston at that time was both forward and large scale. Its spirit was very appealing, as were the substantial resources offered by the State. "All this makes the new school very appealing; something to think about", I said. Cheves shifted his weight, smiled slightly, and continued:

> There are many aspects to this venture, both positive and negative, but I'd like to gloss over them for the moment. I gathered a considerable amount of information about you. First I learned that you and your department might be interested in relocating, primarily because of philosophical differences between you and the new executive director. I also know that these differences of opinion between your group and the new director are with respect to the role of basic sciences in clinical medicine. I was intrigued by your proposal of an 'integrated, basic/clinical approach to teaching' and impressed by your research contributions and the ease with which you have secured financial support from national agencies.

Here I could not resist, and laughingly interrupted him, "Looks like Darrell Ward has been busy talking about me and my department." Cheves also started laughing, "Well…" he said, "I also did some homework." With this statement he got up and asked, "Would you like to come to my office?

We drove the now familiar short distance from the Shamrock to the Texas Medical Center while Cheves continued his commentary. "At this moment the school doesn't have its own building, there is only the Dean's suite in the Jones Library Building." As he talked, we turned into a park-like setting with many trees and a large complex of buildings one of which was the Hermann Hospital, and another small attractive building was the Jones Library. We parked under one of the trees and walked into the library where the school offices were located. On the first floor was a desk occupied by an attractive blond, slim woman who Cheves introduced as Ms. Sondra Ives. He then introduced me to a handsome, slightly graying man who was Dr. Robert (Bob) Tuttle, Associate Dean of Academic Affairs and Mr. Richardson, Associate Dean for Fiscal Affairs. Cheves cracked another smile, and turning towards me said, "This is it; this is the current Medical School."

I was becoming more and more intrigued as we went into his office and closed the door. It was a small spartan space with papers and books scattered everywhere. Cheves perched on one corner of his desk and looking at me steadily announced: "There are many problems and many obstacles but, believe me, it will be a great deal of fun building this school." After this preamble, I got a large dose of history, politics, and stories of greed, as well as other issues related to the Hermann Hospital.

I was horrified when I glanced at my watch; it was 10:20. I had been so engrossed in conversation with Cheves that I'd totally forgotten that my plane for Denver was departing at 12:30. Cheves, however, was unperturbed, "Don't worry; I'll drive you to the airport. It's only a 45 minute ride." On our way to the airport Cheves decided that there was time for him to show me one of Houston's nicest residential areas, the Memorial Area. It was only 30 minutes from the Medical Center and turned out to be a beautiful, wooded neighborhood consisting of several townships nestled in a pine forest. It was a charming suburb with attractive homes on large wooded lots. As I left, I promised Cheves I would seriously think about it.

As I rushed off the plane in Denver, I could see the girls and Ania waiting for me. Soon I had all three hanging on my neck and I was barraged with questions about Houston. Ania and the girls all spoke at the same time wanting to know all about Texas. I promised I would tell all once we had boarded the bus to the Arapaho Ski Basin, one of the oldest ski areas Colorado. After an easy ride, we arrived at the Arapahoe Lodge in time to rent our ski equipment and enjoy a nice dinner.

I was still feeling the powerful impression made by Cheves, and struggled to come up with a bottom line that summarized my feelings, impressions, and reactions. What I had seen in Houston hadn't borne out the purely subjective ideas I'd had based on limited exposure to movies and books, and off-hand remarks by acquaintances claiming some knowledge of Texas. Houston appeared to be a modern and attractive city, the little I'd seen of it, a city that would compare well to any large city in America. What impressed me most was the pulse, tempo and energy I'd sensed all around me. As I spoke about it, I realized that I was quite excited and very positive about Texas and Houston. The girls reacted with excitement while Ania had a big question mark on her face.

When we returned to Philadelphia the world around me exploded. Everyone wanted to see me and talk to me about our move. There were two messages from Cheves Smythe, Al Kaplan was camping on my doorstep, and Sam Ajl called several times to inquire if I had returned from the trip. I wanted to get the department together at noon the following day to summarize my trip to Houston. Everyone showed up and I tried to provide an evenhanded analysis of my experiences at Baylor College of Medicine and later, surprise, surprise, at the UT Medical School. As I talked I quickly realized that I was biased. Emotionally I favored UT due, in large part to the mesmerizing effect Cheves Smythe had had on me. While I tried to describe the two schools, and the two offers, my colleagues were focused primarily on the issue of Texas as the location.

When I finished talking, there were few seconds of silence followed by pandemonium; everyone wanted to express their opinions and ask questions. I couldn't believe my eyes and ears. The meeting broke into small discussion groups dealing primarily with questions about Texas itself rather than with the desirability of moving to one of the schools there. I tried not to influence the discussions; I just moved between the groups and listened. By the end of the afternoon I had gained a fairly clear idea about the faculty response to the possibility of our move to Texas. Harold would not under any circumstances consider a move "down south" and his associate, Dr. Zuckerman, agreed. Jack simply couldn't physically do it because his research depended so heavily on field studies and his "field" was at the ammunition depots in Western Pennsylvania (where he had his population of woodchucks). Miguel was torn because his wife, a psychologist and professor at Hahnemann University Hospital, had an extensive research program and clinical practice. The rest of the faculty was actually excited about the possibility of moving to Texas.

Within a week of my return from Colorado, I had a call from the Chairman of the Ob-Gyn Department at Baylor inquiring whether I had any further questions concerning the position and which other faculty members would be interested in moving with me. At the same time I had had a letter from Dean Smythe acknowledging our meeting and asking for convenient dates for my return visit and possible visits by the rest of my faculty. I could only smile at the wording of his invitation which implied that my move to Houston was all agreed upon, with only details to be discussed.

The mood at Korman Research Building was subdued but anxiety pervaded the faculty. I had a prolonged discussion with Sam Ajl and shared with him my experiences in Texas as well as the feelings of my faculty. Sam was optimistic as always. He felt that Mr. Sigmond's philosophy was only a brief detour on the part of AEMC and that it would soon find equilibrium. "You know, Emil, the commitment of the Board towards basic research remains steadfast." This was a mantra he had repeated often over the past several months.

Unexpectedly I had another phone call from Texas. Dr. Smythe called to invite me to a faculty meeting to be held the following week at the Flagship Hotel in Galveston. He suggested I bring Ania and other interested faculty members and offered to pick us up at the airport and drive us to the hotel. I accepted this invitation fully cognizant that we would have to make up our minds regarding the move soon. I felt I owed Cheves a definite answer by the end of this next visit. Another faculty meeting was in order.

The outcome of our meeting was an understanding that if I decided to go, Ania, Keith Smith, Jim Lloyd and Drs. Chowdhury would join me while the others would have to find jobs elsewhere. It was a very sad meeting. The group had worked so well together and had become close socially as well. I fully understood everyone's personal feelings about the break up that this move would cause and promised not to make any final decisions until after the Galveston meeting.

Galveston was a barrier island connected to the Texas mainland by a long causeway. The Flagship hotel was built on a pier extending from the beach into the Gulf of Mexico. It was tall, modern and very elegant, and the room assigned to us was beautiful. Dr. Smythe announced that we would meet in a small private bar at the hotel so everyone could get acquainted, then walk over to Guido's Seafood Restaurant for dinner. I was surprised by how small the group was: the dean; two associate deans; Dr. Ruiz, the current chairman of the Department of Ophthalmology at Hermann Hospital; Dr. Joe Wood, recruited from San Antonio to head up the Department of Anatomy; Dr. William Fields, a neurologist; and Ania and me. The agenda for next morning's meeting not yet available but it was very exciting to be in this group of pioneers. We shared a spirit of adventure and optimism as well as the excitement of creating something new. It was this spirit that had initially attracted me and was strengthening my conviction that we should join the organization. However, I could tell that Ania was still not convinced.

The meeting commenced the following morning promptly at 8:00 AM. The first item on the agenda was the curriculum. "Gentlemen," started the Dean, "I am proposing a unique curriculum for our new Medical School, and our Dean for Academic Affairs fully agrees with it. I propose that during the first two years we have a fully integrated basic and clinical curriculum, and that in order to facilitate this effort we have 'programs', rather than 'departments'. Each program will be headed by a director rather than by a chairman.

I remembered hearing this statement before; Sam Ajl established this type of programs and directors at AEMC. After having lived with this system for ten years, I had many concerns about it but decided not bring them up here but just listen. I looked at Ania, and she nodded her head, following my thoughts.

The Dean mentioned programs combining microbiology and infectious diseases or reproductive medicine and biology as examples. A lively discussion ensued and it became clear that those present were very much attuned to this idea. Then the discussion moved on to fiscal issues. Mr. Richardson, the Associate Dean for Fiscal Affairs, took over and explained that the UT System mandated that all faculty be paid by state appropriation. He also explained the fiscal structure of the school and expressed great optimism since very few medical schools in the country had such arrangements with their states. "This," he said, "should add to the stability of the school and its ability to recruit new faculty."

Here again I developed an uneasy feeling. Never having been attracted to the politics of organizations, or the political aspects of their financial structures, I was naïve. I was willing to secure funds for my Department and my faculty salaries. The fiscal situation at UT, as presented, sounded good but my uneasiness persisted.

That evening Ania and I had a long talk. This would be the turning point; I had to give Dr. Smythe a decision. Our position at AEMC was academic but offered a great deal of autonomy and freedom from direct supervision by any medical school bureaucracy. However, it required each department to secure its own funding. At UT the supplies, equipment and salaries were guaranteed by the school via state funding. Thus the situation at these two institutions differed significantly. Then there was the "Dean Smythe factor." I trusted him and very much wanted to participate in his great experiment, the integrated curriculum.

There also might have been a subconscious, literally childish influence at work and talking to Ania about it made us laugh. It dealt with nostalgia dating to my childhood days in Poland, when most of us inhaled short, trashy novels about the wild west, the redskins and the cowboys in the far away land of America. Every boy imagined that he would have his own mustang, cowboy hat and spurs as well as a Colt revolver. As I expounded on these memories to Ania, she doubled over with laughter. "Where are the prairies?" she inquired. "I haven't seen a single cowboy! Houston looks like any large modern city but has a warm climate in the winter." Here I interrupted her. "Oh, yes" I exclaimed, "That's the 'clincher', nice warm weather in the winter! I'm tired of the ice and snow. When we want to ski, we can fly to Colorado." "OK, OK" she said "but we'll see how nice the warm weather in Houston is when the summer comes!" That put a damper on my enthusiasm and we both remained quiet for a long time deeply engrossed in our own thoughts. Finally she got up, walked over to me, slowly put her arms on my shoulders and whispered, "Let's do it."

After returning to Philadelphia and once again conferring with my faculty, I called Dean Smythe and accepted his offer for Ania and me. He instantly responded that, in that case, he would like me to try to attend the monthly faculty meetings in Houston. I told him that several other members of the group might also wish to join the faculty but prior to making up their minds, would like to visit Houston and meet with him. He was completely receptive to that idea.

The tempo of our activities increased remarkably. First, I went to Sam to inform him of our decision and it wasn't a pleasant meeting. I also advised those who might wish to join me in Houston to contact the Dean and arrange a visit with him before making their own decisions. I hoped that some of my colleagues, who were also close personal friends, would join us in Houston. I also knew that many of them were attached to the Northeast and would not consider a move to Texas.

They all secured good positions elsewhere. Harold moved to the University of Pennsylvania, Miguel to Hahnemann Hospital, and Zuckerman to the University of Delaware. Jack Christian joined University of New York in Binghampton, New York which was close to a large tract of forested land with lots of wild life were he considered retiring. Everyone was planning to vacate the premises by end of June and I was very sad. We had spent a large segment of our lives together, built a great department, collaborated on many scientific projects, and become good friends. However, I had to focus on the limitless horizons of our new opportunities, including the chance to build a new medical school and, hopefully, an even greater department.

Most of our laboratory equipment had been acquired through our research grants, so we were given permission by NIH to move it to Houston. Jim Lloyd, who had elected to move with us, had to deal with the most complex logistics. He was engaged in population density studies in the laboratory rather than in the field. He had designed a huge system of cages in which he had bred a large population starting with one pair of mice in order to follow its growth and the factors affecting it. We wanted to move the entire cage system including the mice and that required careful planning to prevent the animals from dying in transport.

Our next visit to Houston to attend the monthly faculty meeting fell on the last day of February. The weather in Houston was perfect; sunny blue skies contrasted with green lawns and trees, and temperatures in the upper 60s. What a contrast to Philadelphia, where we were still sliding on sheets of ice! During this visit I also planned to have discussions with the dean regarding his impressions of the other faculty who had visited with him Houston. The rest of our time would be devoted to house hunting.

Since the faculty meeting was not scheduled to start until 4:00, I decided to see the Dean first thing in the morning. We also wanted his recommendation for a real estate agent. He was very prepared for this request since over the past couple of months he had made several such recommendations for other incoming faculty. He made an appointment for us with an agent named Mr. Creed who was to pick us up by noon. Cheves suggested that we stay in the office until then to discuss additional issues.

He was eager to tell me about his meetings with the other faculty from Philadelphia; apparently they had gone well. We then broached the question of temporary housing for the school and its first permanent structure, the John H. Freeman Building. It would be a two-story structure erected in a partly wooded area just north of the Jones Library occupied primarily by the clinical departments. Most basic science instruction and some clinical teaching was to be conducted in space leased in the near by Center Pavilion Hospital, as well as at Hermann Hospital. The immensity of this task was starting to dawn on me.

Precisely at noon Mr. Creed appeared in the Dean's Office. He was an average size, middle-aged man with graying temples and a pleasant smile. He suggested that we start with lunch so that we could get acquainted and he could find out what we were looking for in our new house. We went to a terrific seafood restaurant, one that would compare well to any of the top seafood restaurant on the Chesapeake Bay. After a martini, we plunged into our house business, pausing only briefly to discuss our food order with the waiter. After hearing my brief description of our current house in Philadelphia, Mr. Creed began promoting the River Oaks neighborhood. "It is," he rhapsodized in his rich velvety baritone, "the most exclusive part of town, it's where the elite of the city live." I looked at Ania with a bemused look, and she responded with a mischievous smile. I knew precisely what she was thinking.

After looking at few houses in the River Oaks, it became obvious to us that this neighborhood was much too rich for our blood. The next best alternative was to look at the lovely wooded area Cheves had driven me through on my previous visit, called Memorial. We soon found a beautiful contemporary house on Coloma Lane with an attractive swimming pool and we instantly fell in love with it. A recently widowed faculty member at UT was eager to sell it; however, the asking price seemed out of reach for us based on our projected incomes. At the urging of our agent, we bravely made an offer that by any standard would have been considered unrealistically low, and returned to Philadelphia disappointed that we probably couldn't buy that house.

The next morning proved to us once again that life holds many surprises! Early in the morning, while we were still sound asleep, I answered a telephone call and, according to Ania, said in a mumble, "Oh? Yes…really? OK." I hung up and immediately went back to sleep. Later that morning, she asked, "Who called us so early?" I hesitantly replied, "I think it was the real estate agent from Houston. I think our offer for that house we liked was accepted, and that we need to sign some papers to finalize the purchase. I think we got the house, but I need to call him back to make sure that it actually happened, and that I wasn't dreaming." We both burst into laughter, "You think you purchased a house in your sleep?" she said, "You better call him back to make sure." It was in fact real. We were to become the proud owners of a wonderful house in Houston originally built by an architect for his own family. We were on our way to Texas!

CHAPTER 12

THE FINAL CHAPTER (BY ANNA STEINBERGER)

Emil and I completed our move to Houston in July 1971. Inette was to join us a month later after finishing her summer job as a camp councilor. Pauline remained in Philadelphia to complete her education at the Pennsylvania Academy of Fine Arts. Saying goodbye to her was very painful for us as it was the first time our little family was to be separated.

Most of our belongings were transported by a commercial moving company, but we decided to pack a few plants and personal belongings into our car and make the trip leisurely over several days. This would give us a chance to do a bit of sightseeing along the way.

We arrived in Houston on the evening of July 4th. The air temperature must have been in the high 90's with humidity close to 100 %! We could hardly catch our breath and wondered if we had made the right decision to move here. It was a harsh introduction to Houston's summer heat. However, the city was in full swing celebrating Independence Day with music and glorious fireworks. We viewed this festive spirit as a good omen as well as a nice welcome to Texas! As soon as we arrived in our new home we turned on the air-conditioning and took a dip in the pool, which immediately relieved our discomfort. After that we felt happy and full of anticipation about beginning this exciting chapter in our lives.

The very next morning we experienced some of the famous Texas hospitality. A neighbor, a middle age, attractive woman whom we had never met before, came by with a basket filled with all kinds of goodies, home made soup, biscuits, cookies, etc. She introduced herself and casually handed us the keys to her house. "My husband and I are leaving tomorrow for our farm and will be gone for over a week. I noticed that you arrived yesterday but didn't have your furniture delivered yet, so please feel free to stay at our house until the rest of your belongings arrive. I've put clean linens on the beds, and there is lots of milk and juice in the refrigerator. You'll be much more comfortable there."

We were stunned! What an incredibly generous offer from a total stranger! At that moment we became convinced that we would love living in this neighborhood. We declined her gracious offer, explaining that we'd brought several sleeping bags anticipating a delay in the arrival of our belongings. We wanted to stay in the house in order to have it fully functional and ready by the time our things were delivered. This friendly and memorable gesture made us feel very welcome in the neighborhood and was the beginning of a lasting friendship with our neighbors on Coloma Lane. We lived there for about seven years before moving to within a few blocks of the Medical Center in order to avoid the long commute to work on the expressways.

One of our major challenges now was to better understand "Texacan". It is still considered English but with a distinct Texas twist, like the cheerful goodbye: "Y'all come back now, ya hear?" Quite often as I drove away from a gas station, I would find myself looking around and wondering who "all" was in the car with me.

Establishing the Division (later renamed Department) of Reproductive Medicine and Biology at the UTMSH was a daunting and tremendously challenging task. It would be unique in providing clinical care and conducting basic and clinical research on the functions and disorders of both male and the female reproductive systems. This was a concept Emil had envisioned years ago and had been striving to achieve. This division became the first in the world to do so.

We were busy planning our laboratory and office facilities as well as developing the curriculum for the incoming class of medical students in September. Moreover, we were busy interviewing potential faculty members who Dean Smythe hoped to recruit to the new medical school. We worked long hours, but the challenges were invigorating and the camaraderie that developed among the initial faculty members continued for many years to come. We always remembered this early period of the medical school with great pleasure and nostalgia.

It took nearly two years for the initial medical school building (the John Freeman Building) to be completed on the grounds of the Texas Medical Center. During this period our work proceeded in temporary quarters at the Center Pavilion Hospital on Holcombe Street. Although our facilities were cramped and minimally functional, the enthusiasm of everyone involved in the adventure of creating the school was palpable. The pros and cons of new ideas were discussed at length in the halls, over lunch and in our offices and homes. Long evenings and weekends were spent writing research grant proposals for submission to the NIH, NSF and other granting institutions. These were needed to fund our research projects and we were very fortunate that our requests were most often approved.

We were also busy with organizing and staffing of our Division. This task was simplified by the fact that several of our colleagues from Philadelphia had joined us in the Texas adventure. They provided a good nucleus for the new department. It rapidly expanded to a unit of eleven faculty members plus a number of graduate students, post-doctoral fellows, laboratory technicians, nurses and secretaries. The Department was enriched by the addition of several other scientists including Barbara Sanborn, Robert Tcholakian, Eduard Grotjan, Jerrold Heindel and a physician from Spain, Dr. Luis Rodridguez, MD.

Initially there was some concern over whether my appointment as a faculty member in Emil's Division constituted nepotism and might cause actual, or perceived, favoritism. This problem was promptly solved by Dean Smythe who decided that he, rather then Emil, would determine my salary level and evaluate my performance as a teacher, faculty member and researcher. It was the best and fairest solution. To my knowledge, no one in our unit ever thought that I enjoyed preferential treatment; in fact, they often felt the opposite was more likely the case.

The ensuing years proved most gratifying in terms of our academic accomplishments. They were filled with important scientific breakthroughs and rewarded by the scientific community with much recognition at the national and international level. Also, our course on Human Reproduction, presented during the second year of medical school, was well received by the students who routinely gave it high marks.

Basic and clinical research conducted with various colleagues resulted in the publication of more than four hundred scientific papers and many book chapters. Over fifty post-doctoral fellows from all over the world, including Argentina, Australia, Chile, China, Germany, India, Indonesia, Italy, Israel, Peru, Poland, Spain, Taiwan, and Venezuela, were trained in our Department. Many of them went on to assume prestigious academic positions in their respective countries. We made every effort to maintain contact with them and often participated in the same scientific meetings. Occasionally, we were even able to visit them during our travels abroad and it was immensely gratifying to see them flourish.

Emil and I were frequently invited to present our research findings at national and international meetings, serve on the editorial boards of scientific journals, and assume positions of leadership in various societies, including the Endocrine Society, American Society of Andrology, and the Society for the Study of Reproduction. Since Emil was also a clinician, he was very active in clinical societies like the American Association of Clinical Endocrinologists. We were both privileged to serve on various NIH Study Sections to review grant applications in our areas of expertise.

The clinical research based on patients seen in the UTMS-H clinic led, among other findings, to the development of new concepts on the origins and treatment of hyperandrogenism, acne, obesity and ovulatory dysfunction often associated with infertility in women. Most importantly, applying the concepts of "couples infertility" and "fertility potential", the clinic gained wide recognition for its success in helping couples achieve pregnancy.

My research laboratory became known for developing several in vitro techniques for isolating and culturing specific testicular cells, which was useful for investigating their functions. Using these techniques we provided the first direct evidence that Sertoli cells of the testis secrete Inhibin, a hormone that exerts negative feedback on the production of pituitary gonadotrophins. We also provided experimental models for exploring testosterone production by testicular Leydig cells, and developed models for direct investigation of testicular-pituitary interactions in vitro.

Our interactions with faculty members at the medical school extended beyond our work environment. We often invited our colleagues to sail with us, sometimes as far as the Bahamas. This journey across the Gulf of Mexico around the Florida peninsula to the Grand Bahamas took over one week of continuous sailing. Cheves Smythe was a superb sailor and a great fisherman! I only had to mention that dinner time was approaching, and he would toss out the fishing line. Within minutes he would catch a fresh fish for our dinner. The best part was that he would also clean the fish on deck and hand it to me as boneless fillets ready for the frying pan. In calm weather, when the boat could be steered by the autopilot, we enjoyed our healthy dinner. Occasionally, Cheves would even do the cooking; life was great!

Holiday parties in our Department became very popular among the faculty and in the early years, when the classes were small (fewer then 40 students) we also invited the students. Over the years, as the class size increased to over 200 students, we could no longer accommodate everyone.

Emil and I were often invited to the same scientific meetings and were able to travel together. This made our working trips much more enjoyable and occasionally, whenever it was feasible, we took the girls with us as well. We wanted them to see the world and meet some of our professional colleagues. They enjoyed these trips and we loved having them with us.

One trip in particular became etched in our minds. After a scientific meeting in Krakow, Poland, we decided to show our daughters some of the places where we had lived as children before WWII. We rented a car with a Polish driver and headed first to Tchebinia, a small town near Krakow, where Emil spent his early years. Seeing the house where he used to live and play brought tears to his eyes, especially since the once beautiful house and garden now looked neglected and badly in need of repair. It was now occupied by tenants and housed a small business as did a house near the railroad station where his grandparents had once operated a small grocery store. There were very few Jewish people left in town as most had been put to death by the Nazis. Even the Jewish cemetery was no longer recognizable. We took many photographs and left with sad memories and heavy hearts.

An even sadder emotional experience was our visit to Auschwitz/ Birkenau, the largest concentration camp complex in Poland, near Krakow during WWII. Millions of Jews and other innocent victims died there during the Holocaust. The camp is now a memorial being visited daily by many people of all ages and from all over the world. The crematoria were mostly destroyed by the retreating German army and the wooden barracks have fallen victim to the elements, but one can still visualize the unspeakable horrors that took place there. Many relatives on both sides of our family perished in this place and there are no individual grave sites to mark their final resting place. The Holocaust, during which an estimated eleven million innocent men, women and children were murdered, remains the most outrageous crime ever committed against humanity. Many cities have created Holocaust museums and educational programs to teach current and future generations about the dire consequences of extreme hatred and prejudice. The nagging question remains: will people ever learn to live on this planet in peace and with mutual respect and understanding?

In 1974, Emil initiated a major effort to establish the American Society of Andrology, which was to provide a platform for basic and clinical investigators to share their findings and promote an integrated approach to the treatment of male reproductive system disorders. One year later the American Society of Andrology (ASA) held its first formal meeting at Vanderbilt University in Nashville, Tennessee. There, he was elected to serve as its founding president (ten years later I too was so honored). Subsequently, we each received the ASA "Distinguished Andrologist Award" for our research contributions.

ASA continued to thrive by attracting several hundreds members from the US and abroad and developing its own journal, the "American Journal of Andrology. The programs and workshops at the annual meetings were widely recognized for their timely topics and high quality. Being a relatively small society, it promoted warm personal interactions, research collaboration, and long-lasting friendships among its members. Many of the personal interactions continued after our retirement from the academic activities.

Things were progressing well also on our home front. Pauline completed her studies at the Pennsylvania Academy of Fine Arts in Philadelphia and joined us in Houston. She decided to continue her education at the University of Texas in Austin where Inette attended college and later also the Law School. Both girls loved Austin and their campus life. We enjoyed visiting them there whenever we could get away for a few days. After graduation, both girls found suitable jobs in Houston. It was wonderful to have them close to us again and spend vacations together sailing on Galveston Bay during the summer and skiing in the mountains of Colorado. We were all becoming seasoned Texans; we had acquired some western attire and often had Texas BQ in with colleagues and friends.

By this time, we were proud owners of EPIA V, a 35 foot, two-mast boat that could easily handle longer trips and sleep comfortably six persons. We spent almost all of our free time sailing on Galveston Bay or in the Gulf of Mexico. Before the days when GPS was standard on every boat and in every car, we occasionally sailed close to an oil rig in the Gulf to ask their exact latitude and longitude. This helped us with our navigation and we discovered that we could trade for almost anything if we had beer.

On one memorable trip out of Galveston, heading for Tampa an Atlantic hurricane changed direction and crossed over Florida. We were already out in the Gulf, about a hundred and fifty miles south of the Mississippi River Delta and got hit by the tail end of the storm. The wind howled and the waves were enormous. Our engine, which was powerful enough for most other situations, was simply not powerful enough to control the boat in such heavy weather. After several hours of struggling just to keep the boat headed into the huge waves to avoid being rolled over, a Coast Guard cutter "Pine River "came to our rescue. They wanted to tow us but couldn't get close enough to throw us a tow line. Every time a wave picked up their vessel it created a huge trough into which our boat was being sucked in; a few times we thought we were going to be crushed under the huge cutter. We finally gave up exhausted and frustrated when the captain hailed us on the radio to say that we should just follow in their wake. They flattened the waves enough for us to follow them for many hours into the night. Finally, the next morning we found ourselves at a marina in Grand Isle, Louisiana. Inette had to fly home from New Orleans to return to work in Houston.

Emil and I stayed in the Grand Isle marina to make some repairs to our boat engine and then sailed back home safely. It was the sort of experience sailors love to talk about once it's over! After that experience we decided to purchase in 1984 a bigger sailboat, a 46-foot katch, with a more powerful and reliable engine.

After graduating from Law School, Inette joined a law firm in Houston where she met a nice young man, also an attorney. It took just a few months for them to decide to get married. We were delighted with their decision and in May 1978 celebrated their wedding in a beautiful garden setting at Vargos in Houston. While everyone was enjoying perfect weather and the lovely setting, several colorful peacocks decided to join the ceremony and bear witness to the wedding ceremony with their raucous cries.

Pauline was married in 1983, and moved with her husband to Canada. Three years later she presented us with a most precious gift, a beautiful baby boy named Mathew. As the years flew by, we watched him grow into a rambunctious boy who liked boating, fishing, archery and taekwondo. When Mathew was eight we were happy when they moved back to Houston. We bought him his first computer and he took to it like a duck to water. Computers became his passion, and it evolved into his professional career. It was great for Emil and me to have a personal computer expert to help us with our never-ending technical problems. Unfortunately, we lost this valuable support when Mathew was transferred to Milwaukee, Wisconsin. During his first harsh winter there, he slipped on some ice and fractured his ankle. Listening to Mathew talk about the frigid weather, we were grateful to be living in Houston despite the hot and humid summers. Fortunately for Mathew, after living just one year in Milwaukee, he accepted a position with a computer company in California, and was pleased to escape from the snow and ice.

In January 2001, after devoting nearly forty-five years to caring for patients and conducting research, Emil decided to retire from academic medicine. He had discovered a new challenge for his always-active mind—writing about his amazing life. He would spend hours at the computer converting memories, some still very vivid in his mind and others clouded by the passage of time, into a three part memoir called "The Journey".

Though he had previously authored hundreds of scientific publications, writing about his experiences from memory was something totally new and required a different writing style; one he liked to call "creative non-fiction". Here, there was no scientific data to analyze, no published reports for comparative analysis, and no laboratory in which to duplicate events or verify a hypothesis. There were just memories of his experiences, occasionally refreshed by reference to other sources to verify facts like dates, place names or geographic locations.

This project started almost by chance when our daughters or grandson asked, "Where were you living when the German army was near Moscow?" "Were you scared?" "What did you do when the clothes you had could no longer be worn?" "How did you manage to catch up with your schooling without knowing the language?" "What did you have to eat during the war?" "What do you mean bed bugs wouldn't let you sleep?"

One morning I showed Emil a book, more precisely an album, entitled "Grandparents' Memories". It had a series of questions with space provided to fill in the answers, add photographs and even a blank page for "additional notes". He was interested in sharing this kind of information but such a structured and abbreviated format for recording a life filled with so many unusual experiences did not appeal to him at all! Instead, he decided to write a few pages recounting his story in his own words. Therefore, what started as a brief recollection written in a few pages grew into three full-length books.

One of the most intriguing parts of Emil's writing was the attention he devoted to the small details of his life; often leaving the reader wondering how he could remember them so well when he was only a child or young teenager at the time. When I asked him this same question, his explanation was:

"I really don't have the events clear in my mind until I sit down at the computer and start writing about them. Sometimes, I'm not even sure what I'm going to say until I actually begin to type. Then, as if by magic, a recording goes on in my mind and the events come back as though they happened only yesterday. I begin to see the places where I lived, and hear the voices of people I knew many years ago. It is truly amazing to me how this works, but it does."

He was extremely disciplined about his writing. In the morning, after getting up and exercising for about an hour in the gym or the swimming pool, scanning the daily newspaper while sipping a cup of coffee, and taking a shower, he would begin to write. I would hardly see him until it was time for lunch, after which he would again disappear into his little study, often working until dinner. In the evenings he enjoyed watching the news or an interesting program on the National Geographic or History channel, but invariably he did some additional writing. Writing had become his newest passion and he enjoyed it tremendously. However, writing did not preclude us from taking time off for traveling, sailing, skiing, and many social activities.

We often sailed our EPIA VI all the way from Kemah, Texas all the way to the Bahamas. Occasionally, we preferred to keep the boat in one of Bahamas marinas and fly there for cruising around the islands. This type of sailing was beautiful and much more relaxed then sailing across the Gulf day and night for a whole week!

When Emil started experiencing some symptoms of heart failure, and received a couple of cardiac stents, our trips to the Bahamas became less frequent, and we ultimately decided to sell the boat. It was very difficult to part with our beloved, last EPIA on which we had so many wonderful adventures, but running the risk of additional heart problems in the middle of a sail forced this decision. Afterwards, whenever someone would ask Emil: "If you had an opportunity to live your life over again, what would you have done differently?" I always thought he might have said that he would have married a more agreeable woman; however, his standard answer was, "I would not have sold my boat, and I would have retired from work ten years earlier." I always knew that he loved to sail but that statement also proved to me how much he enjoyed writing his memoirs, possibly even more than all of his earlier academic endeavors.

Volume one of his memoirs entitled "BETWEEN THE DEVIL AND DEEP BLUE SEA," was published in 2005 and recounted the struggles Emil and his family endured during WWII, and the events immediately following as he made his way to "the promised land" via Ellis Island. That book received many favorable responses from readers, many of whom said, "Once I started reading it, I couldn't put it down".

The second book, "THE PROMISED LAND –Woes of an

Immigrant", was published in 2007. In it, Emil continues his story after arriving in the United States and attempting to create a new life here in spite of having no money or knowledge of the English language. He recalls many of the situations he encountered, some strange, interesting often very funny and occasionally disappointing. Nevertheless, he maintained a positive outlook, filled with optimism and enthusiasm though it all. His journey takes the reader through his marriage, his successful completion of medical school, his earliest forays into research and his excitement over becoming the father of two beautiful daughters.

Emil's passion for writing continued with "THE GOLDEN AGE AND ITS IMPLOSION". This final volume of his trilogy completes the "Journey". We follow him through his service in the Navy, completion of his medical training and his professional career. Here he delves into various aspects of medical education, medical training and health care delivery in the United States, including the role of insurance companies in meeting the health needs of patients and the spiraling costs of medical care.

We share his personal and professional experiences as the "woes" of the immigrant from the second book turn into national and international recognition for Emil as an academician, clinician, and researcher. He also knew how lucky he was to have found a perfect life partner often saying, "All of my experiences have been much enriched by sharing them with an important co-worker and life-long collaborator, my wife."

In December 2006, soon after beginning work on this book, Emil received shocking news. He was diagnosed with non-operative lung cancer and had to undergo extensive radiation and chemotherapy, which often left him exhausted. This news came as a huge surprise to us, as he was in overall excellent health, exercising vigorously every morning and feeling well. Receiving this diagnosis was like a lightening bolt out of a clear blue sky, reminding us how unexpected life's events can be… Despite his weakening condition, Emil continued to write, although at a much slower pace, and participated in many book-signing events. Unfortunately, he eventually became too ill to and unable to finish the book. Knowing how important it was to him to complete everything he'd ever started; I decided that with the help of some friends, family and colleagues I could finish it for him.

We also managed to take several interesting trips after his diagnosis, and in between his treatments. In February, 2007 we were on a cruise in Hawaii and in November joined a group of Iowa University alumni for a two-week trip to Vietnam. It was one of the few parts of the world we hadn't previously visited in our extensive travels and it was a truly fascinating trip.

In July, 2008 we travelled to Fiji and Tonga for the coronation of His Majesty King George Tupou V. Tonga is the only remaining independent kingdom in the Polynesian islands and the coronation, which was timed to coincide with the king's 60th birthday on August 1 was an unforgettable event. The entire town of Nuku'alofa (the capital of Tonga) was decorated with huge banners wishing the king a long life, good health and happiness. There were military parades and grand spectacles of native dancing open to the general public and concerts and formal balls for invited guests. Many foreign dignitaries and royalty were in attendance representing their respective nations and fabulous clothing and jewelry abounded at these lavish events.

Proceeds from the Royal Charity Concert by the Symphony Orchestra of China, and several other events held during the coronation festivities, were to benefit the Royal Endocrinology Society, that King George Tupou V had established to improve the health of his people. Creating this society was an important step toward solving some of Tonga's greatest public health problems, particularly Type II diabetes which is prevalent among the local population.

Why were we invited to this historic event? It all began about twelve years earlier. Our close friends, Dina and Gaetano (Nino) Frajese, both physicians practicing in Rome, asked if we would like to join them on a summer vacation in Tonga and Samoa. We had travelled with them previously and always enjoyed their company, so we readily accepted their invitation. Emil, in particular, was always ready to visit far away, exotic places. We had never been to Tonga or Samoa, so it seemed like it would be an exciting adventure; and it was!

It was fascinating to learn more about the history and culture of the Polynesian people. What our Italian friends didn't tell us was that they were carrying gifts from the Vatican for the then reigning King of Tonga, His Majesty King George Tupou IV. They wanted to present these gifts to him in person, so an audience was arranged, and we were all invited to the palace for lunch. The king was a voluminous man with a friendly smile and a kindly manner. He was dressed in traditional Tongan clothes and didn't speak much English or Italian. His son (whose coronation we later attended) was then the crown prince and amazed us with his excellent command of English and several other western languages. His manner and clothes were also much more western than those his father wore. The prince subsequently visited the Drs. Frajese in Rome and later, of course, invited them to his coronation.

Despite having made this earlier acquaintance, Emil and I were thoroughly surprised to be also invited to the coronation ceremonies. It was very tempting to attend this unique event so, despite Emil's deteriorating health condition, we made the long trip to Polynesia. We met Dina and Nino at the Los Angeles Airport and continued our journey together.

We spent the first week in Fiji at a luxurious seaside resort enjoying beautiful scenery, excellent native cuisine, and several evening performances by the native dancers and musicians. Each evening, before sunset, a man dressed in native costume would light numerous torches around the property, giving it a magical appearance and a feeling of great mystery. We created many wonderful memories of beautiful scenery and friendly encounters with the kind people of Fiji. After returning to Houston, we loved to relive our experiences by viewing the photographs and videos Emil took during this trip. Sadly it was the last time we were able to travel with our friends from Rome as Emil passed away a few months later.

In September, Emil participated in a book signing arranged by Barnes and Noble Booksellers for a number of authors from the Houston area. The event was well attended, and Emil happily stayed for hours autographing the first two published books of the "Journey".

Later that month, he received the "Claude Cody Retired Physicians Award" which honored a retired physician for contributions in arts and literature. Emil was honored for his thirty articles, called "Musings", which had been published in a local newspaper, and for the first two volumes of his memoir. The award was presented by Claude Cody IV at an elegant luncheon attended by many friends, both our daughters as well as Emil's sister, Stella, who flew in from California for this occasion. Sadly, this turned out to be the last in a long list of prestigious awards Emil had received during his distinguished career as a physician, educator, scientist, and writer.

His philosophy of life had always been "Work hard and play hard because every day counts!" He accomplished this admirably and did, indeed, live his life to the fullest. He welcomed every challenge, overcame every hardship, maximized every opportunity and savored every happy moment. He passed away peacefully in his sleep on October 12, 2008.

ABBREVIATIONS

AEMC----Albert Einstein Medical Center, Philadelphia, PA
AFSS------American Fertility & Sterility Society
AHA------American Hospital Association
BOQ------Bachelors Officers Quarters
DRH------Detroit Receiving Hospital
ENT-------Ear, Nose & Throat
FDA-------Food & Drug Administration
NIH-------National Institutes of Health
NNMC----National Naval Medical Center
NMC------Navy Medical Corps
NMRI-----Naval Medical Research Institute
PNH-------Portsmouth Naval Hospital
PhD-------Doctor of Philosophy
PX---------Post Exchange
SHI--------Statutory Health Insurance
SSR--------Society for the Study of Reproduction
TEM-------Triethylene melamine
WWII-----World War II

AFTERWORD:
REMINISCENCES OF A YOUNG SCIENTIST

As often is the case in the sciences, the people with whom you train can have a significant influence on the direction of your career. My postdoctoral training mentor, Stanley Korenman, M.D., then at the University of Iowa, was serving on an NIH Study Section panel that reviewed grant applications. On that same panel was a professor who had just accepted a position as Chair of the new Department of Reproductive Medicine and Biology at the University of Texas Medical School in Houston, and who was looking for new faculty, particularly those trained in the study of hormone action. My background in endocrinology, biochemistry, and in the biochemistry of steroid and polypeptide hormone action interested Emil Steinberger and by February 1972 my husband Hugh and I were leaving our winter coats and boots in Cedar Rapids, Iowa, to visit warm, balmy Houston, Texas.

I found the Drs. Steinberger and their group to be quite dynamic; they were focused on male reproduction and were well versed in tissue culture and steroid chemistry. My interest and background was in molecular endocrinology, primarily focused at that time in the female and in particular the uterus, so this appeared to be a good professional opportunity for me. I would have colleagues who could help me learn about the male reproductive tract at a time when molecular endocrinology was in its infancy regarding the male system. My husband also found interesting career opportunities at Rice University that made the move attractive to him too. Therefore, in August of 1972, my husband and I packed up our belongings and moved with our small daughter to Houston.

Those were heady days at UTMSH. The school had started only a few years before and was in the process of implementing a full four-year curriculum. Dean Smythe had wisely chosen to recruit department heads who could bring in established groups that could instantly start producing scientific work of note to quickly put it on the map. Emil's was one such entity, and I was one of the first "outsiders" to join this close-knit group of basic and clinical scientists. Like the research group itself, the field of reproductive medicine represented a synthesis of expertise in male and female reproductive biology and endocrinology.

I rapidly discovered several things: Emil was strong-willed and knew where he wanted to take the department. He had very high standards and an incredible command of the basic and clinical scientific literature related to his discipline. He required and appreciated excellence, but demanded no more of others than he demanded of himself. He was a creative thinker and contributed significantly to the deliberations in those exciting days when the Medical School curriculum was being designed and the character of the school was being determined. With virtually all new faculty and no traditions to fall back upon, we set about inventing our own way of doing things. Since we were few in number, everyone was expected to contribute to this endeavor. Unlike more established institutions, where women often had to overcome traditional views of their roles, female faculty members at UTMSH had equal opportunities to take part in this planning. While many medical schools organized their curriculum based on subject matter, UTMSH championed an emerging trend and provided an integrated approach to systems (such as the reproductive system), bringing together basic and clinical topics. It was an exciting concept and worked for many years until the school decided to return to a more traditional department-based instruction. In my opinion, the integrated approach allowed the students to more fully grasp the breadth of a topic, even if it was logistically more challenging because it required integration and communication between lecturers from different disciplines.

Both of the clinicians with whom I have been associated, Dr. Korenman and Dr. Steinberger, moved seamlessly from basic to clinical thinking. Between them and my previous associations with clinician-scientists during my tenure as a laboratory research assistant at Harvard Medical School prior to enrolling in graduate school, I thought this was natural. I have since come to realize that this is a tremendous and rare gift. Both Stan and Emil had trained as endocrinologists, and this subspecialty of internal medicine, even more so than the parent discipline, attracts those who delight in using deductive reasoning paired with keen observation and a strong basic science foundation to solve complex clinical problems.

Emil's basic science interests were in testicular biology, and he was particularly anxious to know how hormones achieved the development of germ cells. (Parenthetically, answers to some these questions are only now coming to light). He pointed me to studies he had done with W.O. in which he could destroy specific cell types in the testis and study the wave of spermatogenesis that filled in behind the germ cell populations he had eliminated. It was only much later that I learned he had essentially earned a PhD as well as an MD at the University of Iowa.

Anna, a formidable scientist in her own right, had developed methods to isolate and maintain in culture, purified populations of specific testis cells (Leydig cells and Sertoli cells) and small pieces of testis tissue with seminiferous tubule architecture intact. She also developed a separate program culturing cells of the pituitary and studying the control of the production of pituitary hormones. Her seminal findings included some of the earliest evidence for the hormone Inhibin, which exerts negative effects on the production of some pituitary hormones.

It speaks well for Emil and his vision that he put together a group of people with widely differing and complementary expertise that spanned the spectrum from practical clinical and behavioral expertise to molecular expertise, all focused on testicular biology and disease. The work was sustained by a prestigious NIH Program Project grant for a significant time, as well as numerous individual grants and graduate programs.

We met regularly as a group to discuss research results and generate new ideas. To this day, I can say that I have never experienced such an open and free-minded merging of clinical and basic expertise and ideas. Often basic scientists are reductionist in their thinking (I have been accused of this by clinical colleagues) or lack appreciation for the less exact but nonetheless rigorous clinical research approaches, which are inherently constrained by the considerations required when working with human subjects. Conversely, clinicians often feel uncomfortable in the world of focused basic science that may seem far away from the needs of patients. In Emil's relatively small department, however, we got to know and appreciate each other's expertise and to rely on each other's wisdom and unique insights. I also became much more aware of clinical relevancy, a key ingredient in any NIH grant in the current age. As a result, I have been motivated to seek out clinical colleagues throughout my career.

Emil gave me free rein to think about future research projects, but encouraged me to consider working on the control of the Sertoli cell by androgens. I did this, exploring the expression and regulation of androgen receptors (the intracellular mediators of androgen action), other androgen binding proteins, and actions of androgens. Important collaborators along the way, in addition to Emil and Anna, included John Elkington, Dolores Lamb (my first graduate student), Susan Buzek, Yu Hui Tsai and ChunYing Ku, among others.

Emil did many things to help me develop my career. He showed me his successful method of grant proposal organization, a model with which I was immediately successful and that I have used to this day. He partnered with me on some NIH contracts, and then stepped aside as I applied for and obtained independent grant funding. He provided me with my first postdoctoral fellow, John Elkington, when I could not afford to hire one. This increased my productivity and helped both of us to further our careers. He counseled me that "you have to spend money to make money," meaning that strategic investment of resources pays off in enhanced research productivity. This is a lesson I have never forgotten and that I have applied in my own laboratory and in my position as a department head.

Emil recommended me to serve on an NIH special review panel early in my career and later, after I had built my research program, recommended me for membership on an NIH study section. In doing so, I met many scientists and began the networking that has served me well throughout my career. Emil, as Stan Korenman had done before, also introduced me to key leaders in the field and made sure that I had the opportunity to "get noticed" at national meetings. Years later Dr. Griff Ross, former Director of the Clinical Center at NIH, joined the faculty at UTMSH as clinical director under Dean Ernst Knobil. Griff had many sayings, one of which has stayed with me all these years: "When you find yourself in a rowboat and someone hands you an oar, row, damn it!" I realized that that is what I had been doing— taking advantage of opportunities that came my way (many made possible by Emil) and making sure I did a good job at them. One opportunity led to another. Little did I realize, until I read The Promised Land, that

Emil had been repaying all those who had had faith in him by doing the same for an upcoming faculty member. I have tried to pass on that legacy to those who have trained with me or worked in my department as well.

Emil kept close tabs on how I was progressing with obtaining grant funds, publishing my results in good peer-reviewed journals, reviewing manuscripts for journals, and getting invitations to serve on study review panels. He pointed out that all of these things were required for promotion and tenure, and when the time came, I had no problem obtaining both. For a while Emil was a Principal Investigator on an NIH Program Project Grant, a precursor of the current Center Grants. The idea was that although the projects were designed and executed by individual scientists, they were related and through their collaboration and by contributing to a defined research goal and sharing knowledge and resources, they produced a whole that was greater than the sum of the parts. This reflected some of the core beliefs Emil fought for during his career, collaboration among specialists such as Ob-Gyn and Endocrinology, and between clinical medicine and basic research. In addition, Co-Principal Investigators, a category not available when I was in the Department of Reproductive Medicine and Biology, now acknowledges that two people can be equal contributors to the conception and execution of a grant. Similarly, co-equal first authors are now acknowledged on manuscripts. These changes reflect the increasing trend toward collaborative research, even across institutions. Thus, the conduct of science itself is still evolving.

I have always had a great appreciation for what Emil did for my career and for the things he taught me. Nonetheless, it was only years later, after reading his first two books that I understood the dynamics of his past and could imagine what he must have been thinking as he gave me advice. I arrived in Houston pregnant with my second child, not an accident but certainly not the situation in which I had hoped to find myself when starting my first faculty position. Emil looked a bit disappointed when I told him of my pregnancy, but that was the last time I heard about it. This may seem like nothing in today's climate, when discriminating against a woman for being pregnant would be a prosecutable offense (I particularly appreciate this now as a Department

Head), but in 1972 women wanting careers as scientists and faculty members were still greeted with skepticism.

Female scientists had to prove themselves many times over, locally and on the national scheme, but we benefitted from the trail blazing efforts of scientists like Anna and the support of chairmen like Emil. There was no Family Leave Act in those days, and no formal maternity leave. I was writing a grant with Emil when my son was born but he allowed me to continue working on it at home. After a few weeks I was gradually returning to work when I, unfortunately, contracted mycoplasmic pneumonia. Emil was very concerned about my health and, knowing that our family finances were precarious, kept me on full pay and did not press me to return to work. I have often thought of how generous he was in that act, and of the faith that he placed in me even though I had not even completed my first year. It is another example that I have tried to follow in my career as a laboratory leader and now as an administrator.

There was one more lesson that I learned from Emil and Anna. In 1984, the medical school decided to merge the very visible and productive Department of Reproductive Medicine and Biology with the Department of Ob-Gyn. Emil and Anna saw their vision dissolving and, although it was clearly a very difficult time for them, they focused on what could be done, not on what could have been and made plans to move on. It was a lesson in survivorship, and one that was not lost on the rest of us. Later, while reading Emil's books, I realized the poignancy of the circumstances under which he and Anna had honed their survivorship skills.

Those of us in the Department of Reproductive Medicine and Biology all adjusted to what was a difficult transition and eventually went our separate ways inside and outside UTMSH. Emil was offered a position befitting his status within the Medical School, and the rest of the faculty members were offered positions in the Department of Ob-Gyn. Emil, Keith Smith and Luis Rodriguez-Rigau opted instead to open a private clinical practice, the Texas Institute of Reproductive Medicine and Endocrinology (TIRME), which was "devoted to clinical management of general endocrine and nonsurgical reproductive system disorders of the male and female." It is still a very successful entity, and these physicians have helped many men and women achieve reproductive success and/or deal with endocrine disorders. Anna continued to do her research and assumed several senior leadership positions as a Professor in the Department of Ob-Gyn. Only one year after retiring as Professor Emerita, she was recruited as Assistant Dean for Faculty Affairs and became even more active in helping young faculty to advance through the academic ranks and assuring equitable treatment for all faculty, particularly women faculty. I later became a Professor in the Department of Biochemistry and Molecular Biology.

Emil and Anna continued to provide career advice and promote the advancement of former faculty members and students long after leaving UTMSH. They were also major forces for enlightened dialogue in the Houston area and strong supporters of the Houston Holocaust Museum and its programs. One of my last and most lasting memories of Emil is of him dancing with joy and energy at a large joint 80th birthday celebration that he and Anna hosted for relatives, friends from their distant past, friends from UTMSH and others. Emil's approach to life, in spite of its ups and downs or perhaps because of having survived so many of them, is summed up in the best definition I have ever found for the Hebrew expression L'Chaim! (on www.dummies.com, of all places):

> The phrase is not to a good life, to a healthy life, or even to a long life. It is simply to life, recognizing that life is indeed good and precious and should always be celebrated and savored.

Barbara M. Sanborn, Ph.D.,
Professor and Head,
Department of Biomedical Sciences,
Colorado State University

About the Author

Emil Steinberger was one of the most colorful and influential pioneers in the medical and scientific field of male reproduction. This book captures his dynamic forceful, dominating personality, his optimism and determination, charm and courage, successes and sacrifices. Emil had great passion – love for his wife, children, and for sailing, skiing, and adventure. He enjoyed good fortune, luck, world-wide recognition, and happiness, and lived life to the fullest. His life story gives valuable insights into the ways of academic politics. This is also the story of the proverbial penniless immigrant who conquered all. I had the privilege of knowing Emil and his life-partner, Anna, and working in sufficiently closely related fields so that I can personally relate to his experiences as a medical resident in Detroit, a young physician at Naval Medical Research Institute, an aspiring researcher in Philadelphia, and at his typical breakneck speed, as department chairman in Houston. This book is thoroughly enjoyable reading, and should be inspirational to many young people in clinical medicine, biomedical research and most any field of endeavor. Very heartwarming!

David Rodbard MD
Biomedical Informatics, Potomac MD

LaVergne, TN USA
16 October 2010
201076LV00003B/3/P